POLICY IMPLICATIONS OF

INTERNATIONAL GRADUATE STUDENTS AND POSTDOCTORAL SCHOLARS IN THE UNITED STATES

Committee on Policy Implications of International Graduate Students and
Postdoctoral Scholars in the United States

Committee on Science, Engineering, and Public Policy

Board on Higher Education and Workforce

Policy and Global Affairs

THE NATIONAL ACADEMIES

THE NATIONAL ACADEMIES PRESS
WASHINGTON, D.C.
www.nap.edu

THE NATIONAL ACADEMIES PRESS 500 Fifth Street NW Washington, DC 20001

NOTICE: The project that is the subject of this report was approved by the Governing Board of the National Research Council, whose members are drawn from the Councils of the National Academy of Sciences, the National Academy of Engineering, and the Institute of Medicine. The members of the committee responsible for the report were chosen for their special competences and with regard for appropriate balance.

Support for this project was provided by the National Science Foundation under grant number 0342159; the National Institutes of Health, under contract number 1-OD-4-2137 Task Order 137; and the National Academies. Any opinions, findings, conclusions, or recommendations expressed in this publication are those of the authors and do not necessarily reflect the views of the organizations or agencies that provided support for the project.

International Standard Book Number 0-309-09613-8

Committee on Science, Engineering, and Public Policy, 500 Fifth Street NW, Washington, DC 20001; 202-334-2807; Internet, http://www.nationalacademies.org/cosepup. ,

Additional copies of this report are available from the National Academies Press, 500 Fifth Street NW, Lockbox 285, Washington, DC 20055; (800) 624-6242 or (202) 334-3313 (in the Washington metropolitan area); Internet, http://www.nap.edu.

THE NATIONAL ACADEMIES
Advisers to the Nation on Science, Engineering, and Medicine

The **National Academy of Sciences** is a private, nonprofit, self-perpetuating society of distinguished scholars engaged in scientific and engineering research, dedicated to the furtherance of science and technology and to their use for the general welfare. Upon the authority of the charter granted to it by the Congress in 1863, the Academy has a mandate that requires it to advise the federal government on scientific and technical matters. Dr. Ralph J. Cicerone is president of the National Academy of Sciences.

The **National Academy of Engineering** was established in 1964, under the charter of the National Academy of Sciences, as a parallel organization of outstanding engineers. It is autonomous in its administration and in the selection of its members, sharing with the National Academy of Sciences the responsibility for advising the federal government. The National Academy of Engineering also sponsors engineering programs aimed at meeting national needs, encourages education and research, and recognizes the superior achievements of engineers. Dr. Wm. A. Wulf is president of the National Academy of Engineering.

The **Institute of Medicine** was established in 1970 by the National Academy of Sciences to secure the services of eminent members of appropriate professions in the examination of policy matters pertaining to the health of the public. The Institute acts under the responsibility given to the National Academy of Sciences by its congressional charter to be an adviser to the federal government and, upon its own initiative, to identify issues of medical care, research, and education. Dr. Harvey V. Fineberg is president of the Institute of Medicine.

The **National Research Council** was organized by the National Academy of Sciences in 1916 to associate the broad community of science and technology with the Academy's purposes of furthering knowledge and advising the federal government. Functioning in accordance with general policies determined by the Academy, the Council has become the principal operating agency of both the National Academy of Sciences and the National Academy of Engineering in providing services to the government, the public, and the scientific and engineering communities. The Council is administered jointly by both Academies and the Institute of Medicine. Dr. Ralph J. Cicerone and Dr. Wm. A. Wulf are chair and vice chair, respectively, of the National Research Council.

www.national-academies.org

COMMITTEE ON POLICY IMPLICATIONS OF INTERNATIONAL GRADUATE STUDENTS AND POSTDOCTORAL SCHOLARS IN THE UNITED STATES

Principal Project Staff

LAUREL L. HAAK, Study Director
PETER H. HENDERSON, Collaborating Board Director
JAMES A. VOYTUK, Collaborating Senior Program Officer
ALAN ANDERSON, Consultant and Senior Writer
NORMAN GROSSBLATT, Senior Editor
SHADEEQUA MILLER, Program Assistant
JUDY GOSS, Senior Program Assistant
SARAE BAUSCH, Christine Mirzayan Science & Technology Policy
    Graduate Fellow
CHRISTINA TAT, Christine Mirzayan Science & Technology Policy
    Graduate Fellow
ERIC ZIMMERMAN, Christine Mirzayan Science & Technology Policy
    Graduate Fellow
M. CRINA FRINCU, Christine Mirzayan Science & Technology Policy
    Graduate Fellow
RACHEL MACCOSS, Christine Mirzayan Science & Technology Policy
    Graduate Fellow
RICHARD YEH, Christine Mirzayan Science & Technology Policy
    Graduate Fellow
MAIKE C. RENTEL, Christine Mirzayan Science & Technology Policy
    Graduate Fellow

COMMITTEE ON SCIENCE, ENGINEERING, AND PUBLIC POLICY

HUGO SONNENSCHEIN, Charles L. Hutchinson Distinguished Service Professor, Department of Economics, University of Chicago, Chicago, Illinois

SHEILA E. WIDNALL, Abby Rockefeller Mauze Professor of Aeronautics, Massachusetts Institute of Technology, Cambridge, Massachusetts

WM. A. WULF (Ex officio), President, National Academy of Engineering, Washington, DC

MARY LOU ZOBACK, Senior Research Scientist, Earthquake Hazards Team, US Geological Survey, Menlo Park, California

Staff

RICHARD BISSELL, Executive Director
DEBORAH D. STINE, Associate Director
LAUREL L. HAAK, Program Officer
MARION RAMSEY, Administrative Coordinator

Preface

This report reflects the continuing interest of the Committee on Science, Engineering, and Public Policy (COSEPUP) in the education and training of scientists and engineers in the United States. COSEPUP's 1993 report *Science, Technology, and the Federal Government: National Goals for a New Era* emphasized the importance of human resources to the research enterprise. A second report, *Reshaping the Graduate Education of Scientists and Engineers* (1995), urged institutions to offer graduate students expanded educational experiences and to equip them better to choose from among the broad range of careers now open to scientists and engineers. That concern was extended to postdoctoral scholars in 2000 with *Enhancing the Postdoctoral Experience for Scientists and Engineers.*

Increasing the attractiveness of science and engineering (S&E) careers gained importance in the late 1990s as fewer US citizens enrolled in advanced training in S&E, a trend accompanied by a substantial rise in the proportion of international graduate students and postdoctoral scholars in US institutions. An unrelated but equally pressing trend that is likely to affect the quality of US S&E education is the recognition by nations around the world of the value of S&E to their economies and societies. From the advanced industrial societies of Europe and Japan to the newly emergent world powers of China and India, nations have launched efforts to compete for the most talented scientists and engineers worldwide.

In an effort to address the complex conditions affecting the relative standing of US S&E, the National Academies charged COSEPUP to address the following questions:

1. What is known about the impact of international graduate students and postdoctoral scholars on the advancement of US science, US undergraduate and graduate educational institutions, the US and other national economies, and US national security and international relations?

2. What is the impact of the US academic system on international graduate students' and postdoctoral scholars' intellectual development, careers, and perceptions of the United States? How does it differ if they stay in the United States or return to their home countries?

3. What is known about the impact of international student enrollment on the recruitment of domestic S&E talent in the United States? What is the status of working conditions for international graduate students and postdoctoral scholars compared with their domestic counterparts?

4. What are the impacts of various policies that reshape or reduce the flow of international students and postdoctoral scholars (for example, visas, immigration rules, and working conditions)?

5. What findings and conclusions can be drawn from the answers to the preceding questions? What principles should guide national policy regarding international graduate students and postdoctoral scholars?

In considering their charge, the committee encountered difficulties whose solution will require much more public discussion. A persistent hindrance is the lack of accurate and timely data about international graduate students and postdoctoral scholars, a difficulty that is addressed in Chapter 4. In addition, it became clear that the recruitment goals of many academic administrators are often in tension and sometimes contradictory. For example, one of the goals is to recruit the best students possible, regardless of national origin, to maximize research productivity and departmental quality. A second goal, not always in harmony, is to find economical ways to staff academic laboratories and classrooms. Similarly, a goal for many administrators, particularly at state-supported institutions, is to provide educational and research opportunities for students who are from that state and are likely to remain there and contribute to the state's economy after graduation. A goal for policy makers at the national level is to attract larger numbers of US citizens into S&E, especially among women and underrepresented minority groups.[1]

The purpose of this study, therefore, was to recommend measures that would both address those diverse goals and maintain the quality of the nation's S&E enterprise in the face of new trends. Implementing such mea-

---

[1]See, for example, John Hennessey, Susan Hockfield, and Shirley Tilghman. 2005. "Women in science: The real issue." *The Boston Globe* (February 12).

sures will be possible only with mutual understanding and cooperation between those who set national-security policies and those who educate and employ scientists and engineers.

To carry out the work of the study, COSEPUP selected an ad hoc committee made up of people with special expertise in the demographic and personnel aspects of the S&E workforce and with wide research and educational experience in public and private universities, the private sector, professional societies, and government service. The committee heard from numerous experts and participants in diverse educational and research fields, from government agencies, and from persons who provided data on the recruitment, career paths, and motivations of international students. It also discussed in depth the recent effects of post-9/11 federal policy changes on the flow of foreign-born scientists and engineers and on the traditional perception of the United States as a welcoming destination for international students and scholars.

In its attempt to address the diverse trends and conditions embraced by these topics, the committee focused its deliberations on three central questions:

• How can the United States best improve the openness and mobility that characterize scientific activity while addressing concerns about the economy and national security?

• To what extent does the United States depend on international graduate students and postdoctoral scholars to maintain the excellence of its research and development enterprise?

• How can the United States optimize the participation of domestic students and at the same time recruit the best international talent?

The details of the committee's findings and recommendations are found in Chapter 5. Their overall thrust is to provide a basis for clarifying priorities and, where necessary, reshaping the sometimes contradictory policies that govern the movement and activities of international scientists and engineers, particularly with respect to visa and immigration policy. The committee became convinced during the course of its work that such measures are essential to ensure the continued high quality of the US S&E enterprise in the years to come.

In conclusion, I would like to add a personal note of thanks to the dedicated and responsive members of the ad hoc committee responsible for this report. They brought to this project, in addition to long experience and good judgment, an exemplary degree of promptness and thoroughness in responding to staff queries and vetting successive chapter drafts. The accuracy and perspective of the text were further enhanced by the work of an external review committee and by feedback from National Academies staff members with expertise on this topic.

Phillip A. Griffiths, *Chair*
Committee on Policy Implications
of International Graduate Students
and Postdoctoral Scholars
in the United States

Acknowledgments

This report is the product of the efforts of many people. First, we thank those who spoke at our three committee meetings. Their input was invaluable in shaping the findings and recommendations of the report. They were (in alphabetical order):

PHILLIP ALTBACH, Director, Center for International Higher Education, Boston College

BROWNELL ANDERSON, Senior Associate Vice President, Medical Education, Association of American Medical Colleges

JACQUELYN BEDNARZ, Special Advisor, International Policy Office, Border and Transportation Security Directorate, Department of Homeland Security

PEGGY BLUMENTHAL, Vice President for Educational Services, Institute of International Education

HEATH BROWN, Director of Public Policy and Research, Council of Graduate Schools

THERESA CARDINAL BROWN, Director of Immigration Policy, US Chamber of Commerce

PHILIP CHEN, Senior Advisor to the Deputy Director for Intramural Research, National Institutes of Health

GEOFF DAVIS, Director, Sigma Xi Postdoc Survey

TONY EDSON, Managing Director, Directorate of Visa Services, Bureau of Consular Affairs, Department of State

MICHAEL FINN, Senior Economist, Oak Ridge Associated Universities

ADRIA GALLUP-BLACK, Director of Research and Evaluation, Institute of International Education

SUSAN GEARY, Deputy Director, Student and Exchange Visitor Program, US Immigration and Customs Enforcement, Department of Homeland Security

SUSAN GERBI, George Eggleston Professor of Biochemistry and Chair, Department of Molecular Biology, Cell Biology and Biochemistry, Brown University

RALPH GOMORY, President, Alfred P. Sloan Foundation

JEFFREY GORSKY, Legal Advisory Opinion Section, Visa Office, Bureau of Consular Affairs, US Department of State

DAN GUAGLIANONE, Senior Director, Recruiting and Staffing, Merck Research Laboratories

GORDON HAMMES, University Distinguished Service Professor of Biochemistry, Duke University Medical Center

CHRISTOPHER HARTMANN, Staff Officer, Representative Rush Holt's Office

DIANA HICKS, Chair, School of Public Policy, Georgia Institute of Technology

RON HIRA, Assistant Professor of Public Policy, Rochester Institute of Technology

ROSALYN HOBSON, Economic Growth Agriculture and Trade and Office of Education, US Agency for International Development

JANICE JACOBS, Deputy Assistant Secretary of Visa Affairs, Department of State

VICTOR JOHNSON, Director, Public Policy Department, National Association of Foreign Student Advisors: Association of International Educators

DEVESH KAPUR, Frederick Danziger Associate Professor of Government, Harvard University

MARY KAVANAGH, Counselor, Science, Technology, and Education, European Union, Delegation of the European Commission

GEORGE LANGFORD, Professor, Ernest Everett Just Professor of Natural Sciences, Dartmouth College; Cochair, Workforce Committee, National Science Board

JOHN LAWRENCE, Democratic Staff Director, Committee on Education and the Workforce, US House of Representatives

CAROL MANAHAN, Executive Board Chair, National Postdoctoral Association

R.A. MASHELKAR, Director, Council of Scientific Industrial Research and President, Indian Academy of Sciences

KATHIE BAILEY MATHAE, Federal Relations Officer, Association of American Universities

LORD ROBERT MAY, President, Royal Society of London

DENIS MEARES, Senior Consultant, Planning and Research Branch, IDP Education Australia

PATRICK MULVEY, Technical Research Associate, Statistical Research Center, American Institute of Physics

JOHN NORCINI, President and CEO, Foundation for Advancement of International Medical Education and Research

PHILLIP OSDOBY, Chair, Career and Training Opportunities Committee, Federation of American Societies of Experimental Biology

DAVID PAYNE, Executive Director, Graduate Record Examination Program, Educational Testing Service

WILLIAM PULLEYBLANK, T.J. Watson Research Center, IBM Corporation

MARK REGETS, Senior Analyst, Science Resources Statistics, National Science Foundation

FAZAL RIZVI, Professor of Educational Policy Studies at the University of Illinois Urbana-Champagne and Former Pro Vice-Chancellor (International), Royal Melbourne Institute of Technology

DEREK SCHOLES, Chair, International Postdoctoral Committee, National Postdoctoral Association

ADRIENNE SPONBERG, Director of Public Policy, American Institute of Biological Sciences

CRISTIN SPRINGET, Economic Growth Agriculture and Trade and Office of Education, US Agency for International Development

DEBRA STEWART, President, Council of Graduate Schools

C. STEWART VERDERY, Assistant Secretary, Border and Transportation Security Policy and Planning, Department of Homeland Security

JULIA WARNER, Science Policy Fellow, Office of Legislative and Government Affairs, American Chemical Society

JEFF WHEELER, Staffing Market Intelligence, Intel

JIN XIAOMING, Minister, Science and Technology Office, Embassy of the People's Republic of China in Washington, DC

DOROTHY ZINBERG, Lecturer on Public Policy, Kennedy School of Government, Harvard University

Next, we thank the reviewers of the report. This report has been reviewed in draft form by persons selected for their knowledge, expertise, and wide range of perspectives in accordance with the procedures approved by the National Research Council's Report Review Committee. The purpose of this independent review is to provide candid and critical comments that will assist the institution in making the published report as sound as possible and to ensure that the report meets institutional standards of objectivity, evidence, and responsiveness to the study charge. The review comments and draft manuscript remain confidential to protect the integrity of the deliberative process. We wish to thank the following for their participation in the review of this report:

PHILLIP ALTBACH, Director, Center for International Higher Education, Boston College

FRANK BEAN, Professor of Sociology and Director of the Center for Research on Immigration, Population, and Public Policy, University of California, Irvine

JAMES CARAFANO, Senior Fellow, Heritage Foundation

JOSEPH CERNY, Professor of Chemistry, former Dean of the Graduate Division, Vice Chancellor for Research, and Provost, University of California, Berkeley

JOAN FEIGENBAUM, Professor, Department of Computer Science, Yale University

MICHAEL FINN, Senior Economist, Oak Ridge Institute for Science and Education

JOHN GOLLAN, Dean, College of Medicine, University of Nebraska Medical Center

CARL W. HALL, Engineer, Engineering Information Services

DIANA HICKS, Professor and Chair, School of Public Policy, Georgia Institute of Technology

NOEMIE B. KOLLER, Professor of Physics, Rutgers University

IRVING A. LERCH, Director of International Affairs, American Physical Society

B. LINDSAY LOWELL, Director of Policy Studies, Institute for the Study of International Migration, Georgetown University

CATHLEEN MORAWETZ, Professor Emeritus, Courant Institute of Mathematical Sciences, New York University

WILLIAM Y. VELEZ, Professor of Mathematics, University of Arizona

YIXIAN ZHENG, Assistant Investigator, Howard Hughes Medical Institute and Graduate Program Faculty, Department of Embryology, Carnegie Institution of Washington

Although the reviewers had many constructive comments and suggestions about the report, they were not asked to endorse the report, the findings and recommendations of the report, nor did they see a final draft of the report before its release. The report review was overseen by Lester Hoel, L. A. Lacy Distinguished Professor of Engineering, University of Virginia, and Harold Shapiro, president emeritus and professor of economics and public affairs, the Woodrow Wilson School of Public and International Affairs, Princeton University, appointed by the Report Review Committee, who were responsible for making certain that an independent examination of this report was carried out in accordance with institutional procedures and that all review comments were carefully considered. Responsibility for the final content of this report rests entirely with the author committee and the institution.

In addition, we thank the guidance group that oversaw this project:

SAMUEL PRESTON (Chair), Frederick J. Warren Professor of Demography, University of Pennsylvania
BURT BARNOW, Associate Director, Institute for Policy Studies, Johns Hopkins University
JAMES DUDERSTADT, President Emeritus, University of Michigan
RONALD G. EHRENBERG, Irving M. Ives Professor, Industrial and Labor Relations and Economics, Cornell University
DEBRA W. STEWART, President, Council of Graduate Schools
SHEILA E. WIDNALL, Abby Rockefeller Mauze Professor of Aeronautics, Massachusetts Institute of Technology
JOHN D. WILEY, Chancellor, University of Wisconsin-Madison

Finally, we would like to thank the staff for this project, including Laurel Haak, program officer with COSEPUP and study director, who managed the project; Peter Hendersen, the collaborating board director from BHEW; James Voytuk, the collaborating senior program officer from BHEW who provided data analysis support; Alan Anderson, the science writer for this report; Shadeequa Miller and Judy Goss, who provided project support; Christine Mirzayan Science and Technology Graduate Policy Fellows Sarae Bausch, Christina Tat, Rachel MacCoss, and Richard Yeh who provided research and analytic support; S&T Graduate Fellow Eric Zimmerman for his help researching international mobility policies; S&T Graduate Fellow M. Crina Frincu for her work collecting, collating, and analyzing immigration data from the US Departments of State and Homeland Security; S&T Graduate Fellow Maike C. Rentel for her work translating documents and researching and writing report boxes; Alexander Gelber of Harvard University for his analysis and write-up of the Pew Global Attitudes survey; Charlotte Kuh, deputy executive director of Policy and Global Affairs; and Richard Bissell, executive director, and Deborah D. Stine, associate director, of COSEPUP.

Contents

xix

Figures, Tables, and Boxes

FIGURES

TABLES

BOXES

Summary

To maintain excellence and overall leadership in science and engineering (S&E) research, the United States must be able to recruit the most talented people worldwide for positions in academe, industry, and government. That means that the United States must work to attract the best international talent while seeking to improve and invigorate the mentoring, education, and training of its own S&E students, including women and members of underrepresented minority groups. This dual goal is especially important in light of increasing global competition for the best S&E students and scholars.

The US population of scientists and engineers contains a large proportion of foreign-born scientists and engineers, a proportion that has grown rapidly over the last three decades. For example,

- In 1966, 78 percent of S&E doctorates were US-born and 23 percent were foreign-born. In 2000, 61 percent were US-born and 39 percent were foreign-born.[1]
- In 2003, international students earned 38 percent of the US-awarded S&E doctorates and 58.9 percent of the engineering doctorates.[2]

---

[1]Richard Freeman, Emily Jin, and Chia-Yu Shen. 2004. *Where Do New US-trained Science-Engineering PhDs Come From?* (Working Paper 10554). Cambridge, MA: National Bureau of Economics Research.

[2]National Science Foundation. 2004. *Science and Engineering Doctorate Awards: 2003* (NSF 05-300). Arlington, VA: National Science Foundation. Data are available at *http://www.nsf.gov/sbe/srs/nsf05300/tables/tab3.xls.*

- Among S&E postdoctoral scholars, the share of temporary residents has increased from 37 percent in 1982 to 59 percent in 2002.[3]
- More than one-third of US Nobel laureates are foreign-born.[4]
- Nearly half the doctorate-level staff and 58 percent of the postdoctoral, research, and clinical fellows at the National Institutes of Health campus are foreign nationals.[5]
- For S&E occupations, data from the 2000 US Census indicate that about 38 percent of doctorate-level employees are foreign-born, compared with 24 percent in 1990.[6]
- Of the S&E tenure-track and tenured faculty, 19 percent are foreign-born; in engineering fields, foreign-born hold 36 percent of faculty positions.[7]

International graduate students and postdoctoral researchers, many of whom stay in the United States after completing their studies, make substantial contributions to our society by creating and applying new knowledge. Yet the analysis of their contributions to the nation's leadership in science and technology and their effect on the domestic supply of scientists and engineers has not reached any firm conclusions. There is not agreement on (1) the benefits and risks related to our reliance on the many international graduate students and postdoctoral scholars in our research and development enterprise, (2) the appropriateness of current immigration policies that influence the flow of such students and scholars into the country, and (3) the relevance of a large international S&E population to broader concerns about economic and national security. The purpose of this study is to examine the available evidence on these questions and to suggest foundations for sound policy making.

In the advent of increased security concerns after September 11, 2001,

---

[3]National Science Foundation. 2004. *Survey of Graduate Students and Postdoctorates 2002*. Arlington, VA: National Science Foundation.

[4]Chronology of Nobel Prize winners in Physics, Chemistry, and Physiology or Medicine Web site. *Nobel e-Museum–The Official Web Site of the Nobel Foundation, http://www.nobel.se/index.html.*

[5]Philip Chen, Senior Advisor to the Deputy Director for Intramural Research, NIH, presentation to committee, Washington DC, October 12, 2004. The legislative authorities in the Public Health Service Act permit NIH to "employ" citizens from any country. Other national laboratories are limited by appropriations law to employ only US citizens or nationals of an "aligned" nation (such as a NATO country).

[6]US Census 1990 and 2000 Public Use Microdata Samples (PUMS).

[7]National Science Board. *Science and Engineering Indicators, 2004* (NSB 04-1a). Arlington, VA: National Science Foundation, Table 5-25. Data are available at *http://www.nsf.gov/sbe/srs/seind04/pdf/volume2.pdf*. Note that in 2001, 57 percent of those who were foreign-born S&E doctorate holders were US citizens.

the country has made it more difficult for international students and scholars to come to the United States, in part because of the concern of some that they may receive education and training in sensitive US civilian and military technologic fields.[8] Others argue that mobility restrictions will diminish US leadership in higher education and adversely affect American S&E expertise that is critical to national security and the growth of the economy.[9]

International students contribute to US society not only academically and economically, but also by fostering the global and cultural knowledge and understanding necessary for effective US leadership, competitiveness, and security. Some of the world's most prominent leaders were educated in the United States.[10] Secretary of State Colin Powell commented that "international students and scholars benefit from engagement with our society and academic institutions and we benefit enormously from their interaction with our society as they help our citizens develop understanding and knowledge that enriches our lives, increases international cooperation, enhances our national security, and improves our economic competitiveness."[11]

The United States is not alone in seeking talented scientists and engineers. There is a global competition for the best S&E students and scholars. The European Union (EU) and China, among others, are increasing investments in S&E R&D infrastructure. The EU has created explicit regional policies to improve the climate for international scientists and engineers, and individual nations—including the United Kingdom and Canada—actively recruit international graduate students to their universities.

At the same time that the United States faces increasing competition

---

[8]Offices of Inspector General of the Departments of Commerce, Defense, Energy, Homeland Security, and State, and Central Intelligence Agency. 2004. *Interagency Review of Foreign National Access to Sensitive Technology* Report No. D-2004-062. Washington, DC:OIG.

[9]In a speech on the impact of terrorism delivered at the State University of New York, Sherwood Boehlert, chair of the House Science Committee, stated: "Foreign students who remain here are absolutely critical elements of our science and technology workforce, and those who return home often increase the goodwill toward the United States in their home countries." (Speech to SUNY Presidents on the Impact of Terrorism on R&D, *http://www.house.gov/science*). Also, President George W. Bush has stated: "The United States benefits greatly from international students who study in our country. The United States Government shall continue to foster and support international students." Homeland Security Presidential Directive 2, October 29, 2001.

[10]US educational and exchange programs have produced over 40 Nobel prize honorees, among them current UN Secretary Kofi Annan; 46 current and 165 former heads of government and chiefs of state came here to study as exchange visitors. Allen E. Goodman. 2002. "Rethinking Foreign Students." *National Review* (June 18).

[11]Statement from Colin L Powell, Secretary of State regarding International Education Week, November 15-19, 2004, Washington, DC. Available at *http://exchanges.state.gov/iew/statements/powell.htm*.

from abroad, its own students are increasingly turning to non-S&E careers. Numerous studies have indicated several factors, often field-specific, that can influence domestic students' career choices: the length of graduate education, whether postdoctoral training is necessary, lack of growth of tenure-track faculty positions and uncertainty in research funding, and more attractive career opportunities in other fields. Little is known about the interaction between the flow of international talent to the United States and the decisions of US citizens and permanent residents to choose S&E careers. Students in Europe and in countries that have almost no foreign students—including China, India, and Singapore—are increasingly choosing fields of study outside S&E, a trend ascribed to declining job opportunities for classically trained scientists and engineers in these countries.[12]

Student and postdoctoral training has become part of the larger phenomenon of globalization of science and technology R&D that brings its own questions: How essential is it for the United States to maintain its broad leadership in S&E? To introduce incentives to increase the interest of its own students in S&E fields? To remain the destination of choice for the best international students?

As the tide of S&E expertise rises around the world, it is in the nation's interest to understand better the contribution of international scientists and engineers to the US economy and national security, create policies that can sustain this contribution, and find ways to attract more US citizens to careers in S&E.

FINDINGS AND RECOMMENDATIONS

In general terms, the committee believes that it is essential to the national interest of the United States to maintain its excellence and overall leadership in S&E research and education so that it can maintain its own comparative advantage with respect to global knowledge production. Talented people are a critical input in such a knowledge-driven economy. At present, the strategy of the United States is to draw heavily from international human resources. However, as other nations have built up their S&E infrastructure, there is now more competition for these talented people.

In such a world, what policies might best serve the interests of the

---

[12]See, for example, N. Jayaram. 2004. "Higher Education in India." In: *Asian Universities: Historical Perspectives and Contemporary Challenges*, eds. P. G. Altbach and T. Umakoshi. Baltimore: Johns Hopkins Press, p. 94; and Weifang Min. 2004. "Chinese Higher Education." Ibid, p. 55. Jayaram writes, "The fact that good students are no longer taking basic science courses has seriously affected the academic programs of well-reputed scientific institutions such as the Indian Institute of Science (Bangalore), which has now come out with incentive schemes to urge meritorious students to take basic sciences at the graduate level."

United States and of S&E research in general? What actions can the US government and research universities take immediately to create such policies or to implement them?

The committee offers the following findings and recommendations in response to its charge:

1.   What is known about the impact of international graduate students and postdoctoral scholars on the advancement of US science, US undergraduate and graduate educational institutions, the US and other national economies, and US national security and international relations?

Finding 1-1: International students and scholars have advanced US science and engineering (S&E), as evidenced by numbers of patents, publications, Nobel prizes, and other quantitative data.

Finding 1-2: International graduate students and postdoctoral scholars are integral to the US S&E enterprise. If the flow of these students and scholars were sharply reduced, research and academic work would suffer until an alternative source of talent could be found. There would be a fairly immediate effect in university graduate departments and laboratories and a later cumulative effect on hiring in universities, industry, and government. There is no evidence that modest, gradual changes in the flow would have an adverse effect.

Finding 1-3: Innovation is crucial to the success of the US economy. To maintain excellence in S&E research, which fuels technologic innovation, the United States must be able to recruit talented people. A substantial proportion of those people—students, postdoctoral scholars, and researchers—come from other countries.

Recommendation 1-1: The United States must maintain or enhance its current quality and effectiveness in S&E. A principal objective should be to attract the best graduate students and postdoctoral scholars regardless of national origin. The United States should make every effort to encourage domestic-student interest in S&E programs and careers. A study should be undertaken to examine the best policies and programs to achieve that end.

Recommendation 1-2: The overarching goal for universities and other research institutions should be to provide the highest-quality training and career development to both domestic and international graduate students and postdoctoral scholars of truly outstanding potential. Graduate admissions are directed toward fulfilling a variety of objectives, among which the education of the next generation of researchers should have the highest priority. This educational process will include research and sometimes a teaching experience. Admissions committees should keep in mind career and employment opportunities, in academe and elsewhere, when making admissions decisions. Moreover, data concerning employment outcomes should be readily available to both students and faculty.

2. What is the impact of the US academic system on international graduate students' and postdoctoral scholars' intellectual development, careers, and perceptions of the United States? How does it differ if they stay in the United States or return to their home countries?

Finding 2-1: The education and training provided by US institutions afford international students the opportunity to do high-quality, frontier research and to gain the experience needed to compete for employment in S&E occupations in the United States and abroad.

Finding 2-2: Many international students and scholars who come to the United States desire to and do stay after their studies and training are completed. Those who return home often maintain collaboration with scientists and engineers in the United States and take with them a better understanding of US culture, research, and the political system.

Recommendation 2-1: Universities should continue to encourage the enrollment of international students by offering fellowships and assistantships. Universities that have large international student and scholar populations should conduct surveys to evaluate existing services provided by the institutions. Universities that do not already do so should offer orientation days for international students, train teaching assistants, update Web services, and provide professional development training for administrators staffing international student and scholar offices.

Recommendation 2-2: International postdoctoral scholars make up a large and growing proportion of the US S&E workforce, but there are no systematic data on this population. A high priority should be placed on collecting and disseminating data on the demographics, working conditions, and career outcomes of scholars who earned their doctoral degrees outside the United States. When combined with current data collected by the National Science Foundation (NSF) and professional societies, this should make possible a more complete picture of the US S&E workforce. Funds should be allocated for this purpose by Congress to the NSF or by nonprofit foundations to other organizations.

3. What is known about the impact of international student enrollment on the recruitment of domestic S&E talent in the United States? What is the

status of working conditions for international graduate students and postdoctoral scholars compared with their domestic counterparts?

Finding 3-1: Recruiting domestic S&E talent depends heavily on students' perceptions of the S&E careers that await them. Those perceptions can be solidified early in the educational process, before students graduate from high school. The desirability of a career in S&E is determined largely by the prospect of attractive employment opportunities in the field and, to a lesser extent by potential remuneration. Some aspects of the graduate education and training process can also influence students' decisions to enter S&E fields. The "pull factors" include time to degree; availability of fellowships, research assistantships, or teaching assistantship funding; and whether a long postdoctoral appointment is required after completion of the PhD. The evidence that large international graduate-student enrollment may reduce enrollment of domestic students is sparse and contradictory but suggests that direct displacement effects are small compared with pull factors.

Finding 3-2: There are substantial differences among S&E fields in training and career patterns. For example, in engineering, a bachelor's or master's degree is sufficient to begin a professional career; in the life sciences, doctorates customarily spend over 4 years as postdoctoral scholars before entering the workforce. In the physical sciences[13] and engineering, most students obtain careers in industry; in the life sciences, most work toward positions in academe. Such field-specific variations are not reflected in aggregate data.

Finding 3-3: International and domestic academic postdoctoral scholars express similar satisfaction with their training experience. But access to funding sources and employment opportunities is limited by residence status. There are variable discrepancies in stipends that favor domestic postdoctoral scholars in all fields.

Finding 3-4: Multinational corporations (MNCs) hire international PhDs in proportions similar to the output of university graduate and postdoctoral programs for their US research laboratories and often hire US-trained PhDs for their nondomestic laboratories. The proportion of international researchers in several large MNCs is around 30-50 per-

---

[13]The physical sciences include physics, chemistry, earth sciences, mathematics, and computer science. In each of those subfields, there can be divergent career interests among graduates; but taken as a whole, a position in the industrial sector is the predominant career destination among recent graduates, whether or not it was the desired career at inception or completion of a doctoral program.

cent. MNCs appreciate international diversity in their research staff and pay international and domestic researchers the same salaries, which are based on degree, school, and benchmarks in the industry.

Recommendation 3-1: So that students can make informed decisions about advanced training in S&E, career outcomes of recent graduates should be communicated to prospective students by university departments and faculty advisers. In addition to intensive focused research work, graduate education should encompass career preparation and the development of varied skills for successful careers in S&E. Universities should develop graduate education and postdoctoral programs that prepare S&E students and scholars for the diversity of jobs they will encounter. When it is appropriate, funding agencies should provide career-transition grants for early-career researchers. The committee encourages discussion among universities, industry, and funding agencies to explore how to expand graduate fellowships and encourage women and members of underrepresented minorities to consider education and training in S&E.

4. What are the impacts of various policies that reshape or reduce the flow of international students and postdoctoral scholars (for example, visas, immigration rules, and working conditions)?

Finding 4-1: The flow of international graduate students and postdoctoral scholars is affected by national policies. Among them, changes in visa and immigration policies since 9-11 have adversely affected every stage of the visa-application process for graduate students and postdoctoral scholars in S&E. Interagency cooperation and a willingness to work with members of the S&E community have helped to reduce some bottlenecks and improve procedures, but unfavorable perceptions remain and additional steps need to be taken. Some policies contribute to anxieties among international students and scholars and a perception that the United States does not welcome them. International sentiment regarding the US visa and immigration processes is a lingering problem for the recruitment of international students and scholars. Those environmental factors discourage international students and scholars from applying to US colleges and universities and discourage colleagues who would otherwise send their students to the United States. Recent improvements in processing time and duration of Visas Mantis clearances are a positive step, but extending visa validity periods and Mantis clearances commensurate with a period of study has not been uniform across nationalities.

Finding 4-2: Large drops in international applications in the 3 years after 9-11 caused considerable concern in the university community, but their effects on numbers of first-time enrollments of international S&E graduate students were modest.

Finding 4-3: The flow of international graduate students and postdoctoral scholars is affected by institutional policies. Universities have been responsive to the needs of international students. Many have offices dedicated to international students, and several offer orientation sessions before the start of the school year and teaching-assistant training and English-language courses. Steps taken by educational and exchange institutions have mitigated some of the adverse effects of visa and immigration policies by creating resources for international applicants and establishing earlier acceptance notifications to allow more time for visa-processing. Some universities have begun to reimburse admitted graduate students the $100 Student and Exchange Visitor Information System (SEVIS) fee.

Finding 4-4: Exogenous factors, many of which predate 9-11, affect the flows of international graduate students and postdoctoral scholars. Other countries are expanding their technologic and educational capacities and creating more opportunities for participation by international students. The natural expansion of education in the rest of the world increases the potential supply of talent for the United States and at the same time increases competition for the best graduate students and postdoctoral scholars. Economic conditions—including availability of university-sponsored financial support and employment opportunities—can affect student mobility, as can geopolitical events, such as war and political instability.

Finding 4-5: The inadequacy of data on international graduate students and postdoctoral scholars limits our understanding of the composition of the S&E workforce and of how it might respond to economic or political changes. Moreover, the lack of timeliness and coverage of data on US-trained and internationally trained scientists and engineers hinders our examination of trends and relationships among student flows, enrollments, economic cycles, and other factors. Congress and administrative agencies need better data and more analysis to craft better policies.

Recommendation 4-1: The United States needs a new system of data collection to track student and postdoctoral flows so that it can understand the dynamics and effects of shifting sources of talent. Funds should be provided to the NSF or other institutions to collaborate internationally to create a data system similar to a balance-of-trade account to track degree production, student and postdoctoral movement between countries, push-pull factors affecting student choice at all degree levels, and employment outcomes.

Recommendation 4-2: If the United States is to maintain overall leadership in S&E, visa and immigration policies should provide clear procedures that do not unnecessarily hinder the flow of international graduate students and postdoctoral scholars. New regulations should be carefully considered in light of national-security considerations and potential unintended consequences. Research institutions and the Departments of State (DOS) and Homeland Security (DHS) should continue their discussion on these matters.

a. Visa Duration: Recent policies to extend the duration of Visas Mantis clearances for some students and scholars is a positive step. We strongly encourage DOS and DHS to continue working toward applying those provisions to students and scholars from all countries.

b. Travel for Scientific Meetings: Means should be found to allow international graduate students and postdoctoral scholars who are attending or appointed at US institutions to attend scientific meetings that are outside the United States without being seriously delayed in re-entering the United States to complete their studies and training.

c. Technology Alert List: This list, which is used to manage the Visas Mantis program, should be reviewed regularly by scientists and engineers outside government. Scientifically trained personnel should be involved in the security-review process.

d. Visa Categories: New nonimmigrant-visa categories should be created for doctoral-level graduate students and postdoctoral scholars, whether they are coming to the United States for formal educational or training programs or for short-term research collaborations or scientific meetings. The categories should be exempted from the 214b provision whereby applicants must show that they have a residence in a foreign country that they have no intention of abandoning. In addition to providing a better mechanism for embassy and consular officials to track student and scholar visa applicants, the categories would provide a means for collecting clear data on numbers and trends of graduate-student and postdoctoral-scholar visa applications.

e. Reciprocity Agreements: Multiple-entry and multiple-year student visas should have high priority in reciprocity negotiations.

f. Change of Status: If the United States wants to retain the best students, procedures for change of status should be clarified and streamlined.

Maintaining and strengthening the S&E enterprise of the United States, particularly by attracting the best domestic and international graduate students and postdoctoral scholars, will require the cooperation of government, universities, and industry to agree on an appropriate balance between openness, mobility, and economic and national security. Making choices will not be easy, but the recommendations provided here define priorities, data, and analyses needed to determine substantive steps that will advance the vitality of US research and attract the talented people necessary to perform it. The key is to endow our research institutions and S&E labor force with the flexibility needed to respond to rapid changes in the landscape of our nation's S&E enterprise.

Introduction

Aknowledge-based society depends on the quality of its human resources, especially the scientists and engineers who discover and develop applications for knowledge. The education and training of scientists and engineers constitute one of the most vital tasks of a knowledge-based society. The quality of students and researchers determines a nation's innovative capacity and is the basis of economic competitiveness and national security.[1]

ATTRACTING THE BEST AND BRIGHTEST

Since World War II, the numbers of international students in US institutions of higher education have grown, although there have been dips and surges related to economic cycles, changes in immigration policy, and international political restructuring. In 1952, the student nonimmigrant F and J visa classes were established. Two years later, 34,232 international students were studying in the United States (1.4 percent of the total higher-education enrollment). A half-century later that figure reached 547,867 (3.9 percent

---

[1]National Research Council. 1993. *Science, Technology, and the Federal Government: National Goals for a New Era.* Washington, DC: National Academy Press; National Science Board. 2004. *Science & Engineering Indicators 2004* (NSB 04-1). Arlington, VA: National Science Foundation, Chapter 6.

of enrollment).[2] Among science and engineering (S&E) graduate students, the percentage rose from 20 percent in 1982 to 35 percent in 2002, and it is over 50 percent in some fields of engineering.[3] Recent estimates indicate that over half the postdoctoral scholars in the United States are on temporary visas, and almost half those scholars had obtained their doctorates outside the United States.[4] Thus, about one-fourth of US postdoctoral scholars have been trained in overseas universities.

Talented international graduate students and postdoctoral scholars are drawn to the United States because of the high quality of our research universities, the availability of stipends and research funding, the opportunities for employment after schooling, and an "open-door" immigration policy that allows foreigners to obtain nonimmigrant visas for study and in many cases to convert their student status to longer-term residence once their studies are completed. Through the years, international scientists and engineers have made substantial and often disproportionate contributions in high-technology firms, universities, national laboratories, and other sectors throughout society.[5] **Chapter 1** of this report presents data on graduate enrollments, postdoctoral appointments, entrance examinations, stay rates, stipends, and funding mechanisms that illustrate the often-complex interplay between student choices, educational opportunities, politics, and government policies.

OPEN BORDERS, SECURE BORDERS

Several events in the last few years, some of them shocking, have suggested that the nation's S&E enterprise might be weakened by declining enrollments and that such declines could occur rapidly. At first glance, for example, the terrorist attacks of September 11, 2001, appeared to have

---

[2]Hey-Keung Koh. 2002. *Trends in international student flows to the United States.* New York: Institute of International Education. The IIE, funded by the Department of State, collects data on educational exchange between the United States and other nations and annually publishes its *Open Doors* report based on responses from over 2,700 institutions.

[3]National Science Board. 2004. *Science and Engineering Indicators 2004* (NSB 04-1). Arlington, VA: National Science Foundation, Chapter 2.

[4]Mark Regets, senior analyst, Division of Science Resource Statistics, National Science Foundation, presentation to committee, July 19, 2004. Estimates based on *NSF Survey of Doctoral Recipients 2001* and *NSF Survey of Graduate Students and Postdoctorates 2001*; Geoff Davis, Director, Sigma Xi Postdoctoral Survey, comments to committee November 11, 2004.

[5]Paula E. Stephan and Sharon G. Levin. 2005. "Foreign scholars in US science: Contributions and costs." In: *Science and the University*, eds. R. Ehrenberg and P. Stephan, Madison, WI: University of Wisconsin Press (forthcoming).

disrupted at least parts of the international student flows on which the United States depends.

The awareness that at least a few of those responsible for the actions of 9-11 had enrolled as students in US institutions caused additional concern in many quarters of government and academe, generating calls for tighter controls on international student exchanges and proposals to restrict access of students from particular regions to specific kinds of research. The heightening of security consciousness, in turn, created a perception that the United States was not "a welcoming place" and raised a broad set of security issues that have long been debated in this country. Those issues were especially troublesome during the Cold War, when scrutiny of scientists and engineers doing research in "sensitive" fields, such as nuclear physics, prompted passionate debates about the proper balance between national security and the open communication on which scientific research depends.[6] The effects of visa and immigration policies on the global movement and work of scientists are the subject of **Chapter 2.**

SIGNS OF A BROADER TREND

The impact on international student interest in US graduate and postdoctoral programs caused by 9-11 and other recent events is still being debated. Recent enrollment figures do not indicate a lasting effect of those short-term disruptive events, and they coincide with much broader changes that began to appear long before 9-11. The changes reflect the strong desire of other nations to strengthen their own educational and research capacity in S&E, the effects of which can already be seen. For example, the US share of international students decreased from 36.7 percent of the world's total higher-education enrollment in 1970 to 30.2 percent in 1995.[7] The reasons for the shift are varied and include internal and external factors that are discussed in detail in **Chapter 3.** If this trend persists, the United States will be in a different, more complex world, where knowledge and human resources are shared much more widely with other countries.

---

[6]Jessica Wang. 1999. *American Science in an Age of Anxiety.* Chapel Hill, NC: The University of North Carolina Press; Board of Directors of the American Association for the Advancement of Science. 1954. *Science,* 120: 958; Committee on Loyalty in Relation to Government Support of Unclassified Research. 1956. "Loyalty and research" *Science,* 12: 660.

[7]Hey-Keung Koh. 2002. Ibid, p. 3. It should be noted that numbers of international students in the United States rose steadily between 1955 and 2002, so the decrease in the US market share indicates a large increase in demand for higher education.

ACCESS TO THE BEST TALENT

The issue for the United States, as for other nations, is that a knowledge-driven economy is more productive if it has access to the best talent regardless of national origin. Overdependence on international students may, however, leave the United States vulnerable to geopolitical and other shocks that interrupt international mobility. It is neither possible nor desirable to restrict US S&E positions to US citizens; this would reduce industries' and universities' access to much of the world's talent and remove a substantial element of diversity from our society. As discussed in **Chapter 4,** one way to explore the importance of international scientists and engineers is to imagine the ramifications of a gradual or drastic decrease in their numbers. A global system for tracking international flows of graduate students, postdoctoral scholars, and S&E researchers is critical for effective policy making.

Clearly, the issue extends beyond 9-11 in both substance and scope. This report attempts to address the longer-term question of how the United States can best compete with other leading nations that are already adopting national policies to attract more international scientists and engineers. **Chapter 5** summarizes the committee's findings on what we know and how much more we need to know, and it provides recommendations to policy makers for ways to maintain the nation's strength in the critical sphere of S&E.

DEFINITION OF TERMS

Several terms used throughout this report—*foreign-born, temporary resident, foreign,* and *international* students and postdoctoral scholars— refer to overlapping populations but are not entirely interchangeable.

Foreign-born: Graduate students and postdoctoral scholars born outside the United States. Some of these students and scholars may have become naturalized US citizens before or during their graduate studies and would thus be included in the "US citizens or permanent residents" sections of graphs. Permanent residents qualify for the same citizen-restricted federal grants as do US-born students and postdoctoral scholars and can be hired to work in industry and at national laboratories.

Temporary resident: Graduate students and postdoctoral scholars in the United States on temporary visas, usually F-1, J-1, or H-1b visas. These students and scholars are not eligible for citizen-restricted federal grants and in most cases cannot be employed as staff at national laboratories. Because F-1 and J-1 visas have work restrictions, people holding these visas have less flexibility in their employment opportunities than US citizens and permanent residents.

Foreign: Graduate students and postdoctoral scholars from different countries than where they are studying. Foreign students do not necessarily have to have obtained degrees outside the United States; the fact that they require visas to study in the United States qualifies them as foreign.

International: Graduate students and postdoctoral scholars who study in more than one country. This term is used throughout the report to indicate graduate students or postdoctoral scholars who have obtained at least high-school degrees or their equivalent outside the United States and have come to the United States to obtain graduate education or postdoctoral training. International students and scholars require temporary visas to enter the United States. The term is not restricted to students in the United States, however, and can apply to any students or scholars studying outside their home countries. With the trend toward studying in two countries and then settling in a third, the term seems to fit the current situation better than *foreign.*

1

International Science and Engineering Graduate Students and Postdoctoral Scholars in the United States

S ince World War II, the United States has experienced a steadily growing inflow of students and postdoctoral scholars from throughout the
world, most rapidly during the 1990s.[1] The increases have taken
place despite evidence that US graduate schools give preference to domestic
applicants.[2] From the 1970s, the strongest inflow of graduate students has
been from Asian countries (see Table 1-1). From 1985 to 2001, students
from China, Taiwan, India, and South Korea earned more than half the
148,000 US science and engineering (S&E) doctoral degrees awarded to
foreign students, 4 times the number awarded to students from Europe.

Scholarly visitors gained clear legal status in 1952, when the Immigration and Nationality Act first offered the F visa for those pursuing academic
studies and the J visa for exchange visitors. Today, the total number of
foreign citizens studying in the United States (including undergraduates)
has passed the half-million mark. The percentage of foreign representation
is highest at the doctoral level in S&E fields; in 2002, some 130,821, or
nearly one-third, of all graduate students enrolled at US universities came
from abroad (see Figure 1-1).

---

[1]National Science Board. 2004. *Science and Engineering Indicators 2004* (NSB 04-1).
Arlington, VA: National Science Foundation, p. O-12.

[2]Gregory Attiyeh and Richard Attiyeh. 1997. "Testing for bias in graduate school admissions." *Journal of Human Resources* 32(3):524-548. See discussion later in this Chapter.

TABLE 1-1 Number of US S&E PhDs Awarded by Selected Country of Citizenship, 1966, 1976, 1986, 1996, and 2003[a]

	1966	% of Total	% of Temporary Residents	1976	% of Total	% of Temporary Residents
China	84	0.7	5.2	20	0.1	0.7
India	338	3.0	20.8	532	2.9	19.3
S. Korea	73	0.6	4.5	147	0.8	5.3
Taiwan	168	1.5	10.3	544	3.0	19.8
Japan	51	0.4	3.1	91	0.5	3.3
Pakistan	42	0.4	2.6	29	0.2	1.1
Total: Asia 6	756	6.7	46.5	1363	7.5	49.6
Germany (*)	28	0.2	1.7	36	0.2	1.3
United Kingdom (#)	83	0.7	5.1	123	0.7	4.5
Italy	7	0.1	0.4	24	0.1	0.9
France	9	0.1	0.6	35	0.2	1.3
Israel	60	0.5	3.7	80	0.4	2.9
Ireland	3	0.0	0.2	7	0.0	0.3
Total: Europe 6	159	1.4	9.8	262	1.4	9.5
Total PhDs Awarded	11334			18250		
Total PhDs Awarded to Temporary Residents	1627	14.3		2750	15.1	

aData from National Science Foundation. 2004. *Survey of Earned Doctorates 2002.* Arlington, VA: National Science Foundation. (*) Germany includes East Germany, West

Despite the growing presence of international S&E graduate students and postdoctoral scholars, the data gathered by different sources on their numbers and activities are difficult to compare (see Box 1-1), permitting only an approximate picture of their career status and contributions. For example, few analyses accurately describe their impact on higher education, their research contributions to US industry (if they stay in the United States), or their accomplishments abroad (if they do not stay).[3] Nonetheless, the

---

[3]Terence K. Kelly, et al. 2004. *The U.S. Scientific and Technical Workforce: Improving Data for Decisionmaking.* Santa Monica, CA: RAND Corporation.

1986	% of Total	% of Temporary Residents	1996	% of Total	% of Temporary Residents	2003	% of Total	% of Temporary Residents
223	1.2	5.3	3074	11.3	38.8	2559	10.2	30.9
524	2.8	12.6	1324	4.9	16.7	801	3.2	9.7
417	2.2	10.0	987	3.6	12.4	972	3.9	11.7
809	4.4	19.4	1198	4.4	15.1	478	1.9	5.8
113	0.6	2.7	153	0.6	1.9	187	0.7	2.3
65	0.4	1.6	92	0.3	1.2	34	0.1	0.4
2151	11.6	51.5	6828	25.0	86.1	5031	20.0	60.8
63	0.3	1.5	171	0.6	2.2	196	0.8	2.4
84	0.5	2.0	116	0.4	1.5	114	0.5	1.4
48	0.3	1.1	75	0.3	0.9	111	0.4	1.3
38	0.2	0.9	70	0.3	0.9	89	0.4	1.1
92	0.5	2.2	80	0.3	1.0	55	0.2	0.7
16	0.1	0.4	29	0.1	0.4	26	0.1	0.3
262	1.4	6.3	341	1.3	4.3	591	2.4	7.1
18450			27275			25121		
4174	22.5		7929	29.1		8276	32.9	

Germany, and East and West Berlin. (#) UK includes Wales, Great Britain, Scotland, Northern Ireland, and England.

high level of participation of foreign-born scientists and engineers in US laboratories and classrooms warrants increased efforts to understand this phenomenon and to ensure that policies regarding their movement and activities are adequate. This chapter summarizes some of the effects of international scientists and engineers on the US S&E enterprise, economy, national security, and other national interests.

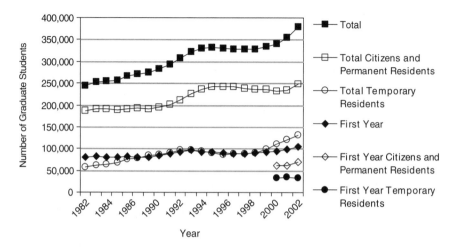

FIGURE 1-1 Total full-time and first-year S&E graduate enrollments, 1982-2002. SOURCE: National Science Foundation. 2004. *Survey of Graduate Students and Postdoctorates in Science and Engineering 2002.* Arlington, VA: National Science Foundation. Enrollment numbers include medical fields.

TRENDS IN INTERNATIONAL GRADUATE-STUDENT ENROLLMENTS AND POSTDOCTORAL APPOINTMENTS

The total number of S&E graduate students in US institutions has grown consistently over the last several decades; within that trend, the share of international graduate students has risen from 23.4 percent in 1982 to 34.5 percent in 2002 (see Figure 1-1). In 2002, international students received 19.5 percent of all doctorates awarded in the social and behavioral sciences, 18.0 percent in the life sciences, 35.4 percent in the physical sciences, and 58.7 percent in engineering[4] (see Figure 1-2).

A recent study further delineates the changing demographics of graduate students in US institutions. In 1966, US-born males accounted for 71 percent of science and engineering PhD graduates, and 6 percent were awarded to US-born females; 23 percent of doctoral recipients were foreign-born. In 2000, 36 percent of doctoral recipients were US-born males,

---

[4]Data are from the National Science Foundation. 2004. *Survey of Graduate Students and Postdoctorates in Science and Engineering (GSS) 2002.* Arlington, VA: National Science Foundation. Taxonomies are those of the GSS. Life sciences include biological sciences, agricultural sciences, and health fields; social sciences include psychology; and physical sciences include physics, chemistry, mathematics, computer science, and earth sciences.

BOX 1-1
Data Sources on Graduate Enrollment and
Postdoctoral Appointments

At least four organizations conduct graduate-enrollment surveys, but their results are difficult to compare. The National Science Foundation (NSF) fields the Survey of Graduate Students and Postdoctorates in Science and Engineering (also known as the Graduate Student Survey, or GSS). The Department of Education fields the Integrated Postsecondary Education Data System (IPEDS); the International Institute of Education (IIE), the Open Doors survey; and the Council of Graduate Schools (CGS), the Graduate Enrollments and Degrees Survey. The surveys use different sampling methods and request different information. IPEDS uses institutional and student self-reported data. NSF, CGS, and IIE use institutional questionnaires; questions cannot be easily compared. The definition of *graduate student* differs: IIE reports on all master's, doctoral, and first professional degrees; CGS includes only master's and doctoral degrees and differentiates by field, degree, and institutional type; IPEDS provides similar but more comprehensive data. NSF surveys graduate departments and counts only master's and doctoral program enrollment and doctoral degrees. Institutional coverage differs between surveys. Separate fields of study cannot be compared, because some surveys do not report on specific fields, and surveys that do may use different taxonomies. The most recent complete data from IIE are on the graduate class that entered in 2003; 2002 data are available from NSF, CGS, and IPEDS. For this report, we are using enrollment data available from the NSF Division of Science Resources Statistics WebCASPAR database system, *http://caspar.nsf.gov*. We used the IPEDS Completion Survey to examine master's degree recipients.

Numbers of postdoctoral scholars are available from the GSS. That survey does not provide much demographic information and it provides no information on where the scholars received a doctoral degree. The NSF Survey of Earned Doctorates (SED) provides some information on the proportion of graduate students who intend to go on to postdoctoral appointments, and the NSF Survey of Doctoral Recipients (SDR) provides longitudinal information on careers and conversion to citizenship. However, both the SED and the SDR follow only postdoctoral scholars who earned their PhDs in the United States. For postdoctoral scholars who came to the United States after earning a degree elsewhere—which some estimate at about 50 percent of the total postdoctoral population—there is very little information. We turned to the Sigma Xi National Postdoctoral Survey to get information on this population, but the survey was fielded only in 2004, so longitudinal data are not available.

---

25 percent US-born females, and 39 percent foreign-born.[5] Among postdoctoral scholars, the participation rate among temporary residents

---

[5]R.B. Freeman, E. Jin, and C-Y. Shen. 2004. *Where Do New US-trained Science-Engineering PhDs Come From?* (Working Paper Number 10544). Cambridge, MA: National Bureau of Economics Research.

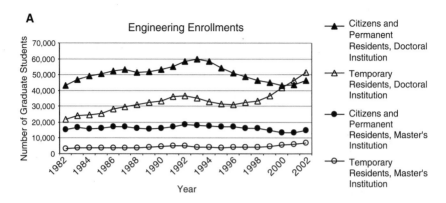

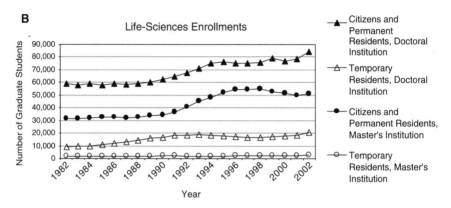

FIGURE 1-2 Enrollments by field, citizenship, and institutional type.
SOURCE: National Science Foundation. 2004. *Survey of Graduate Students and Postdoctorates in Science and Engineering 2002.* Arlington, VA: National Science Foundation.

has increased from 37.4 percent in 1982 to 58.8 percent in 2002 (see Figure 1-3). Similarly, the share of foreign-born faculty who earned their doctoral degrees at US universities has increased from 11.7 percent in 1973 to 20.4 percent in 1999. In engineering fields, the share increased from 18.6 percent to 34.7 percent in the same period.[6]

---

[6]National Science Board. 2004. *Science and Engineering Indicators 2004* (NSB 04-2). Arlington, VA: National Science Foundation, Appendix Table 5-24. Available at *http://www.nsf.gov/sbe/srs/seind02/append/c5/at05-24.xls.*

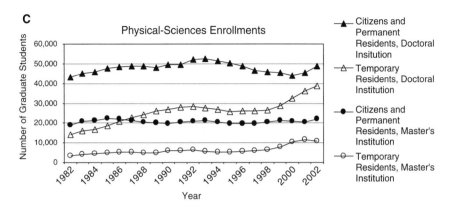

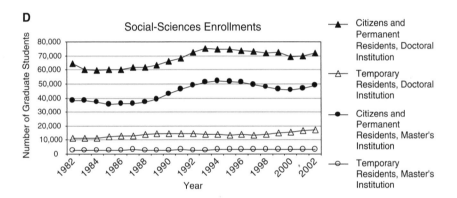

FIGURE 1-2 Continued

Quality of International Graduate Students

How can quality of international graduate students be assessed? Several factors play a substantial role in graduate-student admissions decisions. Among them are selectivity of the institution, applicant Graduate Record Examination (GRE) scores and undergraduate grade point average, undergraduate major, prior research experience, and quality of the applicant's undergraduate institution. The match between the research interests of the applicant and those of departmental faculty also plays a role. Studies show that many admissions committees make implicit adjustments in the GRE verbal score for applicants from non-English-speaking coun-

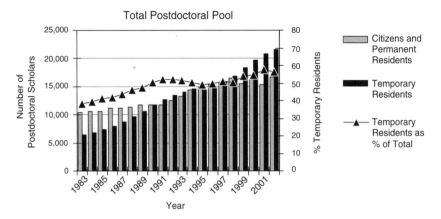

FIGURE 1-3 Academic postdoctoral-scholar appointments in S&E, 1983-2002.
SOURCE: National Science Foundation. 2004. *Survey of Graduate Students and Postdoctorates in Science and Engineering 2002.* Arlington, VA: National Science Foundation. Medical fields are included, but postdoctoral scholars with medical degrees (presumably acting as physicians) are excluded from the analysis.

tries.[7] Furthermore, GRE scores offer admissions committees a way to compensate when other measures of quality may not be readily available.[8] Whether GRE scores predict success in graduate programs is a subject of some debate. GRE test scores and undergraduate grades have been shown to have similar predictive power for first-year academic success but not necessarily beyond that.[9]

One measure is to examine enrollments of temporary residents vs citizens and permanent residents in top-ranked graduate programs, which presumably have their pick of the top-ranked candidates, and enrollments at less highly ranked programs. During the 1990s, when overall domestic-student enrollments in S&E graduate programs were decreasing, were top-ranked programs and less highly ranked programs differentially affected? If

---

[7] Attiyeh and Attiyeh. 1997. Ibid; MaryBeth Walpole, Nancy Burton, Kamau Kanyi, and Altamese Jackenthal. 2002. *Selecting Successful Graduate Students: In-Depth Interviews With GRE Users* (ETS Research Report 02-08). Princeton NJ: Educational Testing Service.

[8] Phillip K. Oltman and Rodney T. Hartnett. 1984. *The Role of GRE General and Subject Test Scores in Graduate Program Admissions* (ETS Research Report 84-14). Princeton, NJ: Educational Testing Service.

[9] Lisa M. Schneider and Jacqueline B. Briel. 1990. *Validity of the GRE: 1988-1989 Summary Report.* Princeton, NJ: Educational Testing Service; RJ Sternberg and WM Williams. 1997. "Does the Graduate Record Examination predict meaningful success in the graduate training of psychologists? A case study." American Psychologist 52(6): 630-41.

domestic students are of higher quality than international students, one would expect (1) proportionately more domestic students in higher-tier graduate programs, which presumably have their pick of students and which students, given the choice, would prefer to attend; (2) a majority of domestic students in higher-tier programs; and (3) under tight supply conditions for domestic students, such as engineering in the late 1990s, an exacerbated difference between higher- and lower-tier programs, so that even fewer domestic students are enrolled in the lower-tier programs.

Using program assessments from the 1995 National Research Council study, *Research Doctorate Programs in the United States: Continuity and Change*,[10] graduate programs in three fields— electrical engineering (EE), biochemistry (BC), and physics (P)—were divided into top-tier (first quartile) and bottom-tier (fourth quartile). Program enrollments from 1992 to 2002 were obtained from National Science Foundation (NSF) data.[11] Means ± standard deviations were calculated among programs in each quartile. In the few cases where graduate programs from the Research Council study did not match the NSF departmental data, these programs were excluded from the analysis. Each quartile included 20-30 programs.

The analysis showed that the difference between top- and bottom-tier graduate programs was not statistically significant. For all three fields examined, both top- and bottom-tier programs started the 1990s with about 60 percent domestic students; the proportions decreased similarly throughout the 1990s. One generalizable difference between first- and fourth-quartile programs was the standard deviation of the domestic-student enrollments. First-quartile program enrollments showed a smaller standard deviation for all years than fourth-quartile programs (EE: 1stQ, 18.3-21.3 percent, 4thQ, 18.4-25.3 percent; BC: 1stQ, 14.0-17.4 percent, 4thQ 21.0-28.4 percent; P: 1stQ 15.7-19.5 percent, 4thQ 17.7-29.0 percent).

Because the percentage of domestic students does not vary with program quality and this was not affected by tight supply, one can argue that the quality of domestic graduate students is not higher than that of international students. A caveat: if graduate programs fix, as a matter of policy, the percentage of admissions of domestic students, the proportions may not be a good measure of student quality. The committee found evidence that graduate-program admissions favor domestic students[12] but found no evidence that outright percentages had been established.

---

[10]National Research Council. 1995. *Research Doctorate Programs in the United States: Continuity and Change.* Washington, DC: National Academy Press.

[11]National Science Foundation. 2004. *Survey of Graduate Students and Postdoctorates in Science and Engineering (GSS) 2002.* Arlington, VA: National Science Foundation.

[12]Attiyeh and Attiyeh. 1997. Ibid.

Other research has shown differences in performance between international and domestic S&E researchers working in the United States.[13] While no significant difference was found in the number of grants, dollar amount of grants, or success rates in obtaining grants, in both normal and fractional count of publications, international scientists were consistently more productive than their domestic counterparts. These differences may be due to a strong incentive among international scientists to engage in research. Even if these international scientists were interested in activities or jobs other than research, their chances of getting them were lower than for domestic scientists.[14]

Recent Trends in International Graduate-Student Enrollments

For doctorate-granting institutions, total enrollment of international S&E graduate students increased dramatically between 2000 and 2002. In 2002, 55.5 percent of international S&E graduate students were enrolled at Research I (R1) universities; R1s also enrolled the highest proportion (26.0 percent) of international students (see Figure 1-4). Institutions enrolling the largest numbers of international S&E graduate students are shown in Figures 1-5 and 1-6. First-time enrollments of international S&E graduate students have been tracked only since 2000 by NSF and since 2002 by CGS, and data from both sources are available only to 2002.[15] It is therefore difficult to ascertain trends after 2002. In 2002, NSF noted a decrease in first-time full-time S&E graduate enrollments among temporary residents, by about 8 percent for men and 1 percent for women.[16] At the same time, first-time full-time S&E graduate-student enrollment increased by almost 14 percent for US citizens and permanent residents—15 percent for men and more than 12 percent for women.

---

[13]S. Lee. 2004. *Foreign-born Scientists in the United States: Do They Perform Differently than Native-born Scientists?* Doctoral Dissertation, School of Public Policy, Georgia Institute of Technology. These data pertain to researchers working in NSF-funded research centers, a specific population that may not be generalizable.

[14]H. Choi. 1995. *An International Scientific Community: Asian Scholars in the United States.* Westport, CT: Praeger; Joyce Tang. 2000. *Doing Engineering. The Career Attainment and Mobility of Caucasian, Black, and Asian American Engineers.* Lanham, MD: Bowman and Littlefield Publishers.

[15]As of April, 2005, CGS has published snapshot data on graduate applications, admissions, and enrollments for 2003 and 2004, and applications for 2005. The complete data for 2003 were not yet compiled, and 2004 enrollment data were not fully collected.

[16]National Science Foundation. 2004. *Graduate Enrollment in Science and Engineering Fields Reaches New Peak; First-Time Enrollment of Foreign Students Declines* (NSF 04-326). Arlington, VA: National Science Foundation.

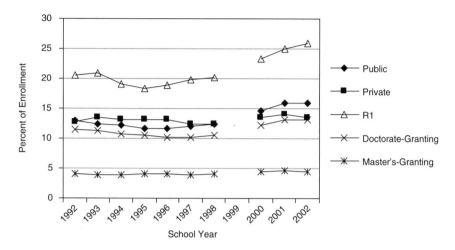

FIGURE 1-4 Enrollment of international graduate students by institutional type. SOURCE: Data are from the Council of Graduate Schools *CGS/GRE Graduate Enrollment and Degrees* annual surveys from 1992-2002. Available at *http://www. cgsnet.org/VirtualCenterResearch/graduateenrollment.htm.* The CGS enrollment numbers include all major S&E fields, as well as business, education, humanities and arts, and public administration and services. The non-S&E fields have 3 and 17 percent enrollment of international students. CGS states, "Institution type was a major differentiating variable in the enrollment of non-US students, reflecting the concentration of international students in doctoral programs in science and engineering."

The decline in first-time international graduate-student applications has stimulated considerable discussion (see Box 1-2) and more than a few warnings that our national S&E capacity may have begun to weaken. The picture for international graduate-student total full-time enrollments is different. For 2002, NSF reported an 8 percent gain in temporary residents enrolled in S&E graduate programs. That gain is smaller than for the previous 2 years (12 percent and 9 percent), but 2002 total full-time enrollment levels exceeded the annual gains for most other years during the last two decades.

What is the meaning of the declining first-time enrollment numbers for international S&E graduate students? Several interpretations seem plausible. First, the decline began from an enrollment peak that followed the atypical economic conditions of the late 1990s. One cause of the rising international enrollment of the 1990s may have been the lure of jobs in dot.com industries. Access to US jobs for foreign-born people is often much better for those who have been educated in the United States. Enrollments

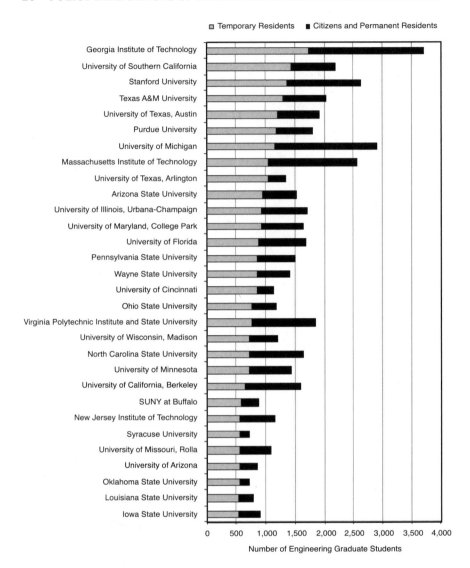

FIGURE 1-5 Top 30 Institutions for enrollment of temporary-resident engineering graduate students, 2002.
SOURCE: Data for Figures 1-5 and 1-6 are from: National Science Foundation. 2004. *Survey of Graduate Students and Postdoctorates in Science and Engineering 2002*. Arlington, VA: National Science Foundation.

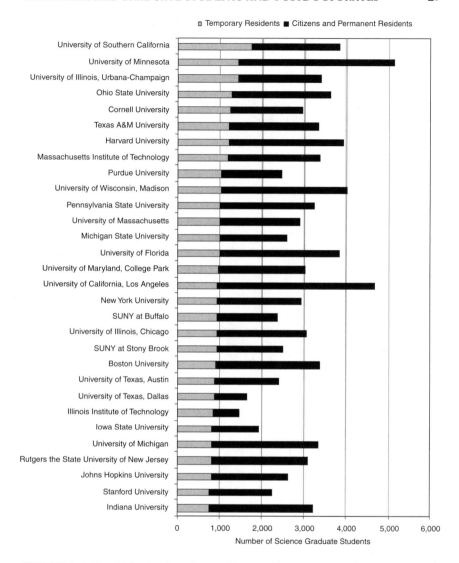

FIGURE 1-6 Top 30 institutions for enrollment of temporary-resident science graduate students, 2002.

BOX 1-2
Post 9-11 Graduate-Student Applications,
Admissions, and Enrollments

Since 9-11, the Institute of International Education (IIE) and the Council of Graduate Schools (CGS) have attempted to quantify the effects of visa and immigration changes on the flow of international graduate students and postdoctoral scholars. Both surveys have limitations but they provide potentially useful insights into recent trends.

IIE, supported by the US Department of State, has been collecting information on international student flows, including enrollments in US graduate schools, since 1950. Its *Open Doors* report[a] provides data on international students in all fields and visiting scholars who are teaching or conducting research on US campuses; it also provides data on US students abroad. IIE reports place of origin, funding sources, and fields of study of graduate students. Its fall 2003 and 2004 enrollment surveys did not break down graduate enrollment by field and included master's and doctoral students in business, engineering, science, and other fields. Retrospective numbers indicate that S&E fields represent about 40 percent of total international enrollments, but it is not possible to gather field-specific information specifically for graduate students from these snapshot surveys.

CGS has been collecting graduate application, admission, and enrollment data since 1986.[b] CGS surveys virtually all PhD-granting institutions in the United States and collects enrollment data by institutional type, ethnicity, sex, and citizenship. CGS gathers information on S&E fields, business, education, humanities and arts, and public administration and services, and it groups together as "other" such fields as architecture, communications, home economics, library sciences, and religion. It performed snapshot applications, admissions, and enrollment surveys in 2003 and 2004, but the most recent complete data publicly available are from 2002.

On the basis of these snapshot surveys, CGS reported substantial decreases in international graduate-student applications and admissions between 2003 and 2004 (see Table 1-2 below).[c] International student applications and admissions to S&E graduate programs were among the hardest-hit. Most graduate students apply to more than program, so the application rate does not correspond with numbers of students. A drop in application rate may reflect the same total number of students applying to fewer schools and does not imply a drop in quality. This interpretation is supported by CGS data, which showed the later decrease in enrollments to be much smaller.[d] Total domestic-student applications and admissions did not change between 2003 and 2004, whereas enrollments decreased by 5 percent. Data from IIE indicate a smaller increase in first-time international-student enrollments than would be expected on the basis of previous trends.[e]

Data from the CGS 2005 survey of graduate-school applications indicate a 5 percent overall decrease in international-student applications between 2004 and 2005. Engineering programs saw a 7 percent decrease, life sciences programs a 1

TABLE 1-2 Change in Applications, Admissions, and Enrollments for International Graduate Students 2003-2004[d,f]

	Total %	Engineering %	Life Sciences %	Physical Sciences %
Applications*	−28 (−5)	−36 (−7)	−24 (−1)	−26 (−3)
Admissions	−18	−24	−19	−17
Enrollments	−6	−8	−10	+6

* 2004-2005 data in parentheses.

percent decrease, and physical sciences a 3 percent decrease.[f] The American Institute of Physics (AIP), concerned about anecdotal evidence that international graduate enrollments were declining after 2001, performed a survey of PhD-granting physics departments in 2003 to complement its annual survey of departments.[g] AIP found that the proportion of international physics graduate students, after rising steadily for several decades to a peak of 55 percent in 2000, declined by 10 percent between 2000 and 2002.

What seems to be driving the decline in enrollments is a mix of reduced applications and reported difficulties in obtaining nonimmigrant visas. For the CGS surveys, the three primary reported causes of the declines in international graduate applications, admissions, and enrollments were increased global competition for students, changed visa policies, and less-favorable perceptions of the United States abroad. In the AIP survey, during the year preceding June 2003, two-thirds of the PhD-granting physics departments and almost half the master's-granting departments reported that they had accepted foreign students who were unable to enroll because of visa difficulties.

[a] The IIE Open Doors report is available at *http://opendoors.iienetwork.org/*.

[b] The CGS graduate enrollment surveys from 1996-2002 are available at *http://www.cgsnet.org/VirtualCenterResearch/graduateenrollment.htm*.

[c] Heath Brown. 2004. Council of Graduate Schools' Report Finds US Graduate Schools Adjusting Policies and Procedures to Address Declines in International Graduate Applications and Admits. Washington, DC: Council of Graduate Schools (September 7).

[d] Heath Brown. 2004. Council of Graduate Schools Finds Decline in New International Graduate Student Enrollment for the Third Consecutive Year. Washington, DC: Council of Graduate Schools (November 4).

[e] IIE. 2004. "Survey of foreign student and scholar enrollment and visa trends for Fall 2004." Open Doors Report on International Educational Exchange, New York: Institute for International Education (November).

[f] Heath Brown and Maria Doulis. 2005. Findings from the 2005 CGS International Graduate Survey I. Washington DC: Council of Graduate Schools.

[g] Michael Neuschatz and Patrick J. Mulvey. 2003. Physics Students from Abroad in the Post-9-11 Era (Pub. R-43). College Park, MD: American Institute of Physics. Available at *http://www.aip.org/statistics/trends/reports/international.pdf*. Note that the small rise in physics enrollment noted by the CGS survey took place the year after the APS survey was fielded.

also may have been influenced by the increases in research assistantship funding for graduate students and postdoctoral scholars during the middle to late 1990s, led by a rapid increase in the budget of the National Institutes of Health (NIH).[17] The current decline, on the other hand, coincides with an economic recession and could be interpreted as a return from an unsustainable peak to a point on a long-term curve that had been rising steadily for many years.

A second possible interpretation is that the recent 3-year decline is the beginning of a long-term downward trend. It may be too early to justify that interpretation or to decide whether such a trend is a sign of weakening in US S&E. For example, there is no evidence yet that the quality of graduate students or the staffing levels in laboratories has suffered. S&E populations have always fluctuated and in ways that are seldom expected; it may simply be too early to discern the causes of the recent decline.[18]

Decline in Students Taking Proficiency Exams

Another factor to consider is the decline in international students taking graduate-school entrance exams (see Figure 1-7). Often seen as early indicators of student intentions, these numbers, too, have been declining recently. The Educational Testing Service (ETS), which administers several leading proficiency examinations for students, reports declines in the volumes of international students using its products. For example, the number of TOEFLs (tests of English as a foreign language) administered to students applying to US graduate schools has declined from a peak in 2002. In addition, the number of Graduate Record Examinations (GREs) taken by international students dropped last year. In India and China, the two largest-volume countries, the number of GRE test-takers fell by about 50 percent from 2003 to 2004. One interpretation of the decline is that fewer international students want to study in the United States. However, the decline in TOEFL volumes is likely to have been influenced by increasing competition from the International English Language Testing System (IELTS). The volume of IELTS users increased from 75,000 in 1997 to 475,000 in 2003,[19] especially as some countries with growing higher-edu-

---

[17]The NIH budget doubled from $13.6 billion in FY 1998 to $27.3 billion in FY 2003.

[18]One review of the NIH budget concluded that the dramatic growth of its budget did not result in an increase in new US doctorates or in the number of US citizens in postdoctoral appointments even while the number of international postdoctoral scholars was rising. Howard H. Garrison, Susan A. Gerbi, and Paul W. Kincade. 2003. "In an era of scientific opportunity, are there opportunities for biomedical scientists?" *FASEB Journal* 17:2169-2173.

[19]IELTS 2003 Annual Review, available at *http://www.ielts.org/library/AnnualReview 2003_v1.pdf.*

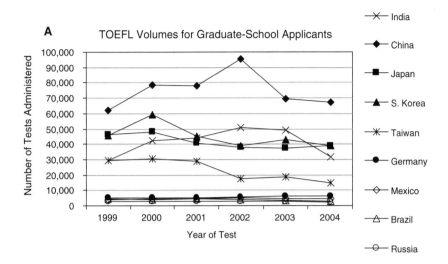

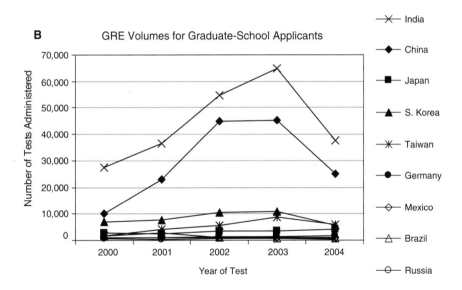

FIGURE 1-7 Graduate school entrance examinations.
SOURCE: Data are from the Educational Testing Service and are available at *http://ftp.ets.org/pub/gre/volumes_00_04.pdf.*

cation sectors, such as Australia, require its use and do not accept TOEFL scores.[20]

GRE volumes decreased in Asia after antifraud measures were taken in October, 2002. ETS learned that verbal portions of the GRE and some of the answers were being posted on Web sites in Asian countries by students who had memorized them. Replacement of the computerized test with paper versions that are changed with each testing date has decreased the number of students taking the test multiple times and may have discouraged some portion of less-qualified students from taking it.[21] In addition, Australia, Canada, and other countries competing with the United States for graduate students do not require applicants to take the GRE.[22]

Initially, some observers had ascribed the decline in volumes of TOEFL and GRE tests to 9/11 visa and immigration policies. However, although these policies may have had an effect, other factors, including competition for other testing services and antifraud measures, probably played a larger role in the decline. A lesson to be learned is that both test-taking and application to US graduate schools can be influenced by factors that may not be apparent at first glance.

International Postdoctoral Scholars

There is less quantitative information about the career paths and experiences of postdoctoral appointees than of graduate students (see Box 1-1 and the discussion of data needs in Chapter 4). Postdoctoral work has become the norm in the physical and life sciences and is becoming more common in other fields. The purpose of a postdoctoral position is to provide a year or more of stipend support to deepen training, complete publications, and otherwise prepare for long-term employment. Most postdoctoral scholars work in academe, and about 10-14 percent in other sectors, chiefly industry and the national laboratories. Little is known about the educational background, motivations, or career paths of either domestic or international postdoctoral scholars.

It is apparent that international postdoctoral scholars play an active and sometimes dominant role in academic S&E research. Their participa-

---

[20]The IELTS is owned, developed, and delivered through the partnership of the British Council, IDP Education Australia, ILTS Australia, and the University of Cambridge ESOL Examinations. IELTS scores are accepted by the majority of higher education institutions in Australia, Canada, Ireland, New Zealand, South Africa, and the United Kingdom and in early 2005 by over 380 universities and colleges in the United States.

[21]David L. Wheeler. 2002. "Testing services says GRE scores from China, South Korea, and Taiwan are suspect." *The Chronicle of Higher Education* (August 16).

[22] David Payne, executive director, GRE Program, Educational Testing Service, presentation to committee, July 19, 2004.

tion varies by field, as does that of graduate students. The most recent numerical analysis of the postdoctoral population in the United States from the GSS shows that the total number of nonphysician academic postdoctoral scholars in S&E fields in US institutions has almost doubled since the middle 1970s, from about 20,000 to 38,000.[23] In the most recent decade for which data are available, the numbers of postdoctoral scholars with temporary-residence visas increased rapidly, rising from 6,472 in 1983 to 21,601 in 2002; the number of US citizens and permanent residents in postdoctoral positions rose much more slowly, from 10,432 in 1983 to 16,715 in 2002 (see Figure 1-3). The growth in postdoctoral positions was largest in the life sciences, where total numbers increased from 9,494 in 1983 to 26,262 in 2002 (see Figure 1-8). Life-sciences postdoctoral scholars in 2002 represented 68.5 percent of the total postdoctoral population. The increasing propensity to take a postdoctoral position is not just attributable to the increased number of PhDs being awarded in the life sciences but also strongly correlated with the increased population of international graduate students,[24] many of whom move into postdoctoral positions.

Where Do International Postdoctoral Scholars Come From?

Two independent estimates indicate that of the 60 percent of academic postdoctoral scholars who hold temporary visas, about four-fifths have non-US doctorates, which means that half of all US academic postdoctoral scholars have non-US doctorates.[25] The scientific society Sigma Xi recently completed a survey of the US postdoctoral population that provides a demographic snapshot for 2004.[26] Sigma Xi found that 53 percent of re-

---

[23]These numbers include postdoctoral scholars in health fields but exclude postdoctoral scholars with medical degrees, who are presumably working as physicians. The figures in this report include only postdoctoral scholars at US academic institutions. In its report *Enhancing the Postdoctoral Experience for Scientists and Engineers* (Washington, DC: National Academy Press, 2000), COSEPUP inferred the NSF figure on academic appointments to be 73% of the total number of postdoctoral appointments.

[24]Paula E. Stephan and Jennifer Ma. 2005. "The Increased Frequency and Duration of the Postdoctorate Career Stage." *American Economics Association Conference, January 7-9, 2005, Philadelphia, PA.* Available at *http://www.aeaweb.org/annual_mtg_papers/2005/0108_1430_1204.pdf.*

[25]Mark Regets, senior analyst, Science Resource Statistics, National Science Foundation, presentation to committee, July 19, 2004. Estimates based on the NSF Survey of Doctorate Recipients 2001 and the NSF Survey of Graduate Students and Postdocs 2001; Geoff Davis, Sigma Xi National Postdoctoral Survey, comments to the committee November 11, 2004.

[26]Geoff Davis, director, Sigma Xi National Postdoctoral Survey Project, presentation to committee, November 11, 2004. Sigma Xi e-mailed a Web survey to 22,178 postdoctoral scholars at 46 institutions, including 18 of the 20 largest academic employers of postdoctoral scholars and NIH. Participants' postdoctoral status was verified by their institutions. 8,392 (38 percent) responded; 6,775 (31percent) completed the 100-question survey. For more information and nonresponse analysis, see *http://postdoc.sigmaxi.org.*

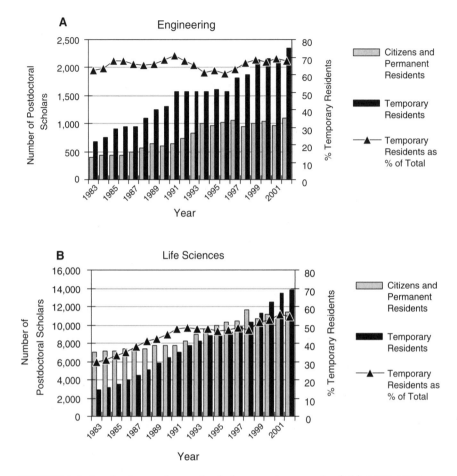

FIGURE 1-8 Academic postdoctoral-scholar appointments by field, 1983-2002. SOURCE: National Science Foundation. 2004. *Survey of Graduate Students and Postdoctorates in Science and Engineering 2002.* Arlington, VA: National Science Foundation. Postdoctoral scholars with medical degrees are excluded from the analysis. *Physical Sciences* include mathematics, earth science, and computer science. *Life Sciences* include biological science, agricultural science, and health fields. *Social Sciences* include behavioral science.

spondents were temporary visitors, 41 percent were US citizens, and 6 percent were permanent residents. Of the total sample, nearly half—46 percent—had received their PhDs abroad (see Figure 1-9). Citizenship and country where PhD was awarded varied by field (see Figure 1-10). Of postdoctoral scholars on temporary visas, almost 80 percent had earned their PhDs outside the United States. Of those with non-US PhDs, the

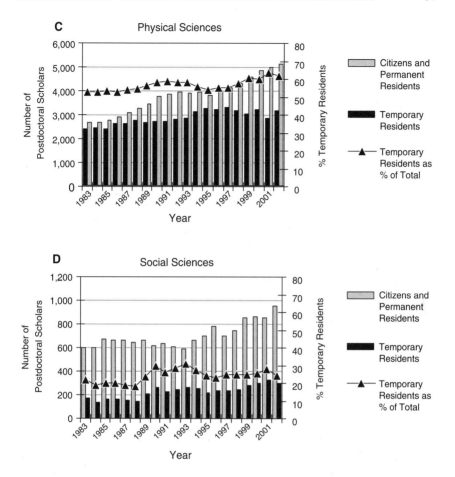

FIGURE 1-8 Continued

highest number came from China (25 percent), followed by India (11 percent), Germany (7 percent), South Korea (5 percent), Canada (5 percent), Japan (5 percent), the UK (4 percent), France (4 percent), Spain (2 percent), and Italy (2 percent). One conclusion that can be drawn from the numbers is that the United States is benefiting from an inflow of postdoctoral scholars who have received graduate support and training elsewhere.

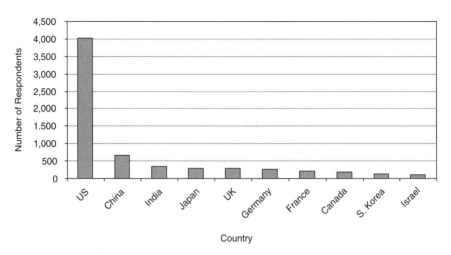

FIGURE 1-9 Where postdoctoral scholars received doctorates.
SOURCE: Data for Figures 1-9, 1-10, 1-11, 1-12, and 1-21 are from the Sigma Xi National Postdoctoral Survey. 22,178 postdoctoral scholars at 46 institutions were contacted, including 18 of the 20 largest academic employers of postdoctoral scholars and NIH. Postdoctoral status was confirmed by the institution. 8,392 (38 percent) responded; 6,775 (31 percent) of the respondents completed the entire survey, which included over 100 questions.

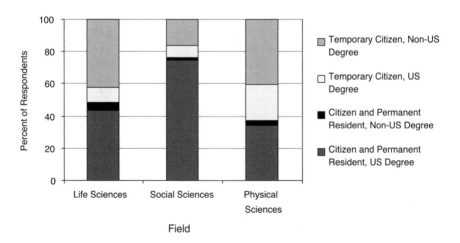

FIGURE 1-10 Postdoctoral-scholar citizenship, field, and country of doctorate.

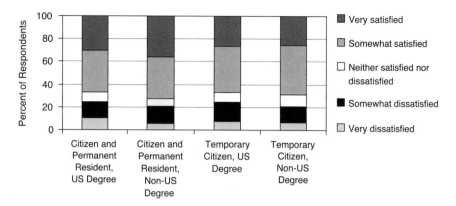

FIGURE 1-11 Satisfaction with postdoctoral experience in the United States.

The Postdoctoral Experience for Temporary Residents

Sigma Xi also collected information on training experience and compensation. International and domestic academic postdoctoral scholars expressed similar satisfaction with their training experience (see Figure 1-11). Temporary residents showed a greater tendency than US citizens to feel that their postdoctoral position was preparing them for an independent research position (see Figure 1-12). Access to funding sources and employment opportunities was more limited for noncitizens, and a significant difference in annual stipend levels was reported. Temporary residents earned 7 percent less than citizens ($37,600 for temporary residents versus $40,400 for citizens). Temporary residents worked longer hours and earned an estimated "hourly wage" ($14.52) that was 11 percent smaller than that of US citizens ($16.29).[27] The difference was noticeable by source of degree: temporary residents with non-US PhDs (41 percent) earned $3,100 less than citizens with US PhDs (43 percent). Similar differences in stipend support are corroborated by data on doctorates with US degrees from NSF's longitudinal Survey of Earned Doctorates (see Figure 1-13).

The Changing Balance of International and Domestic Scientists and Engineers

The numbers of US citizens and permanent resident graduate students in S&E fell between 1993 and 2002 at the same time that the numbers of

---

[27]Neither figure includes the instructional or training component, so they should not be compared with wages for employment.

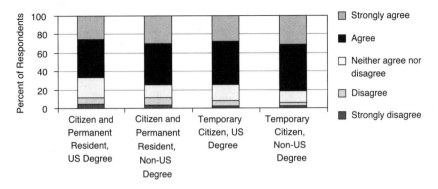

FIGURE 1-12 Preparation for independent position.

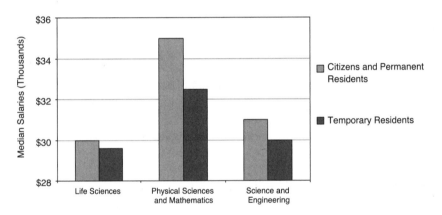

FIGURE 1-13 Median 2001 postdoctoral-scholar stipends by citizenship and field, for the 1999-2000 PhD cohort.
SOURCE: National Science Foundation. 2004. *Survey of Earned Doctorates 2002.* Arlington, VA: National Science Foundation.

international graduate students increased.[28] There is considerable discussion about whether the presence of high numbers of international graduate students in some fields can make those fields less appealing to US students

---

[28]From 1993 to 2001, for example, numbers of US citizens and permanent resident graduate students dropped by 10 percent (with numbers of white males dropping by 26 percent) while numbers of temporary resident graduate students rose by 31 percent. National Science Board. 2004. *Science and Engineering Indicators 2004* (NSB 04-1). Arlington, VA: National Science Foundation, p. 2-16.

and about how to encourage women and members of underrepresented minority groups to pursue careers in S&E.[29]

Some have suggested that students who complete S&E undergraduate work outside the United States are more knowledgeable and better prepared for graduate studies than are US students. Certainly, in many countries the approach is to provide a narrow, focused undergraduate education. International students with bachelor's degrees often take courses only in their major areas, whereas US students are required to take many courses outside their major areas. For example, in nuclear physics, less than 30 percent of US citizens had taken an advanced undergraduate course in nuclear science versus about 60 percent of international students. Furthermore, of US students in doctoral nuclear-science programs, only 5 percent had a master's degree, whereas over 50 percent of international students had completed a master's degree before starting doctoral work in the United States.[30] Even so, it appears that US students catch up in content knowledge by the second or third year of graduate study, and the time to degree does not differ between international and domestic students.

As the numbers of S&E baccalaureate degrees awarded to members of underrepresented minority groups has increased, there has not been a concomitant increase in graduate-school enrollments.[31] However, it is not clear whether women or underrepresented minority-students are being displaced or are choosing other career paths. An empirical study of admissions to graduate schools showed in the aggregate a substantially higher rate of acceptance of US citizens over international applicants, a modestly higher rate of acceptance of women than men in three of the fields studied, and a substantially higher rate of acceptance of members of underrepresented minorities over other US citizens in all five fields studied.[32]

More recent studies also find no evidence of displacement of women and underrepresented minorities in the graduate admissions process. For

---

[29]For example, see Shirley Ann Jackson. 2002. *The Quiet Crisis: Falling Short in Producing American Scientific and Technical Talent.* San Diego, CA: Building Engineering and Science Talent; Donald Kennedy, Jim Austin, Kirstie Urquhart, and Crispin Taylor. 2004. "Supply without demand." *Science* 303:1105; and National Science Board. 2004. *Broadening Participation in Science and Engineering Research and Education* (NSB 04-72). Arlington, VA: National Science Foundation.

[30]See: DOE/NSF Nuclear Science Advisory Committee. 2004. *Education in Nuclear Science: A Status Report and Recommendations for the Beginning of the 21st Century.* Washington, DC: Department of Energy and National Science Foundation.

[31]David R. Burgess. 1998. "Where will the next generation of minority biomedical scientists come from?" *Cancer* (Supplement) 83(8):1717-19.

[32]Attiyeh and Attiyeh. 1997. Ibid. The authors examined biochemistry, economics, English, mathematics, and mechanical engineering admissions at 48 leading graduate schools.

example, one study found no evidence of displacement but marked effects on educational outcomes, describing a negative correlation between the enrollment of temporary residents and US citizens in graduate programs. The most elite institutions saw the largest increases in temporary-resident enrollment and the steepest drops in enrollment of US citizens.[33] Those effects were statistically significant for white males but not for women or underrepresented minorities. It is not clear whether white males were deterred from enrolling by international students or chose other career paths for different reasons. For example, some may have been drawn to business careers during the dot.com and financial-services boom or to other high-paying professions throughout the 1990s, many of which did not require graduate training.

Additional evidence suggests that there is no displacement of US citizens from graduate programs by temporary residents. The number of PhDs granted to undergraduates from US institutions changed little during the 1990s while the number of non-US bachelor's-degree recipients obtaining US doctorates rose sharply. Thus, the large change in the proportion of citizen to temporary-resident graduate students was caused primarily by the expansion of PhD programs, with a majority of the new slots being taken by international students.[34] Another researcher calculated that an increase of one full-time temporary resident student in an S&E graduate department was not associated with displacement of US citizens or members of underrepresented minority groups.[35] Graduate application and admissions data from CGS (see Box 1-2 and Table 1-2) support these findings. In this "natural experiment" following 9-11, the number of international graduate-student applications and admissions fell dramatically. During the same period, domestic-student applications remained flat, and admissions decreased. If international students displaced domestic students, one would have expected to see a rise in domestic admissions instead of a drop.

Another study examining possible displacement of domestic scientists and engineers from S&E describes the importance of several other factors. First, the displacement of US citizen scientists and engineers occurs mostly from "temporary" jobs in academe, not from "permanent" jobs in academe. Thus, US citizens are losing academic positions that are less valued rather than highly valued. Second, the finding that displacement is largest

---

[33]G. J. Borjas. 2004. *Do Foreign Students Crowd out Native Students from Graduate Programs?* (Working Paper Number 10349). Cambridge, MA: National Bureau of Economic Research.

[34]Freeman, Jin, and Shen. 2004. Ibid.

[35]Mark Regets. 2001. *Research and Policy Issues in High-Skilled International Migration,* Bonn: IZA. Drawn from data from the NSF Graduate Student Survey, 1982-1995.

for those in mathematics and computer science suggests that at least in some fields US citizens were not pushed from the academic sector but rather pulled by better opportunities and higher-paying positions elsewhere in the economy.[36]

ECONOMIC IMPACT OF INTERNATIONAL GRADUATE STUDENTS AND POSTDOCTORAL SCHOLARS

Economists have debated whether the inflow of international scientists and engineers has a favorable or unfavorable effect on the US economy. Most of the research has concerned inflows of unskilled workers, who have constituted a rising share of US immigrants in recent decades. Those workers are thought to reduce the wages of domestic unskilled labor and contribute to rising wage inequality.[37] There is less evidence that skilled visitors have that effect.[38] Indeed, some researchers argue that a disproportionate increase in the number of high-skill immigrants will lower the wages of high-skilled US workers, raise the wages of low-skill workers, and thereby reduce income inequality. Although high-skill immigrants may reduce the economic incentives for citizens to enter high-skill fields, they do contribute to technology development and innovation. Furthermore, the researchers argue that children of high-skill parents disproportionately tend to be highly skilled themselves, creating a beneficial fiscal impact on future innovation capacity.[39]

---

[36]Sharon G. Levin, Grant C. Black, Anne E. Winkler, and Paula E. Stephan. 2004. *Differential Employment Patterns for Citizens and Non-Citizens in Science and Engineering: Minting and Competitive Effects* (Working Paper). Available at *http://www2.gsu.edu/~ecopes/foreignscientists/index.htm*.

[37]X. Clark, T. J. Hatton, and J. G. Williamson. 2002. *Where Do US Immigrants Come From, and Why?* (Working Paper Number 8998). Cambridge, MA: National Bureau of Economic Research.

[38]Borjas has indicated that an immigration-induced 10 percent increase in the supply of doctorates in a particular field at a particular time reduces the earnings of that cohort of doctorates by about 3-4 percent. About half this adverse wage effect was attributed to the increased prevalence of low-pay postdoctoral appointments in fields that have softer labor-market conditions because of large-scale immigration. At the same time, he suggests that a benefit of immigration may be the possibility "that the sizable increase in the skill endowment of the workforce accelerates the rate of scientific discovery." George J. Borjas. 2004. "Immigration in high-skill labor markets: The impact of foreign students on the earnings of doctorates." *American Economic Association Conference, January 7-9, 2005, Philadelphia, PA.* Available at *http://www.aeaweb.org/annual_mtg_papers/2005/0108_1430_1201.pdf*.

[39]Thomas MaCurdy, Thomas Nechyba, and Jay Bhattacharya. 1998. "An economic framework for assessing the fiscal impacts of immigration." In: *The Immigration Debate: Studies in the Economic, Demographic and Fiscal Effects of Immigration*. Washington, DC: National Academy Press, pp. 13-65.

Direct Economic Impact

Chapter 3 discusses the rise of global competition for students, especially among countries where English, the language of most scientific conferences and publications, is the dominant tongue. Some of those countries, notably Australia, emphasize the direct economic impact of international students, which, for economies of modest size, can be considerable. By one estimate, the inflow of fees, tuition, and living expenses from international students constitutes Australia's third-ranking services export industry.[40]

Similarly, NAFSA: The Association of International Educators has estimated that higher education for international students accounted for US revenues of $12.87 billion in the 2003-2004 academic year.[41] That figure is often cited in the press,[42] but it requires interpretation. The NAFSA figure applies to all international students at all levels of study and includes not only tuition and fees paid by undergraduates and professional students but also expenditures on travel, food, housing, incidentals, and the cost of supporting a family. The NAFSA number does not reveal the intricacies of subsidies and taxpayer support for graduate education. An accurate revenue and cost estimate would have to take into account not only types of funding but also sources of funding and determinants of tuition waivers.

Tuition and Fees

From the data on annual tuition, fees, and average support in Table 1-3, it is clear that overall, graduate students are receiving more financial support than they are paying in tuition.

State universities may recoup some of the graduate-student support costs by charging out-of-state tuition for international students. Although undergraduate and some master's students usually pay their own tuition through family or other sources, most graduate students do not. At the undergraduate level, international students on F-1 visas generally cannot obtain residence for tuition purposes and are therefore subject to nonresident tuition fees (NRTs) for the duration of their studies. US citizen and permanent-resident out-of-state undergraduate and graduate students are

---

[40]Simon Marginson, "Australian higher education: National and global markets." In: *Markets in Higher Education: Rhetoric or Reality?* eds. P. Teixeira, B. Jongbloed, D. Dill, and A. Amaral. Dordrecht, The Netherlands: Kluwer, pp. 207-40.

[41]NAFSA, the Association of International Educators. 2004. *The Economic Benefits of International Education to the United States of America: A Statistical Analysis.* Available at *http://www.nafsa.org/content/PublicPolicy/DataonInternationalEducation/econBenefits.htm.*

[42]For example, see Joseph S. Nye Jr. 2004. "You can't get here from there," *The New York Times* (November 29).

TABLE 1-3 Annual Revenues and Costs of Graduate Education per Full-Time Doctoral Student, 2000-2001

Tuition/Fees Paid and Average Support Provided per Full-Time Doctoral Student

	Tuition and fees paid[a]	Average support provided[b]
Public (in-state)	$4,243	$29,929
Private	$14,420	$47,129
Average	$8,070	$37,234

	Full-time S&E doctoral enrollment, 2000
Citizens	231,070
Temporary Residents	110,213
Total	341,283

[a]National Center for Education Statistics. 2002. *Digest of Education Statistics, 2002* (NCES 2003060). Washington, DC: US Department of Education, Table 315. Average graduate-student tuition was weighted by fall full-time graduate enrollment. These numbers include all doctoral-degree programs but not professional schools. NOTES: A rough estimate of the total investment in S&E graduate enrollment from state, federal, university, and private sources can be obtained by multiplying average support by S&E enrollment, yielding a figure of $13 billion.

[b]National Center for Education Statistics. 2002. Ibid, Tables 323 and 345. These numbers include all doctoral-degree programs but not professional schools.

frequently granted residence after one year.[43] In comparison, at the graduate level, many public universities grant tuition waivers to nonresident academic student employees, such as teaching assistants (TAs) and research assistants (RAs), but these waivers vary considerably by state, within state campuses, and even by departments within an institution.[44] If funding is available, individual S&E departments also offer to cover tuition charges, using research grant funds, to attract and retain talented international graduate students. Other funding sources include competitive fellowships and scholarships. Table 1-4 shows policies for several of the public universities with the highest numbers of international graduate students (see Figures 1-5 and 1-6).

---

[43]Jim Caufield. 2000. "UC nonresident tuition policy: long on numbers, short on vision." Commissioned by UCLA Graduate Students Association. Available at *http://gsa.asucla.ucla.edu/issues/nonresident.html.*

[44]Scott Smallwood. 2004. "Stipends for graduate assistants, 2003-4." *Chronicle of Higher Education.* (October 15). Available at *http://chronicle.com/stats/stipends/2004/.*

TABLE 1-4 Public University Tuition Waiver Policies for International Graduate Students

Institution	Regulation on Tuition Waivers
State University of New York at Stony Brook	Tuition charges waived[a]
University of Arizona	Tuition charges waived[b]
University of California, Los Angeles	No waiver for TAs; varying amounts of tuition charges waived for RAs depending on percentage of appointment. Nonresident tuition (NRT) is reduced by 75% for PhD students who have advanced to candidacy[a,b]
University of Florida	Tuition charges waived[a]
University of Illinois at Urbana-Champaign	Tuition charges waived for TAs and RAs with a minimum 25% through 67% appointment; the tuition waiver varies between a "base-rate" and a "full" waiver, depending on the graduate program in which the student is enrolled; the base-rate waiver is for the lowest, in-state tuition rate, and the full waiver covers the tuition as assessed, whether resident or nonresident[a,c]
University of Kansas	NRT waived for TAs and RAs with 50% appointments[a,b]
University of Maryland at College Park	No waiver[d]
University of Michigan at Ann Arbor	Tuition charges waived[a,e]

State and Federal Funding Sources

Like domestic graduate students, international graduate students are typically subsidized by federal, state, university, foundation, and other sources. Many are supported by research assistantships (RAs), with funding obtained by a principal investigator from government grants (such as from NSF, NIH, the Department of Energy, the Department of Agriculture, the Department of Education, and the Department of Defense) and corporate contracts. Others are supported by teaching assistantships (TAs) funded by universities, with funds from state legislatures for public universities or tuition and endowment income for private universities. TAs and RAs are working at low wages, so the calculation of how much they are subsidized

TABLE 1-4 Continued

Institution	Regulation on Tuition Waivers
University of Nebraska	NRT waived for TAs and RAs[b]
University of Texas at Austin	NRT waived for TAs, RAs,[a,b] and nonresident or international students receiving competitive scholarships of at least $1000; resident tuition must still be paid[f]
University of Virginia	Tuition waived for TAs and RAs with 50% appointments[a,b]
University of Washington	Tuition waived for TAs with 50% appointments[a,b]
University of Wisconsin, Madison	Tuition charges waived for TAs and RAs with 33.3% or 50% appointments (depending on department)[a,e]

[a]Scott Smallwood. 2004. "Stipends for Graduate Assistants, 2003-4." *Chronicle of Higher Education*. (October 15). Available at *http://chronicle.com/stats/stipends/2004/*.

[b]Jim Caufield. 2000. "UC nonresident tuition policy: long on numbers, short on vision." Commissioned by UCLA Graduate Students Association, *http://gsa.asucla.ucla.edu/issues/nonresident.html*.

[c]Graduate College, University of Illinois, *http://www.grad.uiuc.edu/issues/nonresident.html*.

[d]Personal communication.

[e]Office of Budget and Planning, University of Michigan, *http://www.umich.edu?~urel/gsi-sa/comparison.html*.

[f]Office of Accounting, University of Texas at Austin, *http://www.utexas.edu/business/accounting/sar/waivers.html*.

is further complicated. Smaller numbers of students receive fellowships or scholarships from various sources.[45]

The types of funding are similar for both domestic and international graduate students, but the mix of funding is different (see Figure 1-14), partly because of restrictions on access to specific funding streams. The

---

[45]National Center for Education Statistics. 2000. *NCES 1999-2000 National Postsecondary Student Aid Study* (NPSAS:2000). Washington, DC: US Department of Education. Tuition and fees are discounted for 75-78% of doctoral students supported by teaching or research assistantships. It should be noted that teaching assistantships cover only the 9-10 months of the term during which classes are in session. Research assistantships cover a full calendar year.

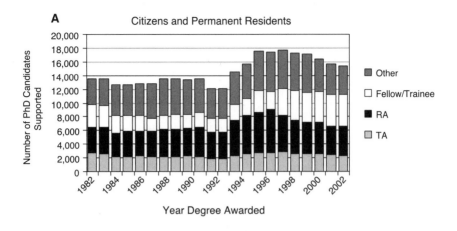

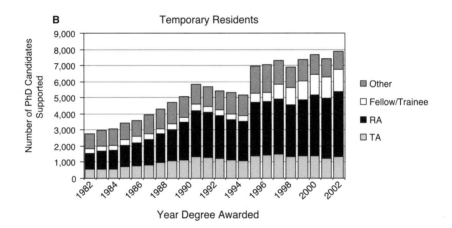

FIGURE 1-14 Primary mechanisms of support for doctoral candidates, 1982-2002.
SOURCE: National Science Foundation. 2004. *Survey of Earned Doctorates 2003.*
Arlington, VA: National Science Foundation. *Other:* support from the student or
scholar's institution of higher education, state and local government, foreign sources, nonprofit institutions, or private industry; *traineeships:* educational awards giv-
en to students selected by the institution or by a federal agency; *research assistantships:* support for students whose assigned duties are primarily in research; *teaching
assistantships:* support for students whose assigned duties are primarily in teaching.

primary support mechanism for postdoctoral scholars is the research grant (see Figure 1-15). Funding numbers for postdoctoral scholars are not reported by citizenship, but restrictions limit the access of international scholars to training grants and fellowships. This has a greater effect in fields with a high proportion of such awards, particularly life sciences and social sciences (see Figure 1-16).

The use of public funding to educate international graduate students has provoked controversy, especially in states whose legislatures have complained that such students may later move to other states or return to their home countries. Critics also list the incremental costs of educating international graduate students, including costs for recruitment, verification of credentials, international-visitor offices, English classes, and for some, early admission to allow time for acculturation.

Stay Rates of International Graduate Students

Clearly, both domestic and international scientists and engineers have an opportunity to make a lasting impact on the US economy. Their impact can be inferred from, if not proved by, their participation in US universities, industries, and national laboratories after they receive their doctorates. In total, foreign-born scientists and engineers were 22.7 percent of the US S&E labor force in 2000, an increase from 12.7 percent in 1980 (Figure 1-17). Representation of foreign-born scientists and engineers in US S&E occupations varies by field and increases with degree level (Figure 1-18 and Table 1-5). Foreign-born doctorates were 37.3 percent of the US S&E labor force, an increase from 23.9 percent in 1990 (see Figure 1-17).

Plans to stay vary by field and by when the PhD was awarded (Figure 1-19). One study found that 45 percent of international students from developing countries planned to enter the US labor market for a time and 15 percent planned to stay permanently; another 15 percent planned to go to a third country.[46] Stay rates appear to be responsive to economic conditions in the United States. For example, during the dot.com boom in the late 1990s, there was a surge of interest among international engineering doctorates in remaining in the United States. Similarly, the propensity for domestic students to enter graduate programs is affected by the job market, as seen by the rapid downturn in domestic physics and engineering graduate enrollments in the late 1990s (see Figure 1-2).

Another study has shown that the stay rate of international doctorate scientists and engineers has increased steadily and substantially in the last

---

[46]N. Aslanbeigui and V. Montecinos. 1998. "Foreign students in US doctoral programs." *Journal of Economic Perspectives* 12:171-182.

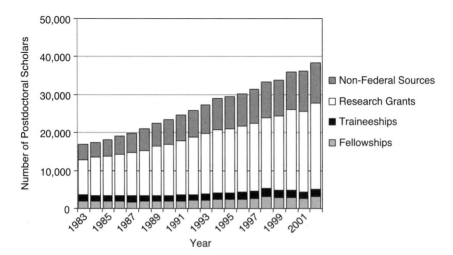

FIGURE 1-15 Primary mechanisms of support for postdoctoral scholars, 1983-2002.

SOURCE: Data for Figures 1-15 and 1-16 are from National Science Foundation. 2004. *Survey of Earned Doctorates 2002.* Arlington, VA: National Science Foundation. *Non-Federal Sources:* support from the institution of higher education, state and local government, foreign sources, nonprofit institutions, or private industry; *research grants:* support from federal agencies to a principal investigator, under whom postdoctoral scholars work; *traineeships:* educational awards given to scholars selected by the institution or by a federal agency; *fellowships:* competitive awards given directly to scholars for financial support of their graduate or postdoctoral studies.

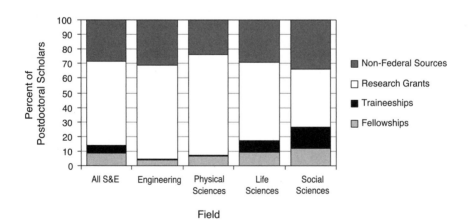

FIGURE 1-16 Mechanisms of support for postdoctoral scholars by field, 1998-2002.

decade.[47] The proportion of foreign-born doctorates remaining in the United States for at least 2 years after receiving their degrees increased from 49 percent for the 1989 cohort to 71 percent for the 2001 cohort.[48] The increased stay rate was due to an increase in the number of PhDs awarded to international students and to an increase in international graduate students deciding to remain in the United States after receiving their PhDs. Stay rates varied by field of study, country of origin, and economic conditions in sending countries. Stay rates were highest among engineering, computer-science, and physical-science graduates. Stay rates varied dramatically among graduate students from the top source countries—China (96 percent), India (86 percent), Taiwan (40 percent), and Korea (21 percent). Decisions to stay in the United States appear to be strongly affected by conditions in the students' home countries, primarily unemployment rate, percentage of the labor force that works in agriculture, and per capita GDP.[49]

Similarly, conversion to US citizenship shows field specificity. In most fields, the percentage of graduate students who were temporary residents at the time their degrees were awarded who later obtain US citizenship has been relatively constant since 1995; in engineering, the numbers of students obtaining citizenship show marked time sensitivity (see Figure 1-20).

The Sigma Xi postdoctoral survey[50] found that the United States was the most attractive place to settle for postdoctoral scholars of all nationalities, regardless of where the PhDs were earned. The exception was European citizens who had earned non-US PhDs, who preferred to return to Europe (see Figure 1-21).

---

[47]Although international student is usually taken to mean a student on a temporary visa, the figures sometimes include students on both temporary and permanent visas to compensate for the large number of Chinese students in the 1990s who became permanent residents under the Chinese Student Protection Act. This issue is discussed in greater detail by Finn (see next footnote), who finds the stay rate for those on temporary and permanent visas almost the same.

[48]Michael G. Finn. 2003. *Stay Rates of Foreign Doctorate Recipients from U.S. Universities, 2001.* Oak Ridge, TN: Oak Ridge Institute for Science and Education (ORISE). The stay rate was defined as remaining in the United States for at least 2 years after receipt of the doctorate, but Finn estimates that these rates do not fall appreciably during the first 5 years after graduation.

[49]D. L. Johnson. 2001. *Relationship Between Stay Rates of PhD Recipients on Temporary Visas and Relative Economic Conditions in Country of Origin* (Working Paper). Oak Ridge, TN: ORISE.

[50]Geoff Davis, director, Sigma Xi National Postdoctoral Survey Project, presentation to committee, November 11, 2004. Survey results available at *http://postdoc.sigmaxi.org.*

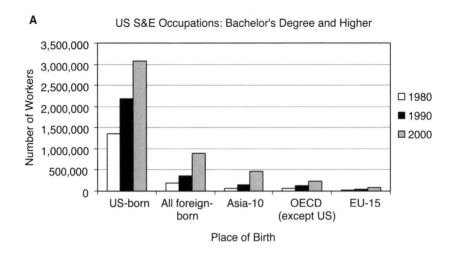

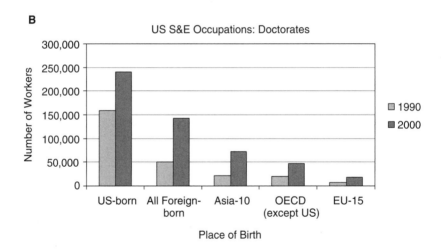

FIGURE 1-17 High-skill workers in US S&E labor force.
SOURCE: Data are from 1980, 1990, and 2000 US Census Public Use Microdata Samples (PUMS).

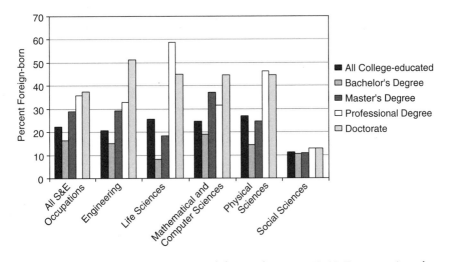

FIGURE 1-18 US Census estimates of foreign-born in US S&E occupations by field, 2000.

SOURCE: Data for figure and table are from 2000 US Census 5 percent Public Use Microdata Samples (PUMS) and include all S&E occupations other than postsecondary teachers, because field of instruction was not included in occupation coding for the 2000 census.

A Positive Impact on Innovation

Skilled migrants may contribute at many levels, as technicians, teachers, and researchers and in other occupations in which technical training is desirable. But some research suggests that they generate economic gains by adding to the processes of industrial and business innovation. Such innovations tend to contribute to future productivity gains of both citizen and immigrant workers, which result in a net increase in real wages. One study provides evidence that the immigration of skilled workers adds to local skills rather than substituting for them.[51] The authors' econometric analyses suggest that a 10 percent increase in the number of international gradu-

[51]G. Chelleraj, K.E. Maskus, and A. Mattoo. 2004. *The contribution of skilled immigration and international graduate students to U.S. innovation* (Working Paper Number 04-10). Boulder, CO: University of Colorado. The authors concluded, "Our results strongly favor the view that foreign graduate students and immigrants under technical visas are significant inputs into developing new technologies in the American economy." Also, immigration rules that permit immigration of the highly skilled, along with education subsidies, are sufficient to ensure new technology adoption, as shown by an exercise in theoretical modeling. P. Chander and S. Thangavelu. 2004. "Technology adoption, education and immigration policy," *Journal of Development Economics* 75(1):79-94

TABLE 1-5 Number of Foreign-Born in US S&E Occupations, 2000

	All S&E	Engineering	Life Sciences	Mathematics and Computer Sciences	Physical Sciences	Social Sciences
All college-educated	816,000	265,000	52,000	370,000	92,000	37,000
Bachelor's degree	365,000	132,000	6,000	197,000	21,000	9,000
Master's degree	291,000	100,000	10,000	146,000	21,000	14,000
Professional degree	25,000	5,000	8,000	6,000	4,000	2,000
Doctoral degree	135,000	28,000	28,000	21,000	46,000	12,000

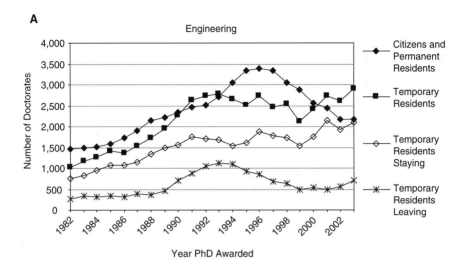

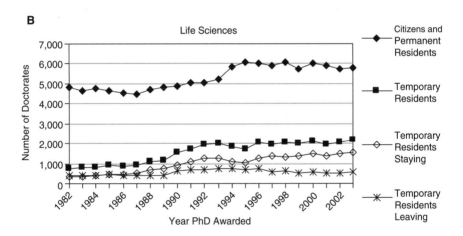

FIGURE 1-19 Plans to stay in the United States after earning doctorate, by field of study.
SOURCE: National Science Foundation. 2004. *Survey of Earned Doctorates 2002.* Arlington, VA: National Science Foundation.

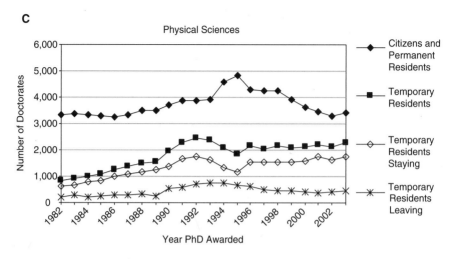

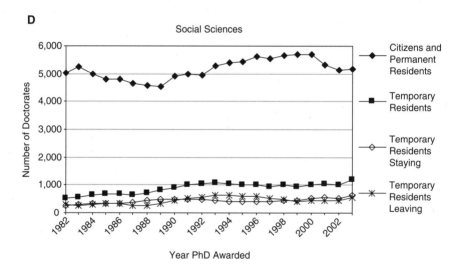

FIGURE 1-19 Continued

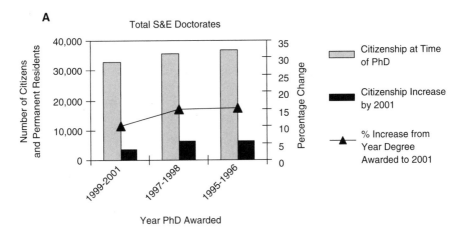

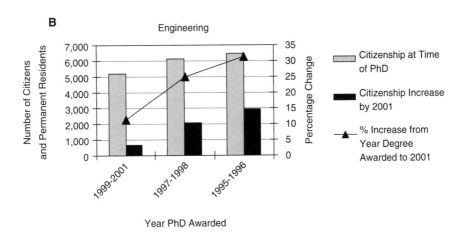

FIGURE 1-20 Changes in US citizenship among US-awarded doctorates in S&E.
SOURCE: National Science Foundation. 2004. *Survey of Doctoral Recipients 2002.*
Arlington, VA: National Science Foundation.

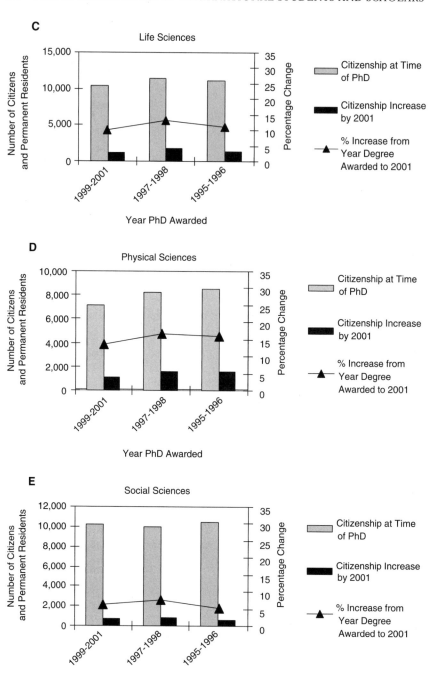

FIGURE 1-20 Continued

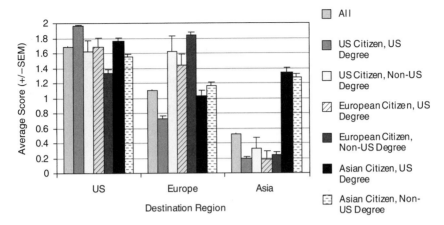

FIGURE 1-21 Plans of postdoctoral scholars to stay in the United States, 2004. SOURCE: Data are final results from 2004 Sigma Xi National Postdoctoral Survey. The question about settlement preference was asked of one-eighth of respondents, who were asked to score their interest on a scale of 0 = not at all, 1 = somewhat interested, and 2 = very interested.

ate students would raise university patent grants by 6.0 percent and nonuniversity patent grants by 4.0 percent. Taken in the aggregate, enrollments of US graduate students had no detectable effect in their model.[52] The authors concluded that bureaucratic hurdles in obtaining student visas may impede innovation if they decrease the inflow of international graduate students.[53]

An Impact Through "Exceptional" Contributions

There is evidence that the foreign-born and foreign-educated, at least in the recent past, have made a disproportionate number of "exceptional"

---

[52]Chelleraj et al. 2004. Ibid, pp. 27-28. The authors state, "Relatively open access to international students has allowed US universities to accept the brightest graduate students in science and engineering from all over the world. In turn, international graduate students contribute to innovation and patenting in S&E while domestic students do not in the aggregate. Presumably this is because international graduate students are more concentrated in such fields as S&E than are domestic students. Further because of work restrictions for international students, domestic students have greater opportunities to be employed in non-research activities in both university and non-university settings."

[53]Chelleraj et al. 2004. Ibid, p. 2.

contributions to the S&E enterprise of the United States.[54] Figure 1-22 shows that since 1990, almost half the US Nobel laureates in science fields were foreign-born; 37 percent received their graduate education abroad. A surprisingly large percentage of foreign-born scientists and engineers working in the United States were educated (at least in part) abroad, suggesting that the United States has benefited from investments in education made by other countries. More recent data (for example, the 2004 elections to the National Academies) suggest that a transition may be under way and that these conclusions concerning the foreign-born may not hold in the future.

Impact on Industry

The impact of international scientists and engineers on US industries, as measured by their presence, seems to be considerable. Skilled immigrants are highly mobile, and one study concludes that most technology industries in which they are concentrated are fast-growing exporters and leading contributors to the nation's economic growth.[55] At IBM Research and Intel, for example, about one-third of the S&E doctoral-level employees are foreign nationals.[56] Up to half the researchers in US automotive industry laboratories are foreign-born.[57]

According to one of the few available studies, 32 percent of all new PhDs with definite plans to work in US industry are temporary residents at the time of graduation. That is about the same as the proportion of temporary residents in the population of new PhDs. The proportion of temporary residents going into industry is highest in mathematics (43 percent), civil engineering (42 percent), electrical engineering (41 percent), mechanical engineering (40 percent), and computer science (38 percent). The largest

---

[54]Paula E. Stephan and Sharon G. Levin. "Foreign scholars in U.S. science: Contributions and costs." In: *Science and the University,* eds. Ronald Ehrenberg and Paula Stephan. Madison, WI: University of Wisconsin Press (forthcoming). The authors use six criteria to indicate "exceptional" contributions (not all contributions) in S&E: individuals elected to the National Academy of Sciences (NAS) and/or National Academy of Engineering (NAE), authors of citation classics, authors of hot papers, the 250 most cited authors, authors of highly cited patents, and scientists who have played a key role in launching biotechnology firms.

[55]AnnaLee Saxenian. 2001. *Silicon Valley's New Immigrant Entrepreneurs* (Working Paper No. 15). San Diego, CA: Center for Comparative Immigration Studies, University of California. Available at *http://www.ccis-ucsd.org/PUBLICATIONS/wrkg15.PDF.*

[56]William R. Pulleyblank, director, Exploratory Server Systems, IBM Research, presentation to committee, July 19, 2004; Jeff Wheeler, staffing market intelligence, Intel, presentation to committee, July 19, 2004.

[57]William Agnew, Director of Program and Plans (retired), General Motors. Summary of interviews with several high-level R&D directors from large global automotive companies, presented to committee, October 8, 2004.

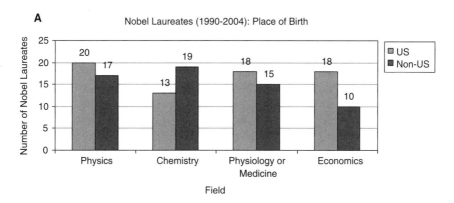

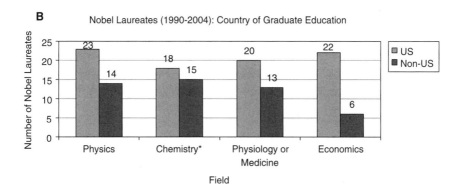

FIGURE 1-22 Exceptional contributions: US Nobel Laureates' place of birth and country of graduate education.
SOURCE: Data from "Chronology of Nobel Prize winners in Physics, Chemistry, and Physiology or Medicine." *Nobel e-Museum—The official Web site of the Nobel Foundation.* Available at *http://www.nobel.se/index.html.* Note that one laureate in chemistry had two PhDs.

number of foreign industrial hires among new PhDs came from China (nearly 10 percent of all industrial hires) and India (more than 8 percent of industrial hires). That is consistent with research that indicates high stay rates of PhDs from China and India.[58]

---

[58]Grant Black and Paula Stephan. "The importance of foreign PhDs to US science." In: *Science and the University*, eds. Ronald Ehrenberg and Paula Stephan. Madison, WI: University of Wisconsin Press (forthcoming).

IMPACT OF INTERNATIONAL GRADUATE STUDENTS AND POSTDOCTORAL SCHOLARS ON NATIONAL SECURITY

As we have seen, the S&E enterprise is increasingly multidisciplinary, interdisciplinary, and global. The US system of higher education that is generally admired by the rest of the world depends on the close interplay between research and education and the broad dissemination of scholarly work. Academic research thrives on the serendipitous discoveries arising from casual access and cross-disciplinary collaboration. The system of competitive peer review, widely acknowledged to promote excellence, requires open and transparent communication. One challenge faced by policy makers is to balance the necessary openness with the need for national security in ways that maintain the productive environment of research and education.

To ensure adequate human resources in fields important for homeland security, in *Making the Nation Safer*, the National Research Council recommended that there be a human resource development program, similar to the National Defense Education Act.[59] National weapons laboratories have instituted specific programs to recruit and hire critically skilled people to staff nuclear-stockpile stewardship programs, for which US citizenship is a primary consideration, including graduate and postdoctoral internship programs, programs involving local high schools and universities, and provision of support for current employees to gain additional training. A recent report indicates these programs are a major reason that these laboratories do not have significant problems locating the necessary people to fill critical-skills positions.[60]

The committee considered additional national security issues but data are not available on what additional risks, if any, an international student may pose versus a domestic student, particularly now that SEVIS and Visas Mantis security screens have been deployed. Certainly, there are inherent risks in relying on international students to fill the nation's critical S&E positions. As we have witnessed with the tightening of US border security (see Chapter 2), the availability of international scientists and engineers for graduate student, postdoctoral, and other research positions can diminish rapidly. In addition, in periods of international tension, students and scholars who are in the United States on temporary visas may decide to leave.

---

[59]National Research Council. 2002. *Making the Nation Safer: The Role of Science and Technology in Countering Terrorism*. Washington, DC: The National Academies Press.

[60]Government Accountability Office. 2005. *National Nuclear Security Administration: Contractors' Strategies to Recruit and Retain and Critically Skilled Workforce Are Generally Effective* (GAO-05-164). Washington, DC: GAO.

Limitations on the access to international students and scholars may have an adverse impact on the ability to attract the best research talent for the basic research underpinning US national security. The presence of international students and scholars in our academic institutions has prompted some funding agencies to attempt to limit who may participate in research projects.[61] Additional concerns are prompted by export-control regulations on research (see Chapter 2). Most university research is published fundamental research that is exempt from export-control restrictions. Any research that is not openly published would be subject to the restrictions and require a license for the involvement of international students and collaborators from some countries and for some technologies. A 2005 NRC report[62] listed visa problems, restrictive contracts, and export controls as particularly critical to US Department of Defense (DoD) research in engineering and the physical, mathematics, and computer sciences, and recommended that National Security Decision Directive 189 be recognized in DoD basic research contracts. Another NRC report has recommended that international postdoctoral scholars be eligible for federal training grants and fellowships.[63]

If restrictions on research and the processes to pursue it become too onerous, international scientists may choose to work in other nations, depriving the United States of their contributions to combat broad threats to national security, such as the spread of infectious disease. The international response to the worldwide epidemic of severe acute respiratory syndrome (SARS) highlighted the globalization of research and the need to maintain the mobility of the best researchers so that they are free to address such challenges.[64] The World Health Organization coordinated an international effort by 13 laboratories in 10 countries that identified in 1 month the new pathogen that caused SARS. Clearly, a feat of such complexity could not have been accomplished without international scientific collaboration and interaction.

---

[61]Julie T. Norris. 2003. *Restrictions on Research Awards: Troublesome Clauses. A Report of the AAU/COGR Task Force.* Washington, DC: OSTP. This report was requested of the Association of American Universities and the Council on Governmental Relations by the Office of Science and Technology Policy and is based on surveys conducted during spring and summer 2003.

[62]National Research Council. 2005. *Assessment of Department of Defense Basic Research.* Washington, DC: The National Academies Press.

[63]National Research Council. 2005. *Bridges to Independence: Fostering the Independence of New Investigators in Biomedical Research.* Washington, DC: The National Academies Press.

[64]Alice P. Gast. 2004. "The impact of restricting information access on science and technology." In: *A Little Knowledge: Privacy, Security, and Public Information after September 11*, eds. Peter M. Shane, John Podesta, and Richard C. Leone. New York: The Century Foundation.

The value of international scientific exchange in our increasingly interdependent world is of utmost importance. The controls used to regulate international travel of students and scholars, including the technology alert list (TAL), export controls, the Student and Exchange Visitor Information System (SEVIS), and Visas Mantis security checks have been implemented to reduce any potential security risks to the United States posed by international visitors. However, such potential gains in security come at a high cost. The controls have created an unwelcoming atmosphere and are eroding trust with our colleagues around the world. Special efforts need to be made to ensure international visitors do feel welcome in the face of these necessary security measures. If the cancellation of conferences and loss of collaborations continues, the United States may lose its traditional role as a convening power, and this would have grave and lasting consequences.[65]

IMPACT ON INTERNATIONAL RELATIONS

The exchange of students among countries is considered a central feature of international relations and foreign policy by US government leaders, as illustrated by the following statements:

> The relationships that are formed between individuals from different countries, as part of international education programs and exchanges, can also foster goodwill that develops into vibrant, mutually beneficial partnerships among nations.[66]

–President Bush, 2001

> America's educational institutions attract talented future leaders from around the world. International students and scholars benefit from engagement with our society and academic institutions and we benefit enormously from their interaction with our society as they help our citizens develop understanding and knowledge that enriches our lives, increases international cooperation, enhances our national security, and improves our economic competitiveness.[67]

–Secretary of State Colin Powell, 2004

[65]See Jane Lubchenco and Goverdhan Mehta. 2004. "International scientific meetings." *Science* 305:1531; and "Organizing an international meeting in the United States." International Visitors Office Web page, National Academies Board on International Scientific Organizations, *http://www7.nationalacademies.org/visas/Organizing_a_Meeting.html.*

[66]George W. Bush. 2001. Statement for International Education Week 2001 (November 13), *http://exchanges.state.gov/iew2001/message.htm.*

[67]Colin L. Powell. 2004. Statement for International Education Week 2004 (October 15), *http://exchanges.state.gov/iew/statements/powell.htm.*

[68]"Foreign Students Yesterday, World Leaders Today." Bureau of Educational and Cultural Affairs, US Department of State. Available at *http://exchanges.state.gov/education/educationusa/leaders.htm.*

According to the committee's analysis of responses to the Pew Global Attitudes Survey (see Appendix C), people who admire US science and technology and who visit the United States improve their attitude toward the United States substantially. Similarly, returnees who assume leadership positions at home may become strong foreign-policy and national-security assets for the United States. Scientists and engineers who have been educated here often return home with an appreciation of the egalitarian values of scientific research, democratic values, and the productivity of a vibrant capitalist economy. For example, among allies who have participated in an educational exchange program in the United States are Afghani President Hamid Karzai, Philippines President Gloria Arroyo, French President Jacques Chirac, King Abdullah of Jordan, Mexican President Vicente Fox, and British Prime Minister Tony Blair.[68] Of course, one may cite examples of foreign students who find US culture offensive or have even become outright enemies of the United States or of Western culture. Historically, however, science has served as a bridge between nations and a means of communication that can transcend political barriers. A notable example was the continuing exchange of American and Soviet scientists throughout the Cold War.[69]

CONCLUSION

The participation of international graduate students and postdoctoral scholars is an important part of the research enterprise of the United States. In some fields they make up more than half the populations of graduate students and postdoctoral scholars. If their presence were substantially diminished, important research and teaching activities in academe, industry, and federal laboratories would be curtailed, particularly if universities did not give more attention to recruiting and retaining domestic students. The next two chapters will consider national policies and exogenous factors that are likely to influence their participation.

---

[69]Joseph S. Nye, Jr. 2004. "You can't get here from there." *The New York Times* (November 29).

2

Shaping the Flow of International Graduate Students and Postdoctoral Scholars: Visa and Immigration Policy

The advancement of modern science and engineering (S&E) requires dynamic functioning of professional networks of colleagues, mentors, and students. Scientific research is now an international endeavor, so these collegial networks must also be international. E-mail and inexpensive telephony have raised international communication to a new level of convenience, but personal interaction continues to be the sine qua non of collaboration and innovation. The healthy functioning of research networks depends on participants' ability to travel across borders and to work and study in other countries.[1]

The free flow of knowledge and people, however, sometimes conflicts with the short-term national interests of states. There is a tenuous balance between protecting information important to national security interests and the sharing of knowledge that may produce scientific and technologic advances for the common good. Technical knowledge can be used for nefarious purposes, as well as for good, and modern terrorists have adapted their own forms of networking and knowledge dissemination. In an age of terrorism, attempts to limit the misuse of technical knowledge must be as sophisticated and international as science itself. The United States, like other nations, now struggles to balance the need to protect technical infor-

---

[1] Alice P. Gast. 2004. "The impact of restricting information access on science and technology." In: *A Little Knowledge: Privacy, Security, and Public Information after September 11,* eds. Peter M. Shane, John Podesta, and Richard C. Leone. New York: The Century Foundation.

66

mation against the need to maintain the openness of scholarship on which its culture, economy, and security depend.

A growing challenge for policy makers is to maintain the flow of people and information to the extent compatible with security needs. This chapter provides a brief picture of how difficult that has become and how easily the modern cross-currents of policies and regulations, particularly those governing visas and immigration, can disrupt the global movement and therefore the productivity of scientists and engineers. The issuance and monitoring of visas may be as important as the education and training experience.

The repercussions that followed the terror attacks of September 11, 2001, have included security-related changes in federal visa and immigration policy. The changes were intended to restrict the illegal movements of an extremely small population, but they have had a substantial effect on international graduate students and postdoctoral scholars already in the United States or contemplating a period of study here. Other immigration-related policies relevant to international student flows are international reciprocity agreements, deemed export policies, and specific acts that grant special or immigrant status to groups of students or high-skill workers, such as the Chinese Student Protection Act of 1992, and the policies enacted shortly after the end of the Cold War to allow scientists and engineers of the former Soviet Union to enter the United States (see Table 2-1).

Recently, the policy environment has favored heightened security. The security environment in turn has had adverse implications for perceptions of the United States as a desirable destination for study and for international scientific gatherings.

NONIMMIGRANT VISA POLICIES AND PROCEDURES

The Immigration and Nationality Act has served as the primary body of law governing immigration and visa operations since 1952.[2] It was amended by the Homeland Security Act of 2002, which created the Department of Homeland Security (DHS). DHS subsumed the activities of the Immigration and Naturalization Service and of several other entities. The act gave the Department of State (DOS) sole responsibility for vetting and issuing documents for travel into the United States and made DHS responsible for setting visa policy and for overseeing the activities of persons once they arrive in the United States. Both agencies coordinate with the Federal

---

[2]The 1952 Immigration and Nationality Act has been amended several times, most recently by the Illegal Immigration Reform and Immigrant Responsibility Act of 1996, the USA Patriot Act of 2001, the Enhanced Border Security and Visa Entry Reform Act of 2002, and the Homeland Security Act of 2002.

TABLE 2-1 Legislation Affecting Visas and Study Plans

Laws	Executive Orders, Advisories, and Directives	Consequences
1952 Immigration and Nationality Act (INA)		Primary body of law governing immigration and visa operations
1954 International Traffic in Arms Regulations (ITAR)	Technology Alert List (TAL) Deemed Export Controls	• Stems proliferation of weapons of mass destruction and missile delivery systems • Controls transfer of sensitive information to foreign nationals studying at US institutions
1979 Export Administration Regulations (EAR)		Controls export of commodities of commercial interest
1992 Chinese Student Protection Act		Provided eligibility for US permanent residency to Chinese students and scholars studying in the United States in 1989, at the time of the Tiananmen Square uprising.
1994 Foreign Relations Security Act		Holds consular officials liable if terrorists obtain a visa
1996 Illegal Immigration Reform and Immigrant Responsibility Act		Defines criminal penalties for consular misconduct; created Coordinated Interagency Partnerships Regulating International Students (CIPRIS), the predecessor to SEVIS
	VISAS Mantis Implemented in 1998 under authority of INA§212(a)(3)(A)(i)(II) governing illegal technology transfer	Consolidation of several Cold War-era nationality-based screening programs, including CHINEX for PRC nationals and SPLEX for USSR and Eastern Europe nationals; uses TAL to screen visa applicants to guard against the export of sensitive goods, technology, and information.

TABLE 2-1 Continued

Laws	Executive Orders, Advisories, and Directives	Consequences
2001 Patriot Act		Created SEVIS and US-VISIT concept
2002 Homeland Security Act		Created DHS; split authority for visas and immigration. DOS vets and issues documents, DHS handles policy and enforcement
2002 Enhanced Border Security And Visa Entry Reform Act (BSA)		Imposed border control (INS) on DHS Mandated increased requirements for US-VISIT program integration, interoperability with other law-enforcement and intelligence systems, biometrics, and accessibility
	VISAS Condor Implemented January 2002 BSA §306	Security screen for nationals of US-designated state sponsor of terrorism
	Biometric Visa Program Began implementation September 2003 BSA §303	All visa applicants must have personal interview with consular official, scan fingerprints, and submit a photograph
	Machine-Readable Passports (MRPs) for Visa Waiver Program (VWP) Countries (September 2005)	All VWP countries must implement MRPs incorporating biometric identifiers; nationals from VWP countries that do not issue such passports need to obtain a visa for US travel for visas issued after September 2005

BOX 2-1
Immigration and Nationality Act Definitions of Student and Exchange-Scholar Visa Classes and the 214b Provision[a]

F-1: An alien having a residence in a foreign country which he has no intention of abandoning, who is a bona fide student qualified to pursue a full course of study and who seeks to enter the United States temporarily and solely for the purpose of pursuing such a course of study consistent with section 214(l) at an established college, university, seminary, conservatory, academic high school, elementary school, or other academic institution or in a language training program in the United States, particularly designated by him and approved by the Attorney General after consultation with the Secretary of Education, which institution or place of study shall have agreed to report to the Attorney General the termination of attendance of each nonimmigrant student, and if any such institution of learning or place of study fails to make reports promptly the approval shall be withdrawn. [INA § 101(a) (15)(F)(i)]

J-1: An alien having a residence in a foreign country which he has no intention of abandoning, who is a bona fide student, scholar, trainee, teacher, professor, research assistant, specialist, or leader in a field of specialized knowledge or skill, or other person of similar description, who is coming temporarily to the United States as a participant in a program designated by the Director of the United States Information Agency, for the purpose of teaching, instructing or lecturing, studying, observing, conducting research, consulting, demonstrating special skills, or receiving training and who, if he is coming to the United States to participate in a program under which he will receive graduate medical education or training, also meets the requirements of section 212(j), and the alien spouse and minor children of any such alien if accompanying him or following to join him. [INA §101(a)(15)(J)(i)]

H-1b: An alien subject to section 212(j)(2), who is coming temporarily to the United States to perform services ... in a specialty occupation described in section 214(i)(1) .... [INA § 101(a)(15)(H)(i)(b)]

Bureau of Investigation, the Department of Justice, and other entities to meet security requirements.

Over the years, a veritable alphabet soup of visa classes has been created, but there are no classes specific to graduate students or postdoctoral scholars. Which visa is used often depends on where students are in their course of graduate study, how long they have been in the United States, and, for postdoctoral scholars, in which sector they are performing research—a national laboratory, a university, or an industrial setting. Most international graduate students and postdoctoral scholars who visit the United States do so using temporary nonimmigrant visas that cover educa-

B-1: An alien (other than one coming for the purpose of study or of performing skilled or unskilled labor or as a representative of foreign press, radio, film, or other foreign information media coming to engage in such vocation) having a residence in a foreign country which he has no intention of abandoning and who is visiting the United States temporarily for business or temporarily for pleasure. Enrollment in a course of study is prohibited. An alien who is admitted as, or changes status to, a B-1 or B-2 nonimmigrant on or after April 12, 2002, or who files a request to extend the period of authorized stay in B-1 or B-2 nonimmigrant status on or after such date, violates the conditions of his or her B-1 or B-2 status if the alien enrolls in a course of study. Such an alien who desires to enroll in a course of study must either obtain an F-1 or M-1 nonimmigrant visa from a consular officer abroad and seek readmission to the United States, or apply for and obtain a change of status under section 248 of the Act and 8 CFR part 248. The alien may not enroll in the course of study until the Service has admitted the alien as an F-1 or M-1 nonimmigrant or has approved the alien's application under part 248 of this chapter and changed the alien's status to that of an F-1 or M-1 nonimmigrant. (Added 4/12/02; 67 FR 18062).

214b: Every alien (other than a nonimmigrant described in subparagraph (L) or (V) of section 101(a)(15), and other than a nonimmigrant described in any provision of section 101(a)(15)(H)(i) except subclause (b1) of such section) shall be presumed to be an immigrant until he establishes to the satisfaction of the consular officer, at the time of application for a visa, and the immigration officers, at the time of application for admission, that he is entitled to a nonimmigrant status under section 101(a)(15). An alien who is an officer or employee of any foreign government or of any international organization entitled to enjoy privileges, exemptions, and immunities under the International Organizations Immunities Act [22 U.S.C. 288], or an alien who is the attendant, servant, employee, or member of the immediate family of any such alien shall not be entitled to apply for or receive an immigrant visa, or to enter the United States as an immigrant unless he executes a written waiver in the same form and substance as is prescribed by section 247(b). [INA ACT 214(b)]

---

a Immigration Classifications and Visa Categories, Bureau of Citizenship and Immigration Services, US Department of Homeland Security. Available at *http://uscis.gov/graphics/services/visas.htm*.

tional activities: F-class ("student") and J-class ("exchange visitor") visas for most graduate students, and J-class or, less often, H-1b ("specialty worker") visas for postdoctoral scholars (see Box 2-1).[3] Some graduate students and postdoctoral scholars are admitted on other types of visas, including O, J-2, TN, and EA visas.[4] In addition, graduate students and

---

[3]The H-1b population, although important, is largely distinct from the graduate student and postdoctoral populations and is not a major focus of this report; see brief section in Chapter 3.

[4]Philip Chen, senior adviser to the Deputy Director for Intramural Research, National Institutes of Health, presentation to committee, October 12, 2004.

postdoctoral scholars who come to the United States for scientific meetings or short-term research collaborations that do not require university enrollment are admitted on B-1 visas, generally considered "business" visas. The process by which graduate students and postdoctoral scholars apply for F and J visas is outlined in Figure 2-1.

In 2003, for F and J visa classes, the primary sending country was South Korea, followed by Japan, Germany, India, and Great Britain (see Figure 2-2). One can see a clear regional difference: European countries send more J-class or exchange visitors, and Asian countries send more F-class or student visitors. The largest numbers of J-visa visitors come from Germany, followed by Great Britain, Russia, France, and Brazil. The largest numbers of F-visa visitors come from South Korea, followed by Japan, India, China, Taiwan, and Mexico. To give a sense of scale, of the 27,849,443 nonimmigrant visitors in 2003, 20,142,909 were tourists, 4,215,714 were temporary business visitors, some 939,216 (3.4 percent) were students and exchange visitors (F-1 and J-1 visa classes), and 360,498 (1.3 percent) were specialty occupation workers and trainees (H-1b visa class).[5]

Although it is tempting to use those issuance numbers as a measure of undergraduate, graduate, and postdoctoral inflow, it is not advisable inasmuch as visa classes contain a heterogeneous mix of people. F-class visas include students from high school through graduate school. J-class visas include graduate students, postdoctoral scholars, au pairs, camp counselors, short-term international faculty visitors, and others (see footnote to Figure 2-3). And, not all visa issuances lead to travel and enrollment.

9-11 and Its Aftermath

Several clear trends can be seen in visa issuances in recent years (Figure 2-3). F-visa issuances showed a strong, long-term upward trend from 1966 through the end of the century. The downturn for Asia in the middle 1990s reflected the adoption of the Chinese Student Protection Act of 1992, which made thousands of Chinese students enrolled in US institutions in 1989 (at the time of the Tiananmen Square uprising) eligible for permanent residence on July 1, 1993. Currency exchange rates have had a substantial impact on stipends, cost of living, and travel expenses for international students. A steep decline in visa issuances began in 2001, and continued

---

[5]Office of Immigration Statistics, "Table 24. Nonimmigrants admitted by class of admission: Selected fiscal years 1981-2003", *2003 Yearbook of Immigration Statistics,* Office of Immigration Statistics, Office of Management, Department of Homeland Security, 2003. Available at *http://uscis.gov/graphics/shared/aboutus/statistics/TEMP03yrbk/TEMPExcel/Table24D.xls.*

F Visas	J Visas

Apply to US Institution

Universities must be designated by the Department of Homeland Security Student and Exchange Visitor Program office	Exchange-program sponsors are designated by the Department of State (DOS) Bureau of Educational and Cultural Affairs

Accepted into program

Designated school official (DSO) enters student information into SEVIS and supplies applicant with I-20 form; DSO required to remark on English proficiency and finances	Responsible program official (RO) enters scholar information into SEVIS and supplies applicant with DS-2019 form

Pay SEVIS fee ($100)

Schedule interview with US embassy or consulate in home country; wait times depend on consular post; student and scholar visas get priority over other NIVs; pay nonrefundable visa application fee ($100)

INTERVIEW
Biometrics taken (fingerprints, provide 2x2 photograph)
Provide the following documents and evidence:
- Proof of visa application fee payment
- Proof of admission (I-20 or DS-2019)
- Proof of SEVIS fee payment
- Non-Immigrant Visa Application, form DS-156
- Contact Information and Work History, form DS-158
- Supplemental Non Immigrant Visa Application, form DS-157, for all male applicants 16 - 45 years old: for all male applicants over 16 from countries listed as state sponsors of terrorism (North Korea, Cuba, Syria, Sudan, Iran, and Libya)
- Evidence of ties to home country (**214(b) screen** to determine intent to immigrate)
- For all Fs and for Js when requested by program sponsor, provide evidence of sufficient knowledge of English and financial support
- Passport valid for travel to United States, validity date at least 6 months beyond intended duration of study

	Consular official determines eligibility for 2-year foreign residence requirement (212e)

Consular official will certify information with SEVIS and other government databases; wait time for visa processing, same day to over 30 days, depends on post and security screens

SECURITY SCREENING
—If program or activity falls under scientific and technical fields listed in Technical Alert List (TAL), the **Visas Mantis** program is invoked, and a security advisory opinion (SAO) must be requested
—In addition, the **Visas Condor** program was established in January 2002 for counter-terrorism purposes. Applies to nationals of countries of concern; if invoked, a security advisory opinion (SAO) must be requested
—Both Mantis and Condor SAOs require input from multiple agencies; DOS must issue a response before visa can be processed; as of Fall 2004, Mantis and Condor programs were consolidated and most SAOs issued within 30 days

Pay visa issuance fee (depends on reciprocity agreement)

At port of entry to United States, provide valid passport and visa stamp, undergo biometric screen (fingerprints, photo); immigration officer will verify information in SEVIS and other government databases

Re-entry depends on reciprocity agreements, visa validity duration varies from 6 months and use twice to 60 months and multiple uses; institution/sponsor must update SEVIS if any change in study program or activities and this may trigger a new SAO.

FIGURE 2-1 Schedule of activities for F and J Nonimmigrant Visa (NIV) applicants.

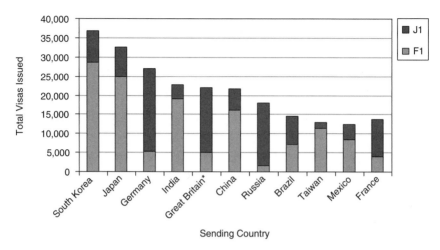

FIGURE 2-2 Top 11 student- and scholar-sending countries, FY 2003.
SOURCE: Data provided by US Department of State and available in its annual publication *Report of the Visa Office*, published by the Bureau of Consular Affairs. Recent editions are available at *http://travel.state.gov/visa/report.html*. (*) Note that Great Britain issuance numbers include UK and Hong Kong.

through 2003. J-visa issuances, mostly to Europeans, followed roughly the same pattern, with a larger rise in the 1990s and a smaller downturn after 2001. To date, the downturn has reflected an increased denial rate more than a decreased application rate. As seen in Figure 2-4, the refusal rate for J-visa applicants rose steadily from 2000 through 2003. The adjusted refusal rate for F-visa applicants peaked in 2002. In 2004, denial rates had decreased considerably and were approaching 1999 levels.[6] It is not possible to obtain visa denial rates by country.

One can track the changes in nonimmigrant-visa issuance rates directly to changes in visa and immigration policies and structures after the terror attacks of 9-11. Implementation of the student-tracking system, the Student and Exchange Visitor Information System (SEVIS) and enhanced Visas Mantis security screening led to closer scrutiny and longer times for visa processing. The effects of the increased security were felt keenly by newly accepted and continuing students, who with university researchers and administrators expressed dismay at the new degree of difficulty in obtaining

---

[6]US Department of State, Immigrant Visa Control and Reporting Division, 1998-2003. See Figure 2-4.

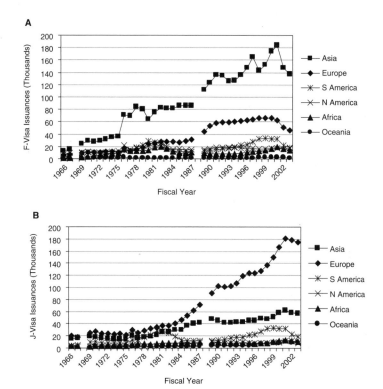

FIGURE 2-3 Visa issuance volumes by region for F and J classes, 1966-2003.
SOURCES: Data provided by US Department of State and are from its annual publication, *Report of the Visa Office*, published by the Bureau of Consular Affairs. Recent editions are available at *http://travel.state.gov/visa/report.html*. No regional data were available for 1968 or 1988. Regions are as defined by Department of State. North America includes Antigua and Barbuda, Bahamas, Barbados, Belize, Canada, Costa Rica, Cuba, Dominican Republic, El Salvador, Grenada, Guatemala, Haiti, Honduras, Jamaica, Mexico, Nicaragua, Panama, Saint Kitts and Nevis, Saint Lucia, Saint Vincent and the Grenadines, and Trinidad and Tobago. Hong Kong statistics are reported with UK. Before 1992, Europe statistics included USSR. In FY 1992, Kazakhstan, Kyrgyzstan, Tajikistan, Turkmenistan, and Uzbekistan statistics are reported with Asia; and Armenia, Azerbaijan, Belarus, Georgia, Moldova, Russia, and Ukraine are reported with Europe.

F and J visa classes were not broken into subclasses until 1984. Data reported here are for all F and all J visas issued. F visas are for students in secondary (high-school) and postsecondary education. J visas are in two categories: Private Sector (foreign physician, au pair, camp counselor, summer work/travel, and trainee) and Government Programs (postsecondary student, college/university student, professor, research scholar, short-term scholar, specialist, teacher, government visitor, and international visitor). Additional subclasses are for spouses and dependents of primary applicants.

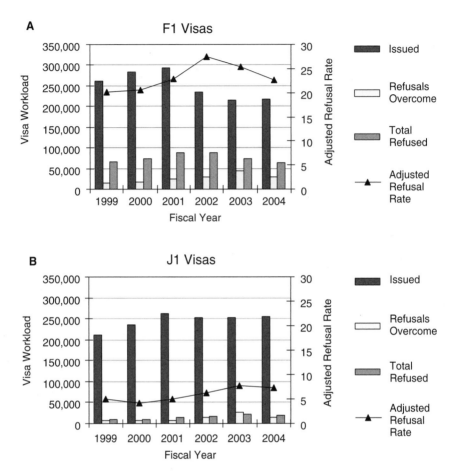

FIGURE 2-4 Visa workloads and refusals: student and exchange visitors.
SOURCE: Data provided by US Department of State and available in its annual publication *Report of the Visa Office*, published by the Bureau of Consular Affairs. Recent editions are available at *http://travel.state.gov/visa/report.html*. The adjusted refusal rate is calculated with the following formula: (Refusals - Refusals Overcome/Waived)/(Issuances + Refusals - Refusals Overcome/Waived).

a visa to study in the United States.[7] In addition, US-based scientific and engineering meetings, conferences, and oversight groups were canceled or unable to go on as planned.[8]

The European press is filled with stories of scholars from China and Muslim countries who were denied re-entry into the United States after brief trips abroad.[9] The press reports concerns about the nontransparent visa application process and seemingly arbitrary visa rejections, again with examples of scholars from non-EU countries.[10] In addition to laments about long delays in obtaining US visas, reports cite rude behavior and long waiting times at US embassies for Asian, Muslim, and European students and scholars.[11] The press is also alarmed that the SEVIS tracking system is akin to parole monitoring for common criminals.[12] In combination, those factors have led to a feeling among Europeans that they are "not welcome in the United States."

The Student and Exhange Visitor Information System (SEVIS)

September 11 accelerated implementation of SEVIS. Mandated by the Immigration Reform and Immigrant Responsibility Act of 1996, SEVIS

---

[7]See, among many examples: "A visa system tangled in red tape and misconceived security rules is hurting America," *The Economist*, May 6, 2004; "Statement and recommendations on visa problems harming America's scientific, economic, and security interests," signed by 22 scientific, engineering, and academic leaders, *The Chronicle of Higher Education*, February 11, 2004; Caroline Alphonso. 2005. "Facing security hurdles, top students flock to Canada." *The Globe and Mail* (February 22).

[8]As one example, Sandia National Laboratories operates numerous government-sponsored programs aimed at reducing the threat posed by unsecured Russian nuclear and other weapons. The programs require scientists from the former Soviet Union to frequently attend government-sponsored conferences and exchanges that are critical to executing nonproliferation objectives. From January 2002 to April 2004, of the 305 scientists invited to attend the conferences, 89 were unable to receive visas in time to attend the Department of Energy-sponsored workshops. That resulted in the delay or cancellation of threat-reduction activities. Some meetings were moved to Western Europe, which increased cost, limited the number of US participants able to attend, and forced workshops to proceed without equipment available at US locations. Sen. Jeff Bingaman, letter to Secretary of State Colin Powell, April 26, 2004.

[9]"Keep out!" *Financial Times Deutschland*, June 24, 2004; "Visa-Probleme halten Gastforscher von USA fern; Strikte Einreiseregelungen aus Terrorangst." *Die Welt*, September 11, 2004; "Outre-Atlantique, la peur de l'etranger pourrait ralentir la recherche." *Le Monde*, June 6, 2003; "Etudiants etrangers, le parcours d'obstacles." *Liberation*, September 11, 2003.

[10]"Les universites americaines font-elees encore recette?" *Le Figaro*, June 30, 2004.

[11]"Studium in den USA—kein Traumziel mehr?" *Neue Zuercher Zeitung*, November 12, 2003.

[12]*Liberation, Le Figaro*, op cit; "Ihr koennt zu Hause bleiben." *Spiegel Online*, April 29, 2004.

became the responsibility of DHS in 2003. It is administered by the Immigration and Customs Enforcement Division and began collecting student-admissions and postdoctoral-appointment data in summer 2003. By July 2004, SEVIS had approved 773,000 student and exchange visitors to study in the United States (F-1, M-1, and J-1 visa categories) and 118,000 of their dependents. It had certified 8,737 schools of many types, from universities to pet-grooming and flight schools, and was receiving about 30 additional requests for certification per day.[13] Despite early challenges[14] and some initial technical difficulties, the system was said to be functioning reasonably well at the time of the present committee's investigation.[15]

SEVIS is both criticized and praised for its role in tracking foreign students once in the United States to verify that they are pursuing their intended courses of study at certified institutions. SEVIS adds a layer of verification not previously available by allowing embassy and consular officers to electronically verify the validity of the I-20 form of a student applicant or the DS-2019 form of an exchange-visitor applicant. The I-20 is provided by a US learning institution to document that a student has been accepted into a course of study; the DS-2019 is provided by a US exchange-visitor program to verify that a graduate student or postdoctoral scholar has been accepted into a designated exchange program (see Figure 2-1).

On September 1, 2004, DHS implemented a $100 fee to help defray the cost of the program, despite criticism that the fee places a substantial burden on students from poor countries. The nonrefundable fee must be paid by all F-1, J-1, and M-1 applicants *before they apply* for an entrance visa and is not refundable if the visa is not issued.[16] The regular visa fee also is not refundable if the visa is declined. There are no data that indicate whether students have been deterred by the $100 fee from applying

---

[13]Susan Geary, deputy director for the Student and Exchange Visitor Program (SEVP), Department of Homeland Security, presentation to committee, July 19, 2004. The number of approved schools has now exceeded 9,000.

[14]Nicholas Confessore. 2002. "Borderline insanity." *Washington Monthly.* Confessore writes about the politics behind implementation of the Coordinated Interagency Partnerships Regulating International Students (CIPRIS), the predecessor to SEVIS.

[15]Government Accountability Office. 2004. *Performance of Information System to Monitor Foreign Student and Exchange Visitors Has Improved, but Issues Remain.* Washington, DC: GAO (GAO-04-690); Government Accountability Office. 2005. *Border Security: Streamlined Visas Mantis Program Has Lowered Burden on Foreign Science Students and Scholars, but Further Refinements Needed* (GAO-05-198). Washington, DC: GAO; Kelly Field. 2005. "Visa delays stemming from scholar's security clearances are down since last year, report says." *The Chronicle of Higher Education* (February 18); Joe Pouliot. 2005. "Boehlert praises improvements to visa processes." House Science Committee Press Office, Washington, DC (February 13).

[16]See the Web site of Immigrations and Customs Enforcement at *http://www.ice.gov.*

for US visas, but some US universities now compensate accepted students for the amount of the fee.

Visas Mantis and Condor

Visas Mantis and Visas Condor programs are intended to provide additional scrutiny for visitors who may pose a security risk. The Visas Mantis process[17] is triggered when a student or exchange-visitor applicant intends to study a subject covered by the Technology Alert List (TAL). The TAL was originally drawn up as a tool for preventing proliferation of weapons technology and was later applied by embassy and consular officials when reviewing student visa applications. The express purpose of the TAL is to prevent the export of "goods, technology, or sensitive information" through such activities as "graduate-level studies, teaching, conducting research, participating in exchange programs, receiving training or employment."[18] If flagged by Mantis, a nonimmigrant-visa application requires a security advisory opinion (SAO), which may involve input from several federal agencies. Initially, Mantis procedures were applied on entry and each re-entry to the United States for persons studying or working in sensitive fields. In 2004, SAO clearance was extended to 1 year for those who were returning to a US government-sponsored program or activity and performing the same duties or functions at the same facility or organization that was the basis for the original Mantis authorization.[19] In 2005, the US Department of State extended the validity of Mantis clearances for F, J, H, L, and B visa categories. Clearances for F visas are valid for up to 4 years unless the student changes academic positions. H, J, and L clearances are valid for up to 2 years unless the visa holder's activity in the United States changes.[20]

In 2002, a new antiterrorist screening process called Visas Condor was added for nationals of US-designated state sponsors of terrorism.[21] That

---

[17]The Visa Mantis program was established in 1998 and applies to all nonimmigrant visa categories, including student (F), exchange-visitor (J), temporary-worker (H), intracompany-transferee (L), business (B-1), and tourist (B-2) applicants.

[18]See *http://travel.state.gov/visa/testimony1.html* for an overview of the Visas Mantis programs and implementation of Condor.

[19]See Department of State cable, 04 State 153587, No. 22: Revision to Visas Mantis Clearance Procedure, *http://travel.state.gov/visa/state153587.html*.

[20]"Extension of validity for science-related interagency visa clearances." Media Note 2005/182. US Department of State, February 11, 2005, *http://www.state.gov/r/pa/prs/ps/2005/42212.htm*; "Overview of state-sponsored terrorism: patterns of global terrorism – 2000." US Department of State, April 30, 2001. *http://www.state.gov/s/ct/rls/pgtrpt/2000/2441.htm*.

[21]Countries designated section 306 in 2005: Iran, Syria, Libya, Cuba, North Korea, and Sudan. See "Special visa processing procedures–travelers from state sponsors of terrorism." *http://travel.state.gov/visa/temp/info/info_1300.html*.

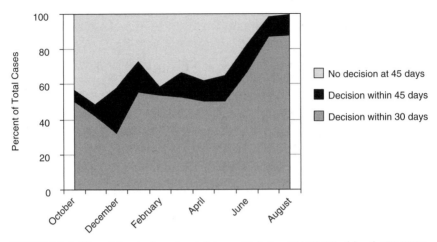

FIGURE 2-5 Visas Mantis Security Advisory Opinion (SAO) Workload, FY 2004
SOURCE: Data presented to committee on October 12, 2004, by Janice Jacobs,
deputy assistant secretary of visa affairs, US Department of State.

addition initially overloaded the SAO interagency process and slowed Mantis clearances, drawing criticism and calls for improvement.[22] The problem of extended waiting times for clearance of nonimmigrant visas flagged by Mantis has for the most part been addressed successfully. [23] In the last year, the proportion of Visas Mantis visitors cleared within 30 days has risen substantially (see Figure 2-5). In October 2003, over 40 percent took 45 days or more to clear; today, virtually none take that long, and fewer than 15 percent take more than 30 days.

OTHER IMMIGRATION POLICIES AND CONDITIONS

Changes in visa policies are only one factor that can affect the mobility of graduate students and postdoctoral scholars. Other immigration policies and conditions related to S&E flows are reciprocity agreements and deemed-exports agreements.

---

[22]Government Accountability Office. 2004. *Border Security: Improvements Needed to Reduce Time Taken to Adjudicate Visas for Science Students and Scholars* (GAO-04-371). Washington, DC: GAO. GAO showed that in April-June 2003, applicants waited an average of 67 days for completion of security checks associated with visa applications.

[23]Testimony provided to committee by Janice Jacobs, deputy assistant secretary of visa affairs, US Department of State, October 12, 2004; Government Accountability Office. 2005. *Border Security: Streamlined Visas Mantis Program has lowered burden on science students and scholars, but further refinements needed* (GAO-05-198). Washington, DC: GAO.

Reciprocity Agreements

A factor that may weigh heavily on those considering US graduate schools and postdoctoral research are the immigration reciprocity agreements between countries. Visa policy in one country that limits visitor entry is matched by the reciprocating country, thus affecting flow in both directions. Reciprocity agreements differ by country and for each class of visa and may include application fees, restrictions on the number of times a person may enter a country on a visa, or the duration of visa validity.[24] For example, a 6-month validity period for F-1 and J-1 visa classes for Chinese citizens means that each time visa holders leave the United States, to return they must reapply for a visa. The 12-month validity period for F-class visas for Russian students can also be problematic.[25] It is promising that China and the United States have agreed to reciprocally extend the visa validity for tourist and business travelers to 12 months and multiple entries.[26]

An analysis of the visa issuance and admissions data from countries with limited-entry visas for students indicates that J-visa holders, who tend to have multiyear multiple-entry visas, take fewer trips per year out of the United States than do F-visa holders (see Figure 2-6). That may be related to Visas Mantis screening. Most S&E graduate students and postdoctoral scholars who wish to re-enter the United States, even those with valid multiple-entry multiyear visas, must be recleared through Visas Mantis procedures—a process that can take over 30 days.

Many graduate students and postdoctoral scholars opt not to travel to international conferences or to visit home to see family, to avoid lengthy disruptions in study or research. A 2004 survey of nonresident postdoctoral scholars working in the United States indicates that about 20 percent of the respondents had curtailed work-related and personal travel in 2003 and 2004 because of concerns that they would have problems re-entering the United States. Of scholars that did travel outside the United States, over 20 percent experienced some problems and 2 percent experienced serious problems on re-entry in both 2003 and 2004 (see Figure 2-7).

---

[24]See the reciprocity tables listed at *http://travel.state.gov/visa/reciprocity/index.htm.*

[25]It should be noted that students are legally in the United States for the duration of their studies (certified by SEVIS), but visa policies may prevent them from returning to complete their studies after travel abroad.

[26]Office of the Spokesman. 2005. "US extends visa validity for Chinese tourist and business travelers." Media Note 2005/56, US Department of State (January 12), *http://www.state.gov/r/pa/prs/ps/2005/40818.htm.*

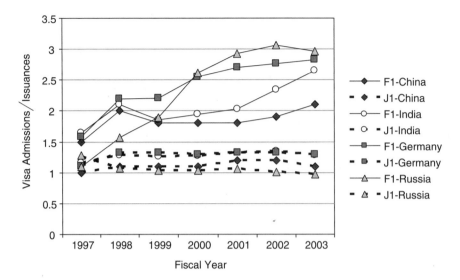

FIGURE 2-6 Student and exchange-visitor trips per year, 1997-2003.
SOURCE: Data on visa issuances from US Department of State. Data on visa admissions are collected at ports of entry and are from Immigration and Customs Enforcement division, Department of Homeland Security. Note that DHS includes mainland China and Taiwan in its admissions reports for China. Department of State issuance numbers for China and Taiwan have been combined for comparability.
NOTES: Student (F) visas are issued for student-college/university and student-secondary (high-school only). Exchange visitor (J) visas are issued for private sector (foreign physician, au pair, camp counselor, summer work/travel, and trainee) and government program (student-college/university, student-secondary, professor, research scholar, short-term scholar, specialist, teacher, government visitor, and international visitor).

Reciprocity schedules dictate validity period of visa and number of times it may be used to enter United States. As of December 2004, reciprocity schedules were as follows: **China:** *F1 and J1* 6 months, two uses; **India** and **Germany:** *F1and J1* 60 months, multiple uses; **Russia:** *F1* 12 months, multiple uses; *J1* 36 months, multiple uses.

Deemed Exports

Export control laws have been a mechanism to control the transfer of goods having *military* applications through the International Traffic in Arms Regulations and have also become a means to limit the export of goods or technologies having *commercial* value through Export Adminis-

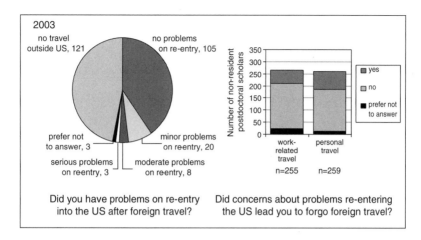

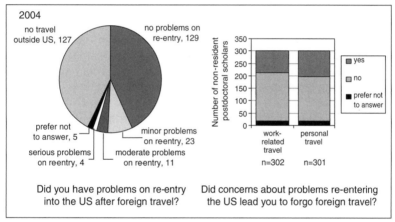

FIGURE 2-7 Re-entry issues for nonresident postdoctoral scholars.

SOURCE: Data are from a November 2004 survey of postdoctoral scholars at the National Institutes of Health carried out by Sigma Xi. Postdoctoral scholars in the United States on temporary visas were asked about their travel in 2003 and 2004. **For the 2003 charts:** Of 305 scholars who responded, 262 scholars were residing in the United States in 2003, 34 were not, and nine preferred not to answer. 260 of the residing scholars indicated whether they had traveled abroad in 2003: 121 had not traveled outside the United States, 136 had, and 3 or fewer preferred not to answer. 135 out of the 136 scholars who had traveled outside the United States indicated whether they had had any problems re-entering the United States. **For the 2004 charts:** 301 of the responding scholars resided in the United States in 2004 and indicated whether they had traveled abroad in 2004. 127 had not traveled outside the United States, 169 had, and five preferred not to answer. 168 out of the 169 scholars who had traveled outside the United States indicated whether they had had problems re-entering the United States.

tration Regulations.[27] Most significant for the international-student and scholar community is the determination that—in addition to the transport of hardware, commodities, and data—a "deemed export" can occur by the transfer of information to a foreign national studying at a US institution, even one who has obtained SAO clearance.

After 9-11, the US government considered whether there were sensitive fields, including fields that have a direct application to the development and use of weapons of mass destruction, to which international students should not be admitted.[28] An analysis of international doctorate recipients showed that of the degrees awarded in 1990-1999, fewer than 11 percent were in sensitive fields, and most of these were in engineering. Students from countries that are now called state sponsors of terrorism constitute 2.0 percent of all PhDs awarded in 1990-1999. Some 79 percent of those students earned degrees in engineering, agriculture, or biological sciences.[29] Universities have reported a substantial increase in situations in which a federal sponsor of research includes award language that restricts the dissemination of research results or the participation of foreign nationals without prior approval on specified research projects.[30] Furthermore, restrictions on travel and study in embargoed countries can impede collaboration and cultural exchange for US students whose dissertation research involves international travel.

The ability to interact freely with and educate international students is preserved by the exemptions granted to universities for fundamental research and educational purposes; however, how these policies are interpreted can affect the ability to interact with students, postdoctoral scholars, and colleagues from other countries. The situation is causing immense frustration and is a subject of current discussion.[31]

---

[27]Export of military hardware and technical data is controlled by the International Traffic in Arms Regulations (ITAR, see *http://pmdtc.org/reference.htm*), dating back to 1954; the export of commodities of commercial interest (and the technical data related to their design, manufacture, and use) is controlled by the Export Administration Regulations (EAR, see *http://www.access.gpo.gov/bis/ear/ear_data.html*), from 1979.

[28]Stephen Burd. 2002. "Bush may bar foreign students from 'sensitive courses'." *The Chronicle of Higher Education* (April 26) A26.

[29]Paula E. Stephan, Grant C. Black, James D. Adams, and Sharon G. Levin. 2002. "Survey of foreign recipients of US PhDs." *Science* 295(5563): 2211-12.

[30]Julie T. Norris, "Restrictions on research awards. Troublesome clauses: A report of the AAU/COGR Task Force". This report was requested of the American Association of Universities and Council on Governmental Relations (COGR) by the Office of Science and Technology Policy. The report is based on surveys conducted during Spring and Summer 2003.

[31]An AAU task force on export controls was established in late 2004. The Bureau of Industry and Security of the Department of Commerce posted an advance notice of proposed rule-making on the "Revision and Clarification of Deemed Export Related Regulatory Requirements" in the Federal Register on March 28, 2005. The public may submit comments, identified by RIN 0694-AD29, at the Federal eRulemaking Portal at *http://www.regulations.gov*.

Section 214(b)

A serious barrier to visits by foreign graduate students is Section 214(b) of the INA, by which an applicant for a student or exchange visa must provide convincing evidence that he or she plans to return to the home country, including proof of a permanent domicile in that country (see Box 2-1). Legitimate applicants may find it hard to prove that they have no intention to immigrate, especially if they have relatives in the United States. In addition, both students and immigration officials are well aware that an F or J visa often provides entrée to permanent-resident status (see Chapter 1 for discussion of stay rates and conversion to permanent residence). It is not surprising that application and enforcement of the 214b requirement can depend on pending immigration legislation or economic conditions.[32]

RECENT EVENTS

At the time of this writing, US visa and immigration policies are in flux. The administration has responded to academic and industry leaders and added staff for visa processing and clearances.[33] DOS has worked to expedite processing of F and J visas at consular posts and embassies.[34] A survey of wait times posted on the DOS Web site indicates that student-visa applicants have a much shorter wait time than other nonimmigrant-visa applicants.[35] DOS has also worked to reduce the time in which an SAO is issued and has extended the SAO validity period.[36] DHS has implemented SEVIS and has just rolled out US-VISIT, another program that may help to provide consular officials independent verification of applicant identity. Universities have increased their efforts to facilitate the immigration and enrollment of graduate students by setting earlier application deadlines, sending earlier notification, offering counseling, and making better use of communication technologies.[37]

---

[32]G. Chelleraj, K.E. Maskus, and A. Mattoo. 2004. *The Contributions of Skilled Immigration and International Graduate Students to U.S. Innovation* (Working Paper Number 04-10). Boulder, CO: Center for Economic Analysis, University of Colorado, p. 18 and Table 1.

[33]"Sanity on visas for students." *New York Times*, February 16, 2005.

[34]US Department of State cable, 04 State 154060, "Student and exchange visitor processing reminder." *http://travel.state.gov/visa/student_exchange_reminder.html*.

[35]See *http://travel.state.gov/visa/tempvisitors_wait.php*.

[36]Stephen A. Edson. 2005. "Testimony on tracking international students in higher education." Before the Subcommittee on 21st Century Competitiveness and Select Education Committee on Education and the Workforce (March 17). *http://travel.state.gov/law/legal/testimony/testimony_2193.html*.

[37]Heath Brown. 2004. *Council of Graduate Schools Finds Decline in New International Graduate Student Enrollment for the Third Consecutive Year.* Council of Graduate Schools, Washington, DC (November 4).

It is difficult to describe the effect of recent changes by field of study, because visa issuances are not categorized in this way. Visa admissions data have such classification, but there can be multiple entries per visa, so it is not an effective measurement tool. Data collected through SEVIS could be very helpful to researchers interested in international student flows, but they too are limited because the data begin in 2003, do not differentiate graduate students from postdoctoral scholars, and do not identify postdoctoral scholars who travel to the United States on H-1b or other nonimmigrant visas.

Little attention has been paid to the plight of graduate students and postdoctoral scholars who wish to attend a scientific meeting in the United States or who are invited to the United States for short-term research collaboration (weeks to a few months) that does not require registration for a university or industrial program. Such scholars do not receive stipends from US sources but may receive honoraria or reimbursement of expenses. Most institutions have been advised by DHS to tell such junior scholars to apply for a B-1 visa, just as for advanced scholars who are invited to institutions and meetings to lecture. However, the B-1 visa class definition (see Box 2-1) appears to exclude such use. The discrepancy is causing substantial confusion for university officials and international students and scholars. In addition, B-1 applicants, particularly students and postdoctoral scholars, are subject to the 214b requirement and can have difficulties in proving they do not intend to immigrate, even though their stays will be short and not US-funded, and they also must plan far in advance of meetings to allow time for the security review process.

CONCLUSION

The United States has long benefited from relatively open visa and immigration policies for international S&E students and researchers. Individuals and institutions that directly rely on or benefit from the presence of international graduate students and postdoctoral scholars, especially the university community, have been concerned that changes in visa and immigration policies after 9-11 jeopardized the flow of international scientists and engineers. In addition, international political views affect students' and scholars' willingness to come to study in the United States.[38] That the

---

[38]Tim Mazzarol and Geoffrey N. Soutar. 2001. *Push-Pull Factors in Influencing International Student Destination Choice* (Discussion Paper 0105). Crawley, WA: Centre for Entrepreneurial Management and Innovation, University of Western Australia; Todd Davis. 2003. *Atlas of Student Mobility.* New York: IIE. Political factors are correlated with stay rates of international graduate students (see: D. L. Johnson. 2001. *Relationship Between Stay Rates of PhD Recipients on Temporary Visas and Relative Economic Conditions in Country of*

consequences were not as great as anticipated can probably be attributed to efforts by the US government to make the nonimmigrant-visa application process work effectively and to measures taken by universities to make the graduate application process responsive to international-student needs.

Student flows respond quickly to alterations in immigration policies. However, the inflow of talented graduate students and postdoctoral scholars is unlikely to be severely affected as long as the world sees the United States as the most desirable destination for S&E education, training, and technology-based employment. If that perception shifts, and if international students find equally attractive educational and professional opportunities in other countries, including their own, the difficulty of visiting the United States could gain decisive importance. Chapter 3 discusses the possibility that such a long-term shift already is occurring.

Origin (Working Paper). Oak Ridge Institute for Science and Education.) and postdoctoral scholars (see: Jurgen Enders and Alexis-Michel Mugabushaka. 2004. *Wissenshaft und Karriere: Ehrfahrungen und Werdegange ehemahleiger Stipendiaten der DFG.* Bonn: Deutsche Forschungsgemeinschaft).

3

The Globalization of
Science and Engineering

The exchange of people and ideas across borders, accelerated in the last 2 decades by perestroika and the emergence of East Asia as a world economic power, has transformed institutions and lands once isolated. Most countries today send bright young people to study abroad.[1] Many of them stay and contribute in lasting ways to their adopted countries. Whether they stay or return home or move on to a third country, these international scholars become part of a rich global network of researchers, practitioners, and educators that provides cultural support for students and scholars whatever their origins.

Since World War II, the United States has been the most popular destination for science and engineering (S&E) graduate students and postdoctoral scholars choosing to study abroad. This nation of about 6 percent of the world's population has been producing over 20 percent of the S&E PhD degrees (see Figure 3-1).[2] Given the fast-rising global tide of S&E infrastructure and training, however, it would be surprising if the current US leadership did not begin to change into a more global network of scientific and economic strength. Indeed, there is considerable evidence that that process has begun.

---

[1]Todd M. Davis. 2003. *Atlas of Student Mobility.* New York: Institute of International Education.

[2]National Science Board. 2004. *Science and Engineering Indicators 2004* (NSB 04-1). Arlington, VA: National Science Foundation, pp. 2-36.

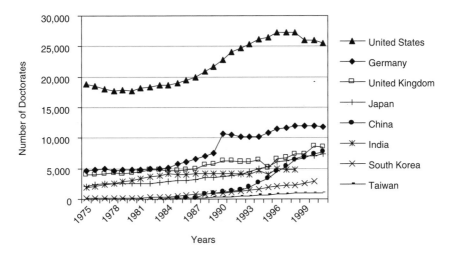

FIGURE 3-1 S&E doctorate production by country, 1975-2001.
SOURCE: National Science Board. 2004. *Science and Engineering Indicators 2004* (NSB 04-1). Arlington, VA: National Science Foundation, Table 5-30.

This chapter will examine the current strengths of the US S&E educational system and S&E enterprise and how they are now challenged by the increasingly global competition for S&E talent.

RELATIVE POSITION OF THE US
SCIENCE AND ENGINEERING ENTERPRISE

By virtually all indicators, the United States leads the world in S&E capacity. The strength of the US S&E enterprise rests on many advantages, including the diversity and stability of its S&E institutions, the strong tradition of public and private support for advanced education and research and development, the quality of its personnel, the prevalence of English as the language of S&E,[3] a relatively open society in which talented people of any background have opportunities to succeed, and the United States' global leadership in providing postdoctoral opportunities.[4] A recent comparison

---

[3]Philip G. Altbach, director, Center for International Higher Education, Boston College, presentation to committee, November 11, 2004.

[4]Because the United States has far more postdoctoral opportunities than any other country and because postdoctoral training is now expected in many biomedical, physical-science, and other fields, the United States automatically attracts some of the world's brightest young people, many of whom choose to stay permanently. Derek Scholes, chair, International Postdoctoral Committee, National Postdoctoral Association, presentation to committee, November 11, 2004.

found that 38 of the world's 50 leading research universities were in the United States.[5]

The strength of the US S&E enterprise is unlikely to falter in the near future, but over the longer term the United States faces challenges in maintaining its leadership. The investment of the United States in S&E education and research takes place in a global environment where other countries compete to produce, retain, and recruit the best S&E talent to strengthen their own research and teaching institutions. During spring 2004, a series of reports and popular articles were published on perceived symptoms of decline in the relative strength of the United States. For example, the *New York Times* reported that "the United States has started to lose its worldwide dominance in critical areas of science and innovation," referring to a decline in the US share of indicators, such as prizes, patents, and numbers of journal papers produced by US citizens and cited by others.[6]

Authorship Trends

Articles and citations are indicators commonly used to assess a country's scientific output. Articles published in internationally recognized journals constitute the key output of scientific research, whereas citations (the number of times an article has been cited) provide a measure of the research's influence. The United States heads the list of nations in the volume of articles published and in citations,[7] accounting for about one-third of all articles in 2001.[8] However, its premier position has eroded over the last 15 years as other countries' publications and citations have grown. From 1988 to 2001, world article output increased by almost 40 percent.[9] Most of the increase can be attributed to growth in article output from Western Europe, Japan, and several emerging East Asian S&T centers (South Korea, Singapore, Taiwan, and China), while the US article output has remained essentially constant since 1992 (Figure 3-2). Since 1997, the European

---

[5]Shanghai's Jiao Tong University Institute of Higher Education, *Academic Ranking of World Universities*, 2004, *http://ed.sjtu.edu.cn/rank/2004/2004Main.htm*. The ranking emphasizes prizes, publications, and citations attributed to faculty and staff, as well as the size of institutions. The *Times Higher Education* supplement also provides international comparisons of universities.

[6]William J. Broad. 2004. "U.S. is losing its dominance in the sciences." *New York Times* (May 3). Journal publications are a key indicator for basic research, and patents are of high significance to the pharmaceutical industry.

[7]David A. King. 2004. "The scientific impact of nations." *Nature*. 430:311-316. King counted internationally co-authored papers more than once (that is, for each country represented in the author list).

[8]National Science Board (NSB) 2004. *Science & Engineering Indicators. 2004* (NSB 04-1). Arlington, VA: National Science Foundation, Chapter 5.

[9]NSB. 2004. Ibid.

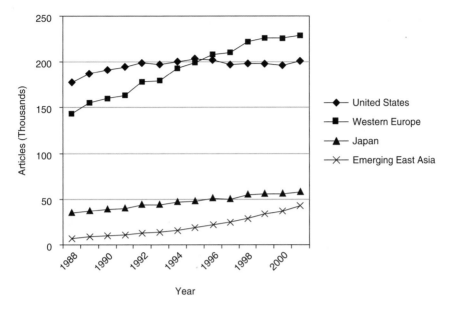

FIGURE 3-2 International authorship trends.
SOURCE: National Science Board. 2004. *Science and Engineering Indicators 2004* (NSB 04-1). Arlington, VA: National Science Foundation, Table 5-30. Note that internationally co-authored articles were counted more than once, for each country represented on the author list.

Union (EU) 15 countries have published more papers than the United States, and the gap in citations has been closing steadily.[10] Since 1993, the EU has matched the United States in citations in the physical sciences, engineering, and mathematics but still lags in the life sciences.[11] The reason for this development remains unknown, but it is more likely due to an increase in the quality and quantity of research abroad than to a decrease in the quantity of US publications.

International collaboration, as assessed by the number of articles with institutional authors from more than one country, more than doubled from 1988 to 2001, leading to an increase from 8 percent to 18 percent of all S&E articles. Even though US institutions participate in most of those collaborations, the US share (but not number) of international papers has fallen since the late 1980s. Collaborative activities between other countries

---

[10]King. 2004. Ibid.
[11]King. 2004. Ibid.

generally grew more rapidly than those of the United States; this suggests that new centers of activity and collaboration are evolving outside the United States. For example, increased ties between the emerging Asian countries and Western European and other Asian countries have led to a decline in the US share of international publications. China, Russia, and several Eastern European countries are an exception to the general trend, with increased US participation in their international articles.[12]

What could be the reason for the substantial increase in international collaboration? Many countries have enhanced their scientific capacity and thereby enlarged their pool of potential collaborators by increasing public support for research and development.[13] However, collaborations between the scientifically most advanced nations are also on the rise, so that cannot be the only reason. A recent study[14] argues that collaborative networks have self-organizing features, a system steered more by individual scientists linking together for enhanced knowledge creation than by structural or policy-related factors. The advantages of collaborations leading to highly cited research articles motivate the urge to collaborate. Consequently, researchers compete with each other for collaborations with the most highly visible and productive scientists in their fields, in their own country or abroad. Facilitating global collaboration could have a considerable impact on knowledge creation and has been promoted, for example, by the EU Framework requirements.

RISING MOBILITY AND BRAIN DRAIN

Students have been leaving their home countries in search of academic opportunities abroad for thousands of years.[15] For scientists and engineers, the trend gained importance with the rise of universities and the need for formal training unavailable at home. As early as the late 19th century, many Americans were drawn abroad to German universities to gain expertise in fast-growing new technical fields.[16] In the following decades, that

---

[12]NSB. 2004. Ibid.

[13]Caroline S. Wagner and Loet Leydesdorff. 2005. "Mapping the network of global science: Comparing international co-authorships from 1990 to 2000." *International Journal of Technology and Globalisation,* (in press).

[14]Caroline S. Wagner. 2005. "Network structure, self-organization and the growth of international collaboration in Science." *Research Policy* (in press).

[15]W. I. Cohen. 2001. *East Asia at the Center: Four Thousand Years of Engagement with the World,* New York: Columbia University Press.

[16]Donald E. Stokes. 1997. *Pasteur's Quadrant: Basic Science and Technological Innovation,* Washington, DC: Brookings Institution, pp. 38-41. Stokes explains the effect of this export and re-importation of science and engineering talent on US universities: "This tide, which was at a flood in the 1880s, reflected the lack of an American system of advanced

trend gradually reversed as US universities gained technical strength and attracted both faculty and students. US universities also benefited from an influx of educated refugees fleeing war-torn Europe during and after World War II.

The globalization of S&E is facilitated by rising international mobility. Political instability, economic changes, and many other factors encourage students to travel abroad for their education, and for many the United States is the destination of choice. China implemented an opening-up policy in 1978 and began sending large numbers of students and scholars abroad to gain skills necessary for the country's economic and social development.[17] Oil profits in Nigeria and other counties support overseas education for thousands of students. In the wake of the Cold War, students and scholars from formerly Communist nations swelled the international flow. India liberalized its economy in 1991 and started encouraging students to go abroad for advanced education and training. Since 2001, the Indian government has been providing money (in FY2005, $5 billion) for "soft loans" to students who wish to travel abroad for their education, and the number of students going abroad increased by 7 percent.[18] In 2002, India surpassed China as the major sender of graduate students to the United States.[19]

The United States has benefited from the inflow of talented students and scholars. Migrants to the United States tend to be more educated than the average person in the sending country, and the proportion of highly educated people who emigrate is high.[20] Many people believe that emigra-

---

studies adequate to the needs of a rising industrial nation, and was a standing challenge to create one. The efforts to fill this gap in American higher education were generously supported by America's economic expansion, particularly by the private individuals who had acquired great wealth in the decades after the Civil War, many of whom had gained a vision of what might be done from their studies in the German universities."

[17]Cui Ning. 2004. "Record number of scholars headed abroad." *China Daily* (December 22). The China Scholarship Council provides information on student flows, state scholarships, financing, and exchange programs. See *http://www.csc.edu.cn.*

[18]R. A. Mashelkar, Director General of the Council of Scientific and Industrial Research, comments to committee, 30 November 2004. See also R. A. Mashelkar, 2005. "India's R&D: Reaching for the top." *Science* 307:1415-17.

[19]*2004 Open Doors Report.* New York: Institute for International Education. Available at *http://www.iiebooks.org/opendoors2004.html.*

[20]See discussion of emigration rates and brain drain in Thomas Straubhaar. 2000. *International Mobility of the Highly Skilled: Brain Gain, Brain Drain, or Brain Exchange?* (HWWA Discussion Paper 88). Hamburg Institute of International Economics. Available at *http://opus.zbw-kiel.de/volltexte/2003/695.*

tion of the technically skilled—"brain drain"—is detrimental to the country of origin. Some effects on the sending country described by scholars are higher domestic wages, lost economies of scale, reduction in specialized skills, and slower resource reallocation to learning-intensive sectors.[21] Others argue that the migration of scholars benefits both sending and receiving countries, providing access to leading research and training not available in the home country and creating transnational bridges to cutting-edge research.[22] In general, the concept of "brain drain" may be too simplistic inasmuch as it ignores many benefits of emigration, including remittances, international collaborations, the return of skilled scientists and engineers, diaspora-facilitated international business, and a general investment in skills caused by the prospect of emigration.[23] Some researchers argue that, as the R&D enterprise becomes more global, "brain drain" should be recast as "brain circulation"[24] and include the broader topics of the international circulation of thinkers, knowledge workers, and rights to knowledge.[25] Such a discussion would include issues of local resources; many countries lack the educational and technical infrastructure to support advanced education, so aspiring scientists and engineers have little choice but to seek at least part of their training abroad, and in many instances such travel is encouraged by governments.

---

[21]Mihir A. Desai, Devesh Kapur, and John McHale. 2005. "The fiscal impact of the brain drain: Indian emigration to the U.S." *Journal of Development Economics* (in press).

[22]Jin Xiaoming, Minister, Science and Technology Office, Embassy of the People's Republic of China, comments to committee, 12 November 2004. See also *Joint Japan/World Bank Graduate Scholarship Program Tracer Study IV*. Washington, DC: World Bank. September 2004, available at *http://www.worldbank.org/wbi/scholarships/*.

[23]Devesh Kapur and John McHale. 2005. "Sojourns and software: Internationally mobile human capital and high-tech industry development in India, Ireland, and Israel." In: *From Underdogs to Tigers: the Rise and Growth of the Software Industry in Israel, Ireland and India*, eds. A. Arora and A. Gambardella. Oxford, UK: Oxford University Press.

[24]OECD. 2002. *International Mobility of the Highly Skilled* (Policy Brief 92 2002 01 1P4). Washington, DC: OECD. Available at *http://www.oecd.org/dataoecd/9/20/1950028.pdf*.

[25]Bogumil Jewsiewicki. 2003. *The Brain Drain in an Era of Liberalism*. Ottawa, ON: Canadian Bureau for International Education. Using Québec as a case study, Jewsiewicki considers the individual's right to choose his or her own career path and the rights of communities to protect their collective investment. He focuses on African and ex-Soviet-bloc academics who discuss their motivations for remaining in Canada. Also see Karine Tremblay. 2004. "Links between academic mobility and immigration." *Symposium on International Labour and Academic Mobility: Emerging Trends and Implications for Public Policy, Toronto, October 22*. Tremblay notes that the percentage of foreign students on OECD campuses rose by 34.9 percent on average between 1998 and 2002 and by 50 percent or more in the Czech Republic, Iceland, Korea, New Zealand, Norway, Spain, and Sweden. In absolute terms, more than 450,000 new individuals crossed borders to study in an OECD country during this short period, raising the number of foreign students enrolled on OECD campuses to 1,781,000.

Supporting the concept of brain circulation is the finding that ethnic networks developed in the United States by international students and scholars help to support knowledge transfer and economic development in both the United States and the sending country. An analysis of patent citations supports the existence of a diaspora effect. One study shows that as the numbers of Indian students and researchers in the United States has increased, the number of US patents issued to ethnic Indians has risen even faster, from 651 (0.9 percent of total) in 1976 to 5,334 (3.2 percent) in 2000.[26] Not only are international researchers contributing to the US S&E enterprise, there is also knowledge diffusion through ethnic channels, with positive economic effects on the sending country.[27]

RISING GLOBAL CAPACITY FOR HIGHER EDUCATION

In concert with increased international mobility is an increased capacity on the part of countries other than the United States to provide higher education. As countries develop knowledge-based economies, they seek to reap more of the benefits of international educational activities, including strong positive effects on GDP growth.[28] One strategy used by emerging economies, such as India and China, is to couple education-abroad programs with strategic investments in S&E infrastructure—in essence pushing students away to gain skills and creating jobs to draw them back.[29] Other countries, particularly in Europe, are trying to retain their best students and also to increase quality and open international access to their own higher educational institutions. An additional element creating competition for US

---

[26]Ajay Agrawal, Devesh Kapur, and John McHale. 2004. Defying distance: examining the influence of the diaspora on scientific knowledge flows. *The Fourth Annual Roundtable on Engineering Entrepreneurship Research Conference (REER), December 3-5, 2004, Atlanta, GA*. Available at *http://mgt.gatech.edu/news_room/news/2004/reer/files/agrawal.pdf*.

[27]William Kerr. 2004. *Ethnic Scientific Communities and International Technology Diffusion*. Working paper. Available at *http://econ-www.mit.edu/faculty/download_pdf. php?id=994*.

[28]The Conference Board of Canada. 1999. *The Economic Implications of International Education for Canada and Nine Comparator Countries: A Comparison of International Education Activities and Economic Performance*. Ottawa, ON: Department of Foreign Affairs and International Trade. Also see AnnaLee Saxenian. 1999. *Silicon Valley's New Immigrant Entrepreneurs*. San Francisco: Public Policy Institute, p. 3. Available at *http://www.ccis-ucsd.org/PUBLICATIONS/wrkg15.PDF*.

[29]R. A. Mashelkar, Director General of the Council of Scientific and Industrial Research, comments to committee, November 30, 2004; Laudeline Auriol. 2004. "Why do we need indicators on careers of doctorate holders?" (DSTI/EAS/STP/NESTI/RD(2004)15). *OECD Workshop on User Needs for Indicators on Careers of Doctorate Holders, September 27, 2004, Paris*. Available at *http://www.olis.oecd.org/olis/2004doc.nsf*.

institutions is the growth of US branch campuses in other countries. The focus of these campuses is generally on undergraduate and professional education, so their impact on the enrollment of international S&E graduate students is minor at this point.

Asia

Only recently has economic development in Asia been linked to higher education. Countries with the most economic success—Japan, South Korea, Singapore, Taiwan, and, more recently, China—have also invested heavily in literacy and in primary and secondary education. As literacy expanded and the middle class developed in the 1980s, demand for higher education increased.[30] As economies have developed, Asian countries have started to invest in higher education and have increased their gross domestic expenditures on R&D (see Figure 3-3). Their investments are reflected by growth in numbers of researchers, papers listed in the *Science Citation Index*, patents awarded, and doctoral degrees awarded.[31]

In China, a key ingredient of the S&E enterprise has been the transfer of technical people.[32] Most of the leading researchers and research managers in China have had experience studying in the United States. The Chinese Science Foundation is modeled on the US National Science Foundation, and peer-review standards and startup packages for junior faculty are also modeled on US standards.[33] As evidence of the growing capacity of China to

---

[30] Philip G. Altbach. 2004. "The past and future of Asian universities." In: *Asian Universities: Historical Perspectives and Contemporary Challenges*, eds. P. G. Altbach and T. Umakoshi. Baltimore, MD: Johns Hopkins University Press, pp. 13-32.

[31] Diana Hicks. 2004. "Asian countries strengthen their research." *Issues in Science and Technology* 20: 75-78. Available at *http://www.issues.org/issues/20.4/realnumbers.html*. The author notes that the number of doctoral degrees awarded in China has increased 50-fold since 1986. "Although in many countries cultural and economic barriers still hamper scientific achievement, foreign science policy goals are clear. Thus, hurdles are likely to be overcome, and scientific progress is likely to accelerate. US scientists will face intensified competition for the best students, corporate research support, space to publish in the top journals, and patents. Inevitably, this will reduce the perceived achievements of younger generations of US scientists. Although they will work far harder than previous generations, they will not command the same dominating position in world science as did their predecessors."

[32] Weifang Min. 2004. "Chinese higher education: The legacy of the past and the context of the future." In: *Asian Universities: Historical Perspectives and Contemporary Challenges*, eds. P. G. Altbach and T. Umakoshi. Baltimore, MD: Johns Hopkins University Press, pp. 53-84; Denis Fred Simon, 2004. "Foreign R&D and the impact of globalization on China's emerging technological trajectory." *Presentation at AAAS S&T Policy Forum, April 2004, Washington, DC*. Available at *http://www.aaas.org/spp/rd/simon404.pdf*.

[33] Jin Xiaoming, Minister, Science and Technology Office, Embassy of the People's Republic of China, comments to committee, November 12, 2004; Executive Summary, DTI Global Watch Stem Cell Mission, September 2004. Available at *http://www.globalwatchonline.com/*

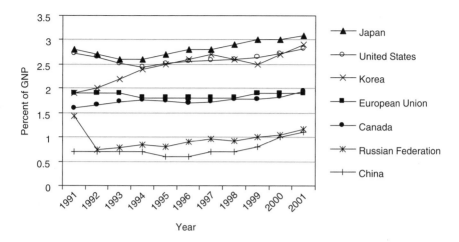

FIGURE 3-3 Expenditure for research and development as percentage of gross national product, 1991–2001.
SOURCE: OECD. 2002. *Main Science and Technology Indicators.* Paris: Organisation for Economic Co-operation and Development.

provide advanced S&E training, 7,300 doctoral degrees were awarded in China in 2000, a 50-fold increase since 1986.[34] An estimated 58 percent of all degrees awarded in 2002 were in engineering and the physical sciences.[35]

China is also beginning to attract substantial numbers of international students to its own universities.[36] For example, at universities in Shanghai,

---

mission/tmsmrep.aspx#life. The DTI Global Watch Mission visited China, Singapore, and South Korea in September 2004 to evaluate scientific excellence and evaluate opportunities for scientific and commercial collaboration.

[34]Hicks. 2004. Ibid.

[35]"President's science council says future health of technology sector is in jeopardy; decline of manufacturing could impact innovation 'ecosystem'." *Manufacturing & Technology News,* 10(18), October 3, 2003. Available at *www.manufacturingnews.com/news/03/1003/art1.html.*

[36]Urmi A. Goswani. 2005. "India fails to mature into learning hub." *Economic Times* (January 13). Available at *http://economictimes.indiatimes.com/articleshow/msid-98027, prtpage-1.cms*; and Cui Ning. 2004. "Record number of scholars headed abroad." *China Daily* (December 22). Ning reports that from 1978 to 2003, China received a total of 620,000 international students. In 2003, China received 78,000 students from 175 countries or regions, who studied primarily liberal arts, medical science, engineering, science, and agronomy. Most students come from the Republic of Korea, Japan, the United States, Viet Nam, and Indonesia. Available at *http://www.chinadaily.com.cn/english/doc/2004-12/22/content_042422.htm.*

more than 19,000 overseas students enrolled in degree courses or short-term training from January to September 2004—a 40 percent increase over the previous year. Still not well developed are opportunities for postdoctoral training.[37]

There are indications that Chinese scholars who were trained in the United States are increasingly considering returning to their home country.[38] A recent survey reported that more mainland Chinese who had studied S&E abroad planned to return home in anticipation of good career opportunities.[39] If such plans materialize, they will represent a huge shift from the existing 96 percent stay rate among Chinese doctorate recipients in the United States.[40] Similar shifts appear to be occurring in India and Taiwan as these countries build up their industrial and educational infrastructure.

Enthusiasm for S&E in Asia appears in many kinds of statistics. For example,

- For the last three decades, about one-third of US college students have earned their first university degrees in S&E; corresponding recent figures are considerably higher for China (59 percent in 2001), South Korea (46 percent in 2002), and Japan (66 percent in 2001).[41]
- Asian countries have designed policies and incentives intended to retain their highly trained personnel, bring them home after training, and otherwise benefit from the skills they acquire in other nations, chiefly the United States.[42]

---

[37]"Focus on Asia-Pacific." *DTI Global Watch Magazine*, November 2004; Executive Summary, DTI Global Watch Stem Cell Mission, September 2004. Available at *http://www.globalwatchonline.com/mission/tmsmrep.aspx#life.*

[38]Sam Dillon. 2004. "U.S. slips in attracting the best students." *New York Times* (Dec. 21), p. A-1.

[39]The survey, conducted by the Chinese Youth Federation and two newspapers in Beijing, polled 3,097 people in October and November 2004. Available at *http://www.straitstimes. com/sub/asia/story/0,5562,291279,00.html?*

[40]Michael G. Finn. 2003. *Stay Rates of Foreign Doctorate Recipients from US Universities, 2001.* Oak Ridge, TN: ORISE.

[41]National Science Board. 2004. *Science and Engineering Indicators 2004* (NSB 04-1). Arlington, VA: National Science Foundation, p. 2-35. The consistent trend masks considerable variation by field. See Fig. 2-11, available at *http://www.nsf.gov/sbe/srs/seind04/c2/fig02-11.htm.*

[42]Jen Lin-Liu. 2002. "Brain gain in Taiwan." *The Chronicle of Higher Education* (October 18); National Science Board. 2004. *Science and Engineering Indicators 2004* (NSB 04-1). Arlington, VA: National Science Foundation, Chapter 4; Jin Xiaoming, minister, Science and Technology Office, Embassy of the People's Republic of China, comments to committee, November 12, 2004; R. A. Mashelkar, director general, Council of Scientific and Industrial Research, New Delhi, comments to committee, November 30, 2004.

• India, through its National Policy on Education (1986) and the New Science and Technology Policy (2003), has focused on R&D and education in S&T. Between 1980 and 2000, Indian S&T doctorate-degree production increased from 2,973 to 5,725.[43]

• China and South Korea are raising their overall S&E spending relative to that of Organisation for Economic Co-operation and Development (OECD) members (see Figure 3-3).

• Asian countries—led by Japan, South Korea, and Taiwan—accounted for over 25 percent of high-technology exports in 2001, up from about 15 percent in 1990.[44]

Europe

The number of young Europeans attracted to careers in S&E is decreasing, and many of the students and researchers who do specialize in S&E emigrate to the United States.[45] To counter that trend and build their S&E workforces, European nations have been working together to internationalize policies and enhance student mobility to "facilitate the creation of a genuine European scientific community." In 1999, the Bologna Declaration laid out a system to harmonize undergraduate- and graduate-degree requirements among EU member countries. To make Europe the most competitive knowledge-based economy in the world, EU governments were urged to raise S&E spending to 3 percent of gross domestic product by 2010.[46] The EU has enacted a "mobility plan" to improve research training, foster collaboration, and increase incentives for knowledge transfer

---

[43]Laxman Prasad. 2004. Employment characteristics of PhD holders in the field of science and technology: Indian experience (DSTI/EAS/STP/NESTI/RD(2004)23). *OECD Workshop on User Needs for Indicators on Careers of Doctorate Holders, September, 27, 2004, Paris.* Available at *http://www.olis.oecd.org/olis2004doc.nsf/*.

[44]National Science Board. 2004. *Science and Engineering Indicators 2004* (NSB 04-1). Arlington, VA: National Science Foundation, Figure 6-9.

[45]In 2000, the EU was ahead of the United States and Japan in the production of S&E graduates. As a proportion of PhDs per 1,000 population aged 25-34, the EU-15 had an average of 0.56, the United States had 0.48 and Japan had 0.24. However, the decline in the number along with the emigration of EU-15 S&E graduates is creating a restriction for European R&D. In the late 1990s, the European S&E workforce accounted for 5.4 per thousand workers, vs. 8.1 per thousand in the United States and 9.3 in Japan. European Commission. 2002. *Towards a European Research Area. Science, Technology, and Innovation, Key Figures 2002.* Brussels: European Commission, pp. 36-38. Available at *ftp://ftp.cordis.lu/pub/indicators/docs/ind_kf2002.pdf.*

[46]Robert M. May. 2004. "Raising Europe's game." *Nature* 430: 831; and Philippe Busquin. 2004. "Investing in people." *Science* 303:145.

between academe and industry.[47] Some examples are the Erasmus and Marie Curie Programmes, designed to create cross-border research opportunities for European and non-European undergraduates, graduate students, and postdoctoral scholars.[48]

Other EU countries, especially those with developed S&E capacity, have implemented strategies to facilitate retention and immigration of the technically skilled. Several OECD countries have relaxed their immigration laws to attract high-skilled students and workers. Some are increasing growth in their international-student populations and encouraging these students to apply for resident status.[49] For example,

- The United Kingdom has implemented a points-based Highly Skilled Migrant Programme on a pilot basis and since the middle 1990s has increased the number of work permits issued to skilled workers.[50]
- In 2000, Germany introduced a "green card" program for information-technology (IT) specialists, with plans to issue 20,000 of these visas per year. The card authorizes a holder to engage in unrestricted employment in Germany for 5 years.[51]
- The Irish government places potential immigrants who are skilled

[47]Commission of the European Communities, 2001. *A Mobility Strategy for the European Research Area* (COM 2001 331 final). Communication from the Commission to the Council and the European Parliament, Brussels, June 20, 2001. Reasons cited by European-born scientists and engineers for wanting to work in the United States included broader work opportunities, better access to leading technologies, and higher salaries. Available at *http:// europa.eu.int/eur-lex/en/com/cnc/2001/com2001_0331en01.pdf*.

[48]Mary Kavanaugh, counselor, science, technology, and education, European Union, Delegation of the European Commission, presentation to the committee, October 11, 2004. But see Maziar Nekovee, "Obstacles to mobility in Europe: Young mobile researchers meet EC policy-makers in Crete." *Science's Next Wave*, November 30, 2000. Available at *http:// nextwave.sciencemag.org/cgi/content/full/2000/11/02/13?ck=nck*.

[49]Karine Tremblay. 2004. Links between academic mobility and immigration. *Symposium on International Labour and Academic Mobility: Emerging Trends and Implications for Public Policy, Toronto, October 22.*

[50]Devesh Kapur and John McHale. 2002. "Sojourns and software: Internationally mobile human capital and high-tech industry development in India, Ireland, and Israel." In: *From Underdogs to Tigers: the Rise and Growth of the Software Industry in Israel, Ireland and India.* Oxford, UK: Oxford University Press.

[51]Green Card Germany Web site *http://www.green-card-germany.com/*; Robert Metzke, "WANTED: 75,000 IT Pros—Germany Considers Green Card Model." *Science's Next Wave*, March 3, 2000. Available at *http://nextwave.sciencemag.org/cgi/content/full/2000/03/02/6*; also see discussion of green cards and brain drain in Thomas Straubhaar. 2000. *International Mobility of the Highly Skilled: Brain Gain, Brain Drain, or Brain Exchange* (HWWA Discussion Paper 88). Hamburg: Institute of International Economics. Available at *http://opus .zbw-kiel.de/volltexte/2003/695.*

workers in IT and biotechnology on a fast track to facilitate intracompany transfers.[52]

- The European Science Foundation has developed a publication to bring together information on funding for new principal investigators.[53]

- Several EU countries and the EU itself have launched programs to facilitate networking among students and researchers working abroad, providing contact information, collaborative possibilities, and funding and job opportunities in the EU. The Deutsche Akademischer Austausch Dienst (DAAD) has launched GAIN,[54] the Italian Ministero degli Affari Esteri has launched DAVINCI,[55] and the EU has its Researcher's Mobility Portal.[56]

Barriers to mobility persist in some European countries, although they are being noted and criticized by those who favor freer flows of scientists and engineers. For example, 29 percent of foreign researchers surveyed recently in Italy reported "high difficulties" with visas, work permits, and other administrative paperwork. Likewise, the efforts of France to recruit highly skilled S&E talent are said to be held back by a "discouraging landscape of administrative convolution, heavy taxes, and inflexible labor legislation".[57] A recent report indicates that the EU is working to improve its procedures for the admission of third-country nationals to perform scientific research.[58]

GLOBAL COMPETITION FOR GRADUATE STUDENTS AND POSTDOCTORAL SCHOLARS

The United States is still by far the leading host country for international students, enrolling some 586,000 foreign-born graduate and under-

---

[52]Expert Group on Future Skill Needs. 2004. *A Model to Predict the Supply and Demand for Researchers and Research Personnel in Line with Ireland's Strategy for Contributing to the European Research Area's 3 percent Initiative.* Dublin: Forfás. Available at *http:// egfsn.forfas.ie/press/reports/pdf/egfsn040906_research_skills_report.pdf.*

[53]Dominique Martin-Rovet. 2003. *Opportunities for Outstanding Young Scientists in Europe to Create an Independent Research Team.* Strasbourg: European Science Foundation.

[54]German Academic International Network Web page, *http://www.gain-network.org.*

[55]Database accessible via the Internet and listing Italian researchers that are not residing in Italy webpage, *http://www.esteri.it/davinci/index.asp?lang=eng.*

[56]Researcher's Mobility Portal Web page, *http://europa.eu.int/eracareers/index_en.cfm.*

[57]Commission of the European Communities; *Snapshots 'Brain drain study.'* Available at *http://europa.eu.int/comm/research/era/pdf/indicators/snap6.pdf.*

[58]Commission of the European Communities. 2004. *On the Admission of Third-Country Nationals to Carry Out Scientific Research in the European Community* (COM(2004) 178 final) Brussels: Commission of the European Communities.

graduate students, more than one-fourth of the world's total.[59] US academic institutions and government laboratories have traditionally attracted high-caliber international graduate students and postdoctoral trainees by providing top-notch research facilities, generous graduate-student scholarships, and student and work visas.[60]

However, the United States must take into account the fact that there is increasing international competition to recruit the best students, particularly in countries where English is the dominant language.[61] A National Science Board (NSB) task force noted that "global competition for S&E talent is intensifying, such that the United States may not be able to rely on the international S&E labor market to fill unmet skill needs."[62] The growth rate of the US S&E labor force would falter if the United States became less successful at attracting immigrant and temporary nonimmigrant scientists and engineers.[63]

How Can the United States Continue to Attract the Best Domestic and International Students and Scholars?

With the increasing competition among countries for international students, there is keen interest in why those students choose to study abroad

---

[59]Simon Marginson. 2004. "Australian higher education: National and global markets." In: *Markets in Higher Education–Rhetoric or Reality?* eds. P. Taxiera, B. Jongbloed, D. Dill, and A. Amaral. Dordrecht, The Netherlands: Kluwer, pp. 207-240.

[60]In a 2004 study of Deutsche Forschungsgemeinshaft (DFG) stipend holders, 72 percent used their award to do postdoctoral training abroad, and of these 66.3 percent went to the United States. Reasons given for choosing the United States included funding, access to equipment, ability to pursue cutting-edge research, research independence, career opportunities in academe and industry, and collaborative opportunities. Jurgen Enders and Alexis-Michel Mugabushaka. 2004. *Wissenshaft und Karriere: Ehrfahrungen und Werdegange ehemahleiger Stipendiaten der DFG*. Bonn: Forschungsgemeinshaft. Available at *http://www.dfg.de/dfg_im_profil/zahlen_und_fakten/statistisches_berichtswesen/stip2004/*.

[6]The Asia-Pacific nations include three of the four largest nations (China, India, and Indonesia) and 10 of the world's 16 cities with populations over 10 million, representing huge concentrations of present and future demand for education. In 2002, almost half the 1.6 million international students worldwide were students from Asian-Pacific countries who invested in education in OECD nations. Majority-English-speaking language countries (MESLCs) enrolled 71.6 percent of all international students from Asia in 2001. OECD. 2003. *Education at a Glance*. Paris: OECD. It should be noted that there are different contexts for flows to non-MESLCs; for example, a different set of circumstances determine flows between French-speaking countries. See Todd Davis. 2003. *Atlas of Student Mobility*. New York: Institute of International Education.

[62]National Science Board. 2003. *The Science and Engineering Workforce: Realizing America's Potential* (NSB 03-69). Arlington, VA: National Science Foundation.

[63]National Science Board. 2004. *Science and Engineering Indicators 2004* (NSB 04-1). Arlington, VA: National Science Foundation, p. 3-39.

and how they then choose destinations and institutions for study abroad.[64] The decision of graduate students and postdoctoral scholars to go abroad for study is a combination of "push" and "pull" factors.[65] Under conditions of increasing capacity among traditional sending countries, the ability of the United States to continue to attract the best students will increasingly depend on its pull factors,[66] including quality, job opportunities, convenience, and perception of being a welcoming place.

Push factors are features of the home environment that are viewed by prospective students as unsatisfactory, such as

- Limited economic wealth.
- Low involvement in the world community.
- Few world-class institutions.
- Few doctoral and postdoctoral programs.
- No availability of a particular specialty.
- Limited access to funding, especially for junior investigators.
- Poor career prospects.
- Adverse social or political conditions.

Pull factors are desirable features of a destination country, such as

- Better academic facilities.
- Better financial support.
- Prestige of a foreign degree.
- Social links and personal recommendations.
- Life in an ethnically diverse culture.
- Better working conditions.
- Better opportunities for employment.
- Willingness of employers to hire well-qualified foreigners.
- Higher salaries, including academic salaries.

---

[64]Anthony Bohm and D. P. Chaudhri. 2000. *Securing Australia's Future: An Analysis of the International Education Markets in India.* Sydney: IDP Education Australia Limited, pp. 150-152. This study reports that although the United States is "an established brand", providing an excellent education across a wide array of characteristics, it performs poorly in affordability and provision of a tolerant and safe environment.

[65]Tim Mazzarol and Geoffrey N. Soutar. 2001. *Push-Pull Factors in Influencing International Student Destination Choice* (Discussion Paper 0105). Crawley, WA: Centre for Entrepreneurial Management and Innovation, University of Western Australia; Todd Davis. 2003. *Atlas of Student Mobility.* New York: IIE. Hubert B. van Hoof and Marja J. Verbeeten. 2005. "Wine is for drinking, water is for washing: Student opinions about international exchange programs." *Journal of Studies in International Education* 9(1):42-61. Similar factors are correlated with stay rates of international graduate students and postdoctoral scholars.

[66]Mazzarol and Soutar. 2001. Ibid, p. 17.

An especially strong US pull factor for graduate students and postdoctoral scholars has been the large increase in research funds, due primarily to growth in the National Institutes of Health budget (see discussion in Chapter 2). Strong job prospects in this country are another strong pull factor.[67] An indicator of job expectations for international graduate students who earned degrees in the United States is the stay rate. In 2001, the percentage of temporary residents who had received PhDs and remained in the United States ranged from 26 percent to 70 percent, depending on the field of the doctorate. This rate has been increasing in recent years[68] (see Figure 1-19). Decisions to return and career outcomes for international graduate students and scholars have been the subject of recent studies.[69]

International and domestic students have different motivations and experience different opportunity costs in pursuing graduate education. Both experience the long time to degree and delayed entry into an independent position. However, especially for students from developing countries, a graduate degree confers a potential to gain employment in the United States that in most cases is otherwise unavailable.[70] Domestic students are not restricted in entering the job market at an earlier stage, and many opt out of graduate education because they can obtain gainful employment without it. It is difficult to measure economic rewards in careers that require a long training period, but one study indicates that the lost earnings for those students who undergo graduate training in life sciences are about $25,000 per year of working life compared with other S&E fields and $62,000 per year of working life compared with professions that do not require as long a training period, such as law.[71] Such professions are not easily accessible to international students.

Most postdoctoral scholars, regardless of residence, would prefer to stay in the United States after their training (see Figure 1-21). Similarly, as

---

[67]Philip G. Altbach, "Higher education crosses borders: Can the United States remain the top destination for foreign students?" *Change.* March/April 2004. See also B. Bratsburg. 1995. "The incidence of non-return among foreign students in the United States." *Economics of Education Review* 14(4):373-83.

[68]Finn. 2003. Ibid.

[69]Deepak Gupta. 2004. "The return choice and careers of foreign-born U.S. S&E Ph.D.s." Doctoral dissertation. Berkeley: University of California; and DOE/NSF Nuclear Science Advisory Committee. 2004. *A Status Report and Recommendations for the Beginning of the 21st Century.* Washington, DC: Department of Energy and National Science Foundation.

[70]Barry R. Chiswick. 2000. *Are Immigrants Favorably Self-Selected? An Economic Analysis* (IZA DP No. 131). Hamburg: Forschungsinstitut zur Zukunft der Arbeit.

[71]Richard B. Freeman, Eric Weinstein, Elizabeth Marincola, Janet Rosenbaum, and Frank Solomon. 2001. *Careers and Rewards in Biosciences.* Washington, DC: American Society for Cell Biology. Available at *http://www.ascb.org/publications/competition.html.*

many as one-third of European visitors to the United States on H-1b visas are thought to stay on permanently.[72] Those rates can be altered by the innovative programs designed by sending countries to attract students home. For example, in some countries, educational loans are forgiven if the student returns to the home country; others designate a job for the returnee. The return rate is higher among postdoctoral scholars who had been awarded prestigious fellowships.[73] Also affecting the return rate are the social ties that a student or scholar has with his or her home country; in many cases, students return home to rejoin family and renew social ties. Those who married while in the United States had a very low return rate.[74]

Declining Domestic Student Interest in Science and Engineering

The committee heard considerable discussion about an apparent decline in interest in S&E careers among US-born students. Graduate-student enrollments are counter-cyclical to economic cycles and show strong field differences (see Figures 1-1 and 1-2). In 2002, in a weak US economy, full-time enrollment in S&E graduate programs reached a new all-time high of 378,800; first-time enrollment also reached a new peak of 104,200. The number of postdoctoral appointments in S&E reached a total of 38,316, also an all-time high.[75] Enrollment trends differ for domestic and international graduate students. Enrollment of US citizens and permanent residents increased more slowly during the 1980s than did enrollment of temporary visa holders and declined from 1994 to 2000. Enrollment in 2002 was 6 percent below the peak year of 1993—a year in which many Chinese students on temporary visas were converted to permanent residents under the Chinese Student Protection Act. The enrollment of S&E graduate students who were US citizens or permanent residents rose by 15,500 in 2002, second only to the 17,100 gain in 1992.[76]

---

[72]Commission on the European Communities. 2004. *Snapshot: Brain Drain Study.* Available at *http://europa.eu.int/comm/research/era/pdf/indicators/snap6.pdf.*

[73]Jurgen Enders and Alexis-Michel Mugabushaka. 2004. *Wissenshaft und Karriere: Ehrfahrungen und Werdegange ehemahliger Stipendiaten der DFG.* Bonn: Deutsche Forschungsgemainshaft. The DFG reports return rates of 85 percent among its fellows.

[74]D. Gupta, M. Nerad, and V. Cerny. 2003. "International Ph.Ds: Exploring the decision to stay or return." *International Higher Education* 31(Spring).

[75]Enrollment numbers include health-science fields; numbers of postdoctoral appointments include health-science fields but not postdoctoral scholars with MD degrees.

[76] Lori Thurgood. 2004. *Graduate Enrollment in Science and Engineering Fields Reaches a New Peak; First-Time Enrollment of Foreign Students Declines* (Info Brief 04-326). Arlington, VA: National Science Foundation.

Among the factors that influence domestic-student interest in graduate work are

- Faculty encouragement or discouragement of student interest.
- Relative postdegree job uncertainty compared with business, law, and medical degree programs.[77]
- Alternative employment opportunities available to bachelor's-degree holders; these are influenced in part by the business cycle.
- Decreased availability of tenure-track positions at universities.
- Long times to degree, especially in biomedical fields, with an average time to degree of 7.5 years.[78]
- The requirement of postdoctoral training
- Long time to first job or scientific independence.
- Relatively low stipends during years of graduate and postdoctoral work compared with salaries available in the private sector or in other professions.

The scarcity of permanent positions can be a large disincentive for undergraduates considering a research career and is cited as a major factor for domestic students choosing other fields of study.[79] This issue is especially acute in fields where postdoctoral work is a job prerequisite and where academe is the predominant career choice of graduate students and postdoctoral scholars,[80] although it is also an issue in fields such as nuclear physics where the predominant career choice is a research position at a

---

[77]See Howard Garrison, Susan Gerbi, and Paul Kincade. 2003. "In an era of scientific opportunity, are there opportunities for biomedical scientists?" *FASEB Journal* 17: 2169-73. It should also be noted that there is flagging student interest in S&E in Europe and Asia which may be tied to lack of jobs with remunerative opportunities comparable with those in finance and law (see Weifang Min. 2004. "Chinese higher education: The legacy of the past and the context of the future." In: *Asian Universities: Historical Perspectives and Contemporary Challenges*, eds. P.G. Altbach and T. Umakoshi. Baltimore, MD: Johns Hopkins University Press, pp. 53-84).

[78]*Doctorate Recipients from United States Universities: Summary Report 2003.* The National Opinion Research Center (NORC) conducts the survey for NSF. Available at *http://www.norc.uchicago.edu/issues/docdata.htm.*

[79]E. Seymour and N. M. Hewitt. 1997. *Talking About Leaving: Why Undergraduates Leave the Sciences.* Nashville, TN: Westview Press; R. Freeman et al. 2001. "Competition and Careers in Biosciences." *Science.* 294:2293-94. See also the discussion of the effects of lower wages on career decisions in physics in Richard Freeman. 2000. *Labor Markets in Action: Essays in Empirical Economics.* Cambridge, MA: Harvard University Press.

[80]National Research Council. 2005. *Advancing the Nation's Health Needs: NIH Research Training Programs.* Washington DC: National Academies Press; and National Research Council. 2005. *Bridges to Independence: Fostering the Independence of New Investigators in Biomedical Research.* Washington, DC: The National Academies Press.

national laboratory.[81] Few career opportunities and a reduced "pull" for scientists and engineers are reflected in lower compensation rates all along the career path.

Studies have suggested ways to encourage US student interest in S&E, including more effective career counseling, closer involvement of the professional S&E communities, placement of limits on time to degree, and better career-data collection and dissemination.[82] Such recommendations are likely to be effective to the extent that they take on high national priority in Congress, the Office of Science and Technology Policy, research-intensive federal agencies, and academic institutions.

The present committee was not charged with examining this issue in detail other than to determine whether large numbers of international graduate students and postdoctoral scholars discourage participation of US citizens, either by crowding out (see discussion in Chapter 1) or by creating a noninclusive environment. Relevant data were limited to conflicting anecdotal reports. Some US students reportedly are hesitant to join a graduate research group that consists largely of international students[83]—this is similar to the "tipping effect" seen in other circumstances.[84] Other students regard such a situation as an opportunity to learn about new cultures and develop international collaborations.

Teaching Assistants

The presence of large numbers of international teaching assistants (ITAs) in US higher education has resulted in concerns about their adequate preparation and supervision. The majority of complaints refer to insufficient language and communication skills, as well as cultural differences.[85]

---

[81]DOE/NSF Nuclear Science Advisory Committee. 2004. *Education in Nuclear Science: A Status Report and Recommendations for the Beginning of the 21st Century.* Washington, DC: Department of Energy and National Science Foundation.

[82]COSEPUP. 1995. *Reshaping the Graduate Education of Scientists and Engineers.*, Washington DC: National Academy Press; COSEPUP. 2000. *Enhancing the Postdoctoral Experience for Scientists and Engineers.* Washington, DC: National Academy Press.

[83]Yudhijit Bhattacharjee. 2004. "Settling in on campus." *Science.* 304:1282-1284.

[84]For more on tipping points, see, for example, Eleanor Wolf. 1969. "The tipping point in racially changing neighborhoods." *Journal of the American Institute of Planners* 29:217-222; Reynolds Farley, Charlotte Steeh, Tara Jackson, Maria Krysan, and Keith Reeves. 1993. "Continuing racial residential segregation in detroit. 'Chocolate City, Vanilla Suburbs revisited.'" *Journal of Housing Research* 4(1): 1-21; Philip Martin. 1999. "Immigration and farm labor: An overview." Available at *http://www.farmfoundatin.org/1999NPPECmartin.pdf.*

[85]L. H. Jacobs and C. B. Friedman. 1988. "Student achievement under foreign teaching associates compared with native teaching associates." *Journal of Higher Education* 59(3): 551-563; Joe Rominiecki. 2005. "North Dakota bill addresses student complaint: I can't understand my prof." *Kansas City Infozine* (February 12), *http://www.infozine.com/news/stories/op/storiesView/sid/5826/;* Scott Stossel. 1999. "Uncontrolled experiment: America's dependency on foreign scientists." *New Republic* (March 29).

Research into the impact of ITAs on student performance, however, fails to provide a clear-cut picture. Some studies revealed an adverse effect of non-native English-speaking ITAs, but others indicated better student performance. For example, two recent publications examining the impact of ITAs on undergraduate economics instruction came to opposite conclusions.[86] In the study that found students were less likely to drop sections led by ITAs, all ITAs had undergone substantive teacher training. Researchers who surveyed talented undergraduates who started out in S&E majors but switched to other fields found no evidence to support the idea that under-graduate attrition from S&E fields was significantly affected by alleged poor tutorial abilities of teaching assistants or linguistic, pedagogic, or social skills of foreign faculty or teaching assistants.[87]

Demographic Challenges

Demographic trends in the United States indicate challenges in maintaining excellence in the S&E workforce. The S&E workforce is aging; a large number of people who received their degrees in the late 1960s and early 1970s are nearing retirement. The rise of the average age of the S&E doctoral workforce is of concern, given historical evidence that many researchers are more productive in their younger years.[88]

Japan and the mature industrial nations of Europe, also facing the challenges of an aging and slow-growing population and declining interest in S&E careers among young people, have created programs designed to attract more women and foreign-born students. The United States is dissimilar in that its overall population is growing and its average age is increasing less rapidly than that of the populations of Europe and Japan.[89] That may not provide immediate advantage, because the US college-age population will shift toward minority groups, especially Hispanics, blacks, and American Indians and Alaskan natives, whose current participation rates in S&E are half or less of those of white, non-Hispanic students.[90]

---

[86]George Borjas. 2000. *Foreign-born Teaching Assistants and the Academic Performance of Undergraduates* (Working Paper 7635). Cambridge, MA: National Bureau of Economic Research; and B. Fleisher, M. Hashimoto, and B. A. Weinberg. 2002. "Foreign GTAs can be effective teachers in economics." *Journal of Economic Education* 33(4):299-325.

[87]Seymour and Hewitt. 1997. Ibid.

[88]Paula E. Stephan and Sharon Levin. 1992. *Striking the Mother Lode in Science: The Importance of Age, Time and Place.* New York: Oxford University Press.

[89]From 2000 to 2015, the Hispanic college-age population is projected to increase by 52 percent. National Science Board. 2004. *Science and Engineering Indicators 2004* (NSB 04-1). Arlington, VA: National Science Foundation, p. 2-11.

[90]National Science Board. 2004. Ibid, p. O-19.

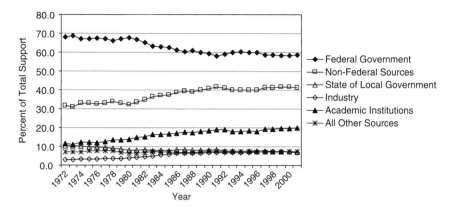

FIGURE 3-4 Percent distribution of US R&D funding, by sector.
SOURCE: National Science Foundation. 2003. *Academic Research and Development Expenditures: Fiscal Year 2001* (NSF 03-316). Arlington, VA: National Science Foundation; NSF/SRS, WebCASPAR database system, *http://caspar.nsf.gov.*

There is some evidence that at least some groups of first-generation Americans may be more likely to enter S&E and this may ease the demographic shift.[91]

Levels of Public Funding

With the increase in international graduate-student enrollment has come a shift in how that research is funded. R&D funding has risen over the years, but the sectors providing the funding are altering their relative contributions. The proportion of funding for research provided by the federal government has declined from about 70 percent in the 1970s to 60 percent in the 1990s while the proportion provided by academic institutions, business, and nonprofits has increased (see Figure 3-4).

Although decreased availability or stagnation of federal academic research funds disproportionately affects temporary residents and can affect graduate-student enrollments[92] (see Figure 3-5), the important role of the

---

[91]Thomas MaCurdy, Thomas Nechyba, and Jay Bhattacharya. 1998. "An economic framework for assessing the fiscal impacts of immigration." In: *The Immigration Debate: Studies in the Economic, Demographic and Fiscal Effects of Immigration.* Washington, DC: National Academy Press, pp. 13-65.

[92]National Research Council. 2001. *Trends in Federal Support of Research and Graduate Education.* Washington, DC: National Academy Press.

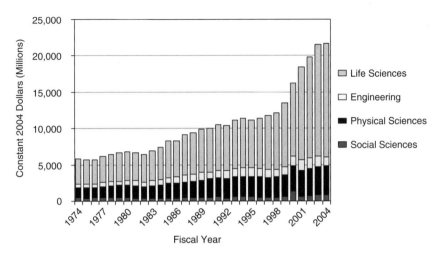

FIGURE 3-5 Federal funding for academic research, 1974-2004.
SOURCE: National Science Board. 2004. *Science and Engineering Indicators 2004* (NSB 04-1). Arlington, VA: National Science Foundation.

states in funding academic research is frequently overlooked in Washington, DC. State funding has decreased as a percentage of university revenues, and higher education is receiving a decreasing percentage of state appropriations. Funding by state legislatures provides the teaching assistantships, scholarships, and other forms of aid on which graduate students depend.[93] States commonly appropriate funds to universities per full-time student. As seen in Figure 3-6, the amount of funding per student has oscillated over time and currently is in decline. That means that public universities have less funding to support graduate students.

One might expect decreased state support for R&D to have an adverse effect on international enrollments at public universities, especially when such funding supports teaching-assistant positions. However, at least at the graduate level there seems to be no negative correlation. From 2000 to 2002, international graduate-student enrollment increased at public universities and decreased at private universities (see Figure 1-4).

The Entrepreneurial Approach to Higher Education

Some countries have begun to view higher education as a way to generate revenues. For example, after the introduction of market-oriented re-

---

[93]Michael Arnone. 2004. "State appropriations for higher education, 2003-4." *The Chronicle of Higher Education* 50(19):A25.

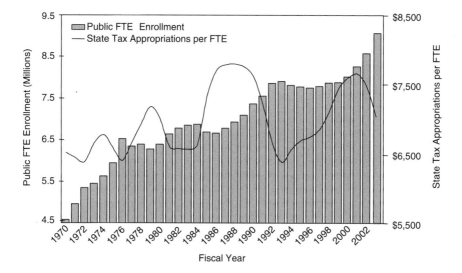

FIGURE 3-6 Enrollment and state tax appropriations per full-time equivalent student (FTE) in constant 2003 dollars.
SOURCE: Paul Lingenfelter. 2004. "The public interest in higher education accountability." *National Accountability Symposium, University of Texas, Austin TX, October 28, 2004.* Available at *http://www.utsystem.edu/cha/acctsymp2004/.* Lingenfelter based his analyses on data from *Grapevine* and NCES *Digest of Education Statistics.* The enrollment and appropriations include both graduate and undergraduate education, but exclude medical education.

forms in Australia, the government reduced its per-student support of higher-education institutions. In an effort to maintain financial solvency, universities began to view education as an exportable economic product and to regard students—primarily undergraduates—as consumers. Those consumers are vigorously sought by marketers, advertisers, and salespeople as sources of revenue. A major strategy has been developing offshore programs of Australian universities, which increased from 25 in 1991 to almost 1,600 in 2003. By 2003, the nation was educating about 210,000 international students, or about 20 percent of the number of its own university-level students. Of the 210,000, 70,000 studied in their own countries[94] through a combination of "offshore," "transnational," or collaborative mechanisms.

---

[94]Fazal Rizvi. 2004. "Offshore Australian higher education." *International Higher Education* 37(Fall):7-9.

For a number of reasons, it is difficult to compare such entrepreneurial educational systems with higher education in the United States, the EU, or Japan. For example, Australia is recruiting tuition-paying undergraduates rather than subsidizing graduate students. For that reason, Australia's international students are almost all in undergraduate or professional programs, and few of them do research; by one calculation, only about 3 percent were in the OECD "research" category in 2004.[95] The entrepreneurial approach has also been criticized for failing to improve the research quality of faculty, and thus for causing an apparent decline in the quality of published research, and for placing proportionately less emphasis on teaching than on such activities as recruitment.[96]

INTEGRATING SCIENCE AND ENGINEERING POLICY WITH FOREIGN POLICY

An aspect of S&E strength deserving brief mention is the challenge in integrating scientific research and educational policies with foreign policy. A familiar, if only occasional, overlap between scientific and foreign policy has been seen in the realm of "big science" such as the multinational particle accelerators and detectors at CERN, large telescopes, and international ocean and geophysical projects. Negotiating big science is seldom easy, partly because of the obvious differences between the realms of science and large-scale political structures. Among the most obvious is that many intergovernment research activities are "top-down," established and monitored by government officials, whereas most research collaborations are "bottom-up," with scientists choosing partners and applying to government for research support. Traditional research linkages create what were long ago called "invisible colleges"[97] of practitioners, below the radar of policymakers. As the globalization of S&E progresses, a better understanding of how to integrate top-down and bottom-up cooperation is needed if nations are to maximize the benefits of their investments in S&E.[98] Scien-

---

[95]Fazal Rizvi, professor, Department of Educational Policy Studies, University of Illinois, presentation to committee, October 11, 2004.

[96]Marginson. 2004. Ibid. Marginson found that "the spectacular growth of higher education in Australia was not grounded in superior quality, but in burgeoning demands, business acumen driven by a combination of scarcity and opportunity, an adequate quality English-language product, a good location and a cheaper price." The program has been, he said, "unable to attract many high-calibre international research students," and "the average quality of published research appears to be in decline."

[97]Derek John de Solla Price, *Little Science, Big Science ... and Beyond,* New York: Columbia University Press, 1963; see also Caroline Wagner and Loet Leyesdorff. 2005. "Network structures, self-organization, and the growth of international collaboration in science." *Research Policy* (in press).

[98]Caroline Wagner. 2002. "The elusive partnership: Science and foreign policy." *Science*

tists and engineers trained to work between cultures may be increasingly important as these negotiations proceed, and US students may benefit from overseas postgraduate training and research experience.[99]

CONCLUSION

Many educational and employment sectors and government agencies have an investment in the activities of international graduate students and postdoctoral scholars, so it is not surprising that the United States has no single government strategy for addressing their activities. The research universities themselves have much to consider. In general, they have invested heavily in the practice of staffing their laboratories and classrooms with graduate students and postdoctoral scholars, about half of whom are temporary residents. As seen in Chapter 2, some of the current policies that most directly influence international flows of scientists and engineers are shaped by concerns over national security and stability considerations rather than by scientific issues: Will this student visitor cause any harm while in the United States? Will that exchange scholar develop or take home knowledge that can be used against US interests?

Clearly, the nation needs flexible policies to deal with international students and scholars, a population that, although small, appears to be highly productive and beneficial. However, to craft effective policies, the federal agencies require a better understanding of the impact of international scientists and engineers on US research and education, economic competitiveness, national security, foreign policy, and international relations.[100] The most reasonable approach is likely to be evolutionary, as policymakers in government, academe, and industry grapple more directly with the questions and findings of the many sources cited in this report.

The primary focus should be on maintaining research excellence. The United States must encourage and attract the most talented people. While continuing to attract the best talent worldwide, the United States should make every effort to encourage domestic student interest in S&E programs and careers. That will require efforts on the part of the faculty to encourage students and the federal government to provide funding for such students to do graduate research.

---

and Public Policy 29(6):409-17; David King. 2004. "The scientific impact of nations." *Nature* 430:311-16.

[99]For example, The National Science Foundation sponsors several research opportunities for graduate students and postdoctoral scholars through its office of international S&E, as does the US Department of State through its sponsorship of the Fulbright program.

[100]Dorothy S. Zinberg, 1991. "Contradictions and complexity: international comparisons in the training of foreign scientists and engineers." In: *The Changing University*, ed. D. S. Zinberg. The Netherlands: Kluwer Academic Publishers, p. 55.

4

Strategies for Improving Policy Decisions

Making sensible policy decisions about the flow of international students and scholars into the United States requires information about its benefits and costs—a sudden stop would be the most serious cost—and about how alternative policies can influence the flow. To the extent that the benefits and costs themselves depend on social and economic circumstances and policies, it is important to understand how the country can enhance the benefits relative to the costs of any given flow.

The benefits to the United States from the inflow of talented students and scholars are clear. Having access to a worldwide pool of talent leads to a higher-quality science and engineering (S&E) workforce than if the country had access only to domestic talent. The flow of international students and scholars also allows the United States to conduct research and education at lower cost than if the country had to rely exclusively on domestic talent. In addition, international students and scholars can help to form international research collaborations and to foster international understanding.

The costs of the flow are indirect. In the job market, a large supply of students and researchers depresses salaries and job opportunities and thus lowers the incentive for domestic students to enter S&E.[1] If international

---

[1]See for example, George Borjas. 2004. *Do Foreign Students Crowd out Native Students from Graduate Programs?* (Working Paper Number 10349.) Cambridge, MA: National Bureau of Economic Research; Mark Regets. 2001. *Research and Policy Issues in High-Skilled International Migration* (DP No. 366). Bonn: IZA.

students and scholars leave the United States, there is the risk that they will work in businesses that compete with those in the United States or use their knowledge in ways inimical to US security. A related but different risk is that international tensions or changes in world conditions will greatly reduce the inflow of overseas talent and diminish our educational and research leadership.

Our knowledge about the flow of international S&E students and scholars to the United States, although limited,[2] allows us to predict with some certainty that in the extreme case a complete cutoff of the flow would create major problems for the US scientific and technologic enterprise. The impact would be felt rapidly by university graduate programs and by researchers who depend on graduate students and postdoctoral scholars. There would be a slower cumulative effect on hiring in industrial, government, and academic sectors.

It is harder to predict how modest changes would affect the scientific workforce, let alone the national well-being, or how larger changes would affect long-term outcomes. Universities might respond by placing more emphasis on the education and mentoring of domestic students. The country might, for example, respond to a drop in the number of international graduate students working as research assistants in laboratories by raising the incentives for US students to take such jobs, by recruiting more international postdoctoral scholars or immigrant scientists and engineers, or eventually by reducing the reliance of research laboratories on graduate students and postdoctoral scholars. Another possible response to increased wages would be to invest in labor-saving research technologies, such as high-throughput molecular biology equipment. With respect to industry, if the United States attracted fewer of the world's most talented scientists and engineers, US firms might shift more R&D activities overseas, maintaining their competitive edge through increased offshoring.

DATA WEAKNESSES

One reason for the uncertainties mentioned above is that the country lacks adequate data for measuring the international flow and career paths of foreign-trained S&E students and postdoctoral scholars (see Box 4-1).

---

[2]See Grant Black and Paula Stephan. 2005. "The importance of foreign PhD students to US science." In: *Science and the University*, eds. R. Ehrenberg and P. Stephan. Madison, WI: Universty of Wisconsin Press (forthcoming); Jeffrey Mervis. 2004. "Many origins, one destination." *Science* 304:1277. This special section reviews experiences of foreign born scientists and engineers working in the United States. Mervis writes, "For all its importance, the relationship between the domestic and foreign born scientific workforce remains an understudied topic."

BOX 4-1
Improving Data Systems for Decision Making

Specific steps for improving data systems for the US S&E workforce are described in a recent report.[a] The following high priority needs are relevant to international S&E flows:

- Current job-market supply and demand conditions— numbers of students by discipline, degree program, career stage, and citizenship status; and job offers, acceptances, and salaries.
- Private-industry data—industry now hires almost 40 percent of US S&E doctoral graduates.
- How domestic students make critical decisions—what they know and value in considering S&E careers during key decision periods.
- Global workforce—numbers and characteristics of foreign S&E students and workers, including those who earned doctorates overseas, by discipline. Why do they choose to study in the United States? What factors influence their decision to stay?
- Data on S&E jobs that US employers have outsourced abroad—what foreign born graduates of US universities do when they leave the United States, and whether those activities are helpful or harmful to US S&E.

---

[a]Terrence Kelly, William P. Butz, Stephan Carroll, David M Adamson, and Gabrielle Bloom, Eds. 2004. The *U.S. Scientific and Technical Workforce: Improving Data for Decisionmaking.* Arlington, VA: RAND Corporation. Available at *http://www.rand.org/publications/CF/ CF194/CF194.sum.pdf.*

The need to improve data on immigration and emigration has been known for at least 20 years.[3] As the flow of scientists and engineers into and out of the United States increased during the 1990s, studies reiterated and expanded on this urgent need.[4]

An understanding of workforce trends is impossible without more frequent counts and timely publication of scientist and engineer populations and of the places in which they have been trained. For example, data on the S&E workforce from the Bureau of Labor Statistics establishment surveys

---

[3]National Research Council. 1985. *Immigration Statistics: A Story of Neglect.* Washington, DC: National Academy Press.

[4] National Research Council. 1996. *Statistics on U.S. Immigration: An Assessment of Data Needs for Future Research.* Washington, DC: National Academy Press; National Research Council. 1999. *Measuring the Science and Engineering Enterprise: Priorities for the Division of Science Resources Studies.* Washington, DC: National Academy Press. This study focused on the Science Resource Statistics division of the National Science Foundation and urged sufficient funding to "continue and expand significantly its data collection and analysis."

include citizenship but not degree level, but the US Census Current Population Survey does have degree data. The counts of foreign trained scientists and engineers working in the United States produced by the National Science Foundational (NSF) throughout the 1990s were estimates based on the 1990 census; by the end of the 1990s, the foreign born share of scientists and engineers was substantially underestimated.[5]

A particular weakness in data concerns the postdoctoral population, in which international researchers make up over half the academic workforce and from which US S&E researchers recruit globally for the laboratory workers that they need. The NSF Graduate Student and Postdoctorates Survey does not collect demographic information, and the Survey of Doctoral Recipients does not include scholars who earned their PhDs outside the United States. NSF's 1997 Survey of Doctoral Recipients had a special section on postdoctoral scholars, but the next similar section is scheduled to appear 10 years later, in 2007. The 1995 retrospective career-history questions that allowed analysis of the duration of the postdoctoral experience are not yet scheduled to be updated. Policies crafted for postdoctoral scholars in the interim are therefore based on outdated assumptions. In the 2003 2004 academic year, Sigma Xi launched a National Postdoctoral Survey.[6] Findings from that survey provide information on postdoctoral scholars previously not available, but it, too, has limitations. The response rate was less than 40 percent, and it is not clear whether the survey will be repeated in successive years to provide longitudinal data.

The inadequacy of data on international graduate students and postdoctoral scholars limits our understanding of the composition of the S&E workforce and of how that workforce might respond to economic or political changes. Moreover, the lack of timeliness and coverage of data on US-trained and internationally-trained scientists and engineers hinders the examination of trends and relationships between student flows, enrollments, economic cycles, and other factors. Congress and administrative agencies need better data and more analysis to craft better policies.

---

[5]The issue of timeliness is addressed by the NSF as follows: "Because the NSF's demographic data collection system cannot refresh its sample of individuals with S&E degrees from foreign institutions (as opposed to foreign born individuals with a new US degree, who are sampled) more than once per decade, counts of foreign born scientists and engineers are likely to be underestimates." National Science Board. 2004. *Science and Engineering Indicators 2004* (NSB 04-1). Arlington, VA: National Science Foundation, p. 3-33.

[6]Sigma Xi contacted 22,178 postdoctoral scholars at 46 institutions, including 18 of the 20 largest academic employers of postdoctoral scholars and NIH. 8,392 (38 percent) responded; 6,775 (31 percent) made it all the way to the end of the 100-question survey. Response rate was increased substantially when a local postdoctoral association was involved (87 percent) and decreased when institutional review boards did not allow Sigma Xi to send multiple reminders (17 percent).

DATA-COLLECTION SYSTEMS FOR MEASURING
INTERNATIONAL STUDENT MOBILITY

The United States needs a new system of data collection to track international student flows and to understand the dynamics and effects of shifting sources of talent. Pulling together existing country-specific data is challenging. A thorough analysis of 25 surveys on the labor market for students and early-career researchers carried out in 21 countries revealed that diverse collection methods often preclude comparison of data.[7] By and large, surveys have been developed to serve national needs and fail to capture such characteristics as international experience and mobility.[8] Clearly, more rigorous and normalized data systems for tracking international graduate students and postdoctoral scholars are required. The United States should partner with other nations to create a truly global system.

One possible model is the US-based international balance-of-trade account for commodities. The US Department of Commerce maintains TradeStat Express, a Web site with extensive data on US merchandise trade that allows the tracing of comprehensive global patterns.[9] Information is compiled from forms and automated reports required by US law to be filed with the US Customs Service and then transmitted to the Census Bureau for virtually all shipments leaving (exports) or entering (imports) the United States (see Box 4-2). To ensure comparability of collected data, the Harmonized Commodity Description and Coding System has been adopted by most countries.

Can such an international tracking system be conceptualized for students and scholars? The Institute for International Education, in collaboration with the British Council and IDP Education in Australia, produced The Atlas of Student Mobility (see Box 4-3), which gives a first glimpse of international student flows. But the picture will need to be refined, particularly with respect to mobility of students in different disciplines and degree

---

[7]Isabelle Recotillet. 2003. *Availability and Characteristics of Surveys on the Destination of Doctorate Recipients in OECD Countries. Statistical Analysis of Science, Technology and Industry Working Paper 2003/9.* Paris: OECD. Available at *http://www.olis.oecd.org/olis/2003doc.nsf.*

[8]Martin Schaaper. 2004. "OECD methodology for tracking doctorate holders and measuring international mobility of HRST." Paper prepared for the sixth Ibero-American and Inter-American Workshop on Science and Technology Indicators, Buenos Aires, September 15-17, 2004. Available at *http://www.ricyt.org/interior/normalizacion%5CVItaller%5CS2_RRHH%5CSchaaperdoc.pdf;* see also: Laudeline Auriol. 2004. "Why do we need indicators on careers of doctorate holders?" OECD Workshop on User Needs for Indicators on Careers of Doctorate Holders, Paris, September 27, 2004. Available at *http://www.olis.oecd.org/olis/2004doc.nsf.*

[9]TradeStat Express home page *http://tse.export.gov/.*

BOX 4-2
Collection of US Foreign Commerce and Trade Statistics[a]

Information on exports of merchandise from the United States to all countries, except Canada, is compiled from copies of Shipper's Export Declarations (SEDs) and SED data from qualified exporters, forwarders, or carriers. Copies of SEDs are required by law to be filed with customs officials at the port of export. Information on US imports of merchandise is compiled primarily from automated data submitted through the US Customs Automated Commercial System. Data are compiled also from import entry summary forms, warehouse withdrawal forms, and Foreign Trade Zone documents as required to be filed with the US Customs and Border Protection Service.

---

[a]See *Guide to Foreign Trade Statistics,* Foreign Trade Division, US Census Bureau, *http://www.census.gov/foreign-trade/guide/index.html.*

BOX 4-3
Project Atlas[a]

One recent project, The Atlas of Student Mobility, illustrates how data on international students can be effectively collated and presented. The atlas synthesizes information from 21 main destination countries and 75 countries of origin by combining publicly available data for the year 2000 from an array of sources. In the first section of the atlas, data on the international student body in each destination country are presented. This includes a map indicating main countries of origin, a pie chart on the economic status of these countries, and a table of leading places of origin for enrolled international students. In the second part of the atlas, each country of origin is analyzed with respect to where its internationally mobile students are enrolled, its higher-education system, and information on relative wealth, government form, and religion. A third section takes a brief look at factors that influence a country's student mobility, taking into account such factors as the human development index, life expectancy, urbanization, civil liberties, and freedom of the press.

---

[a]Todd M. Davis. 2003. *Atlas of Student Mobility.* New York: Institute for International Education.

---

levels, mobility of postdoctoral scholars, career opportunities in different countries, and impact of mobility on workforce productivity. To obtain compatible international data on those issues, systems to capture data on student and postdoctoral-scholar mobility will need to be implemented and harmonized between countries.

BOX 4-4
International Tracking of Doctorates

Recently, the Organisation for Economic Co-operation and Development (OECD), Eurostat, and UNESCO's Institute for Statistics (UIS), sponsored by the US National Science Foundation, embarked on a joint project aimed at international tracking of the careers of doctorate holders. A first meeting, the Workshop on User Needs for Indicators on Careers of Doctorate Holders (CDH) in Paris (OECD, September 27, 2004) set out to gauge interest in this issue, and to explore how different national and methodological approaches might converge to produce internationally comparable indicators on doctorate holder's careers. Central themes were employment characteristics of doctorate holders, postdoctoral experience, and international experience and mobility.[a] Interest proved to be extensive, and a meeting of the "Experts Group on Careers of Doctorate Holders" convened in Montreal (UIS, January 3-February 1, 2005) to determine the type of data currently available and the type of data needed, and to develop an international instrument to help track CDH[b]; a third meeting is planned for May 2005 to discuss the issue further.

---

[a]Emmanuel Boudard. 2004. Developing an integrated information system on the career paths and mobility flows of researchers (DSTI/EAS/STP/NESTI/RD(2004)16. *OECD Workshop on User Needs for Indicators on Careers of Doctorate Holders, Paris, September 27, 2004.* Available at *http://www.olis.oecd.org/olis/2004doc.nsf/.*
    Laudeline Auriole. 2004. Conclusions of the workshop on user needs for indicators on careers of doctorate holders. (DSTI/EAS/STP/NESTI(2004)28). *OECD Workshop on User Needs for Indicators on Careers of Doctorate Holders, Paris, September 27, 2004.*

The atlas has initiated a transnational collaboration, Project Atlas, and has led to agreements on several definitions and constructs. For example, it was agreed that international student should be defined as "a person who physically moves from his or her place of residence for the purposes of study" with nonimmigrant, nonpermanent residence status.[10] Similar harmonization efforts for R&D data are under way among Organization for Economic Co-operation and Development (OECD) countries (see Box 4-4) to build on the 1993 Frascati Manual to function as a "basic international source of methodology for collecting and using R&D statistics." The manual includes a section titled "Measurement of Personnel Devoted to R&D".[11] OECD plans to develop a definition of postdoctoral scholars and to increase the development of data by fields of science.[12]

---

[10]Adria Gallup-Black. 2004. "International student mobility: Project Atlas." *International Higher Education* 37:10-11.
    [11]OECD. 1999. Main *Definitions and Conventions for the Measurement of Research and Development, 5th Edition* Paris: OECD. Available at *http://www1.oecd.org/dsti/sti/stat-ana/prod/eas_fras.htm.*
    [12]Recotillet. Ibid. 2003.

ANALYTIC WEAKNESSES

Data problems aside, the most important reason for our uncertainty about benefits and costs of international student flow is the paucity of analysis of the major behavioral and market factors that shape student and scholar decisions to come to the United States for training and decisions to remain here thereafter. Similarly, little is known about the interaction between the flow of international talent into the United States and the decisions of US citizens or permanent residents to choose S&E careers. Even if a frequent, comprehensive census of the S&E population were done, more is needed than the numbers of students and graduates if we are to understand the factors that influence decisions and how policies can affect outcomes.

The difficulty lies not in choosing the factors at work in the supply of talent but in measuring the effects of the factors. For example, the desire of international students to study in the United States depends on such factors as how the United States education system compares with others; the amount of support available in grants, teaching assistantships, and research assistantships; the probability that studying in the US will lead to permanent residence and possibly citizenship or employment with US firms; and a host of amorphous factors, such as the perceived safety of the country and one's attitude toward the United States. We do not know the degree to which the flow of international students is correlated with those factors, because there has been relatively little analysis of student decisions. Despite the general concern about the decline in the attractiveness of the United States as a destination for students and scholars, the present committee has found no definitive studies on the quantitative effects of policy changes, such as increased security measures or increased fees, on the entry and exit of graduate students and postdoctoral scholars.

For all their importance, moreover, the decisions of foreign-born scientists and engineers with degrees from either US or overseas institutions to immigrate to the United States have not been analyzed in depth. We witnessed a huge influx of immigrant scientists and engineers in the 1990s and saw that the stay rate of foreign-born PhDs in S&E rose during roughly the same period. Were the influx and stay rate primarily responses to the booming US job market of the 1990s, or did they reflect longer-term developments, such as the increased production of S&E graduates overseas, which created a larger global supply of scientists and engineers?

Another analytic weakness is in the understanding of why US students decide to choose S&E careers. Relatively low compensation and long duration of postdoctoral appointments may be deterrents to an S&E career, but these conditions are prevalent only in some fields. The abundance of foreign-trained graduate students undoubtedly contributes to low postdoctoral compensation at least in universities, but we do not know the relative importance of postdoctoral pay in influencing decisions compared with research-career prospects, the length of graduate study, and the attractiveness of options outside S&E research. Nor are there good estimates of how much postdoctoral stipends might rise if the supply of postdoctoral scholars diminished. Answering such questions requires regularly gathered information about annual changes in pay, benefits, and career aspirations of postdoctoral scholars and about opportunities abroad, and it requires creative analysis of the information.

The primary factor affecting students' decisions to major in S&E fields and whether they pursue graduate study may not be postdoctoral compensation but rather their perception of whether S&E degrees will lead to satisfying research careers. Available studies indicate that students are sensitive to labor-market conditions,[13] but where students and scholars learn about the job market, the alternatives they consider, and the effects of their schooling and mentoring experiences on career choices are not well understood. Statistical investigations of the supply behavior of domestic and international students, of the demand behavior and wage responsiveness of US employers to changes in the supply of foreign talent, and of the responsiveness of talented US students to changes in incentives are needed to create an evidence-based policy. Although the charge to this committee does not include an examination of why domestic students enter or avoid S&E, any assessment of policies regarding international students requires knowledge of the decision making of US citizens and permanent residents. The effect of any loss of international talent will be very different if the supply of domestic talent is highly responsive to incentives—monetary or instructional—from what it will be if the supply is barely responsive to incentives.

THE UNKNOWN FUTURE

Policy decisions that affect graduate students also affect supplies of doctorates and postdoctoral scholars several years in the future,[14] so such

---

[13]Richard Freeman. 1971. *The Market for College-Trained Manpower.* Cambridge, MA: Harvard University Press; Richard Freeman. 1980. "Employment opportunities: The doctorate manpower market." *Industrial and Labor Relations Review* 33(2):185-196; and Richard Esterlin. 1993. "Prices and preferences in choice of career: The switch to business, 1972-1987." Discussion Paper 2-1, Williams Project on the Economics of Higher Education, available at *http://www.williams.edu/wpehe/DPs/DP-21.pdf.*

[14]As in previous surveys, students receiving doctorates in 2003 took on the average 7.5 years to complete their degree requirements. National Opinion Research Center. 2005. *Doctorate Recipients from United States Universities: Summary Report 2003.* Chicago, IL: NORC. *http://www.norc.uchicago.edu/issues/docdata.htm.*

policies should be flexible enough to allow for changes in the economy and in demand for S&E workers. But predicting workforce trends is highly problematic.[15] A few years ago, the country was warned of a shortage of information-technology (IT) scientists, so Congress raised the ceiling on H-1b visas to allow a larger flow of qualified IT workers. Not only was the decision based on faulty information, it also was quickly outdated by changes in the market. Today, in part because of the abundance of programmers and computer experts trained in other countries, US enrollments in computer science at the bachelor's level are down sharply. Unemployment rates for computer programmers are high, electrical and electronic engineers face a more difficult labor market than most other professionals, and talk of a shortage has diminished considerably.

Over the years, various institutions and agencies have issued forecasts of shortages or surpluses of scientists and engineers. The accuracy of those forecasts has been weak for three reasons: labor-market researchers lack timely and comprehensive data; many forecasts are issued by groups with a vested interest in the outcome, that is, those who are predisposed to the belief that there should be more or fewer participants;[16] and labor markets can be rapidly affected by various exogenous variables, such as economic expansion or recession, federal budget priorities, war, and immigration policies that are hard to forecast.[17] In the present context, for instance, a slowdown in the growth of federally sponsored R&D could shrink the nation's demand for scientists and engineers, depressing the job market and reducing both international- and domestic-student enrollments. A commitment to double NSF's budget over some period, in contrast, would probably have the opposite effect.

Given those problems, this study has not attempted to forecast labor-market conditions for scientists or engineers. Instead, it has discussed some of the short term variables that influence the flow of international scientists (Chapter 2) and the global context in which more nations strengthen their S&E capacity and compete for the best students (Chapter 3).

---

[15]National Research Council. 2000. *Forecasting Demand and Supply of Doctoral Scientists and Engineers: Report of a Workshop on Methodology.* Washington, DC: National Academy Press.

[16]See, for example, Michael Teitelbaum. 2004. "Do we need more scientists?" In: *The U.S. Scientific and Technical Workforce: Improving Data for Decisionmaking,* eds. T. K. Kelly et al. Arlington, VA: RAND Corporation, pp. 11-20; Donald Kennedy, Jim Austin, Kirstie Urquhart, and Crispin Taylor. 2004. Supply without demand. *Science* 303:1105; Daniel S. Greenberg, "What scientist shortage?" *Washington Post*, May 19, 2004, p. A23.

POLICY SCENARIOS

Input of two kinds is required to improve policy responses to the flow of international students and researchers to the United States. The first kind of input is more and better data specifically designed to answer key analytic questions about the function of the labor market for the S&E workforce. The second kind is the results of rigorous labor-market analyses that can be used to help understand the nation's needs for S&E workers, address the repeated claims of shortages of scientists and engineers, develop strategies that attract high ability US students to S&E, and assess the costs and benefits of such strategies.[18]

Decision-making does not come to a halt in the absence of adequate data or in the absence of adequate modeling of processes. It proceeds with inadequate data and with uncertainty about the effects of policies. In such a situation, it is useful to imagine a series of scenarios and their likely consequences and to at least think through if not simulate counterfactual scenarios—scenarios that involve conditions different from those we see today—and lay out alternatives to decisions under consideration. One can imagine extremely favorable and unfavorable scenarios for the impact of foreign graduate students and postdoctoral scholars on the US S&E enterprise. Figure 4-1 illustrates the inputs and outputs of the US higher-education system for international students. Input filters that may reduce their participation include admission decisions that favor domestic students,[19] visa fees, and security screens. Factors that may favor their participation are networks of former students who have made the United States their home— the diaspora effect—in addition to a number of pull factors, discussed in Chapter 3. Once students complete their degrees, they may stay, go home and collaborate, or leave and compete.

In an unfavorable scenario, large numbers of international students and postdoctoral scholars would discourage US students from participation, and a sudden cutoff of the international flow would in the short term leave the United States with a substantial deficit of researchers and technical

---

[17]Paula E. Stephan. 2004. "What data do labor market researchers needs? A researcher's perspective." In: *The U.S. Scientific and Technical Workforce: Improving Data for Decisionmaking*, eds. T. K. Kelly et al. Arlington, VA: RAND Corporation, p. 45.

[18]Richard B. Freeman. 2004. "Data! Data! My kingdom for data! Data needs for analyzing the S&E job market." In: *The U.S. Scientific and Technical Workforce: Improving Data for Decisionmaking*, eds. T. K. Kelly et al. Arlington, VA: RAND Corporation, p. 33.

[19]Gregory Attiyeh and Richard Attiyeh. 1997. Testing for bias in graduate school admissions. *Journal of Human Resources* 32(3):524-48. The authors found a 5:1 bias in admissions favoring domestic students over international students. See discussion in Chapter 1.

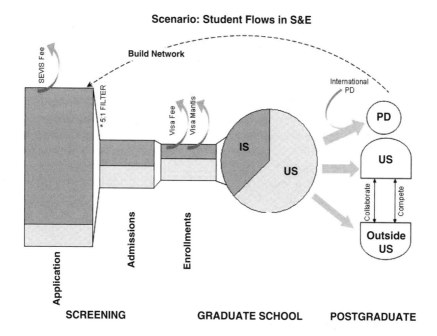

FIGURE 4-1 Outcomes model illustrating the inputs and flows of inernational students (IS), domestic students (US), and postdoctoral students (PD).

personnel. Once home, the returnees would contribute to industries that compete with US based industries or take jobs that are offshored from US multinationals, shifting the locus of scientific and technologic leadership overseas while the United States struggled to replenish its S&E workforce by developing domestic talent. We are nowhere near that extreme, but it may be useful to keep it in mind as a worst-case scenario.

In a favorable scenario, highly skilled international graduate students and postdoctoral scholars enter S&E positions. Those who stay in the United States become permanent residents and citizens; those who eventually return home enter valuable collaborations with US colleagues and become informal ambassadors who communicate the democratic values of scientific research and of the United States. They order US products for their businesses and provide expertise for local divisions of US industries. At the same time, the United States might use graduate-student fellowships, higher postdoctoral pay, and other incentives to increase the flow of the best US talent into S&E. We are not at this extreme either, but it may be useful to keep it in mind as a best case to work toward.

CONCLUSION

Input of two kinds is required to improve policy responses to the flow of foreign-born students and researchers to the United States. The first kind of input is more and better data specifically designed to answer key analytic questions about the function of the labor market for the S&E workforce. The second kind is the results of rigorous labor-market analyses that can be used to help understand the nation's needs for S&E workers, address the repeated claims of shortages of scientists and engineers, develop strategies that attract high ability US students to S&E, and assess the costs and benefits of such strategies.[20]

What can be said is this: there are both benefits and costs to having international graduate students and postdoctoral scholars in the United States. The benefits include increasing the S&E talent pool in the United States, enhancing and diversifying the academic community, lowering the cost of doing research, and enhanced international research collaborations. In short, talented graduate students and postdoctoral scholars constitute a critical input for our knowledge-driven economy. At the same time, having such an open supply of talent has significant costs. It affects job opportunities for all students. Restrictions on international travel or exchange can rapidly affect US research capabilities. International collaborations may lead to enhanced international competition.

At present, the strategy of the United States is to draw heavily on and profit from the international talent pool. However, increased security regulations are restricting entry of prospective international students and scholars and restricting the fields in which they may study. Other nations are fortifying their S&E infrastructure and competing for the best students and scholars. It is in this context that the United States needs to craft policies to maintain its current quality and effectiveness in S&E, including encouraging the interest of domestic S&E students, at the same time that it minimizes the barriers to mobility for international students. Given the lack of control over exogenous events, policies should be crafted to ensure that S&E institutions and the labor force develop enhanced flexibility to respond quickly to changing conditions.

---

[20]Richard B. Freeman. 2004. "Data! Data! My kingdom for data! Data needs for analyzing the S&E job market." In: *The U.S. Scientific and Technical Workforce: Improving Data for Decisionmaking*, eds. T. K. Kelly et al. Arlington, VA: RAND Corporation, p. 33.

5

Findings and Recommendations

In general terms, the committee believes that it is essential for the national interest of the United States that it maintain its excellence and overall leadership in science and engineering (S&E) research and education so that it can maintain its advantage in global knowledge production. Talented people constitute a critical input in such a knowledge-driven economy. The strategy of the United States has been and is to draw substantially from international human resources. However, as other nations build up their own S&E infrastructures, there is increasing competition for these talented people.

In such a world, what policies might best serve the interests of the United States and of S&E research in general? What actions can the US government and research universities take immediately to create or implement such policies?

This chapter presents the committee's findings and recommendations in response to its charge:

(1) What is known about the impact of international graduate students and postdoctoral scholars on the advancement of US science, US undergraduate and graduate educational institutions, the US and other national economies, and US national security and international relations?

The total number of S&E graduate students in US institutions has grown consistently over the last several decades. The share of international graduate students has risen from 23.4 percent in 1982 to 34.5 percent in

2002 (see Table 1-1, and Figures 1-1 and 1-2). The share of temporary-resident postdoctoral scholars has increased from 37.4 percent in 1982 to 58.8 percent in 2002 (see Figure 1-3). In some fields, temporary residents make up more than half the populations of graduate students and postdoctoral scholars.

Despite the growing presence of international S&E graduate students and postdoctoral scholars on US university campuses, the data gathered by different sources on their numbers and activities are difficult to compare[1] (see Box 1-1 and Chapter 4) and yield only an approximate picture of their career status and contributions. The high level of participation of international scientists and engineers in US laboratories and classrooms warrants increased efforts to understand this phenomenon and to ensure that policies regarding their movement and activities are flexible to allow for rapid changes in research and technology.

Students and scholars contribute at many levels—as technicians, teachers, and researchers and in other occupations in which technical training is desirable. They have also been shown to generate economic gains by adding to the processes of industrial or business innovation.[2] And there is evidence that they have made a disproportionate number of exceptional[3] contributions to the S&E enterprise of the United States (see Figure 1-22), although more recent data indicates a transition may be underway.

The S&E enterprise is increasingly multidisciplinary, interdisciplinary, and global. Historically, science has served as a bridge between nations and a means of communication that can transcend political barriers. The exchange of students among countries is considered an element of interna-

---

[1]A. Gallup-Black. 2004. "International student mobility: Project Atlas." *International Higher Education* 37:10-11.

[2]G. Chelleraj, Keith E. Maskus, and A. Mattoo. 2004. *The Contribution of Skilled Immigration and International Graduate Students to US Innovation*, (Working Paper Number 04-10). Boulder, CO: University of Colorado. The authors conclude, "Our results strongly favor the view that foreign graduate students and immigrants under technical visas are significant inputs into developing new technologies in the American economy." pp. 28-29. Also, immigration rules that permit immigration of the highly skilled, along with education subsidies, are sufficient to ensure new technology adoption, as shown by an exercise in theoretical modeling by P. Chander and S. Thangavelu. 2004. "Technology adoption, education and immigration policy," *Journal of Development Economics* 75(1):79-94

[3]Paula E. Stephan and Sharon G. Levin. 2005. "Foreign scholars in U.S. science: Contributions and costs." In: *Science and the University*, eds. Ronald Ehrenberg and Paula Stephan, Madison, WI: University of Wisconsin Press (forthcoming). The authors use six criteria to indicate "exceptional" contributions (not all contributions) in S&E: persons elected to the National Academy of Sciences (NAS) or National Academy of Engineering (NAE), authors of citation classics, authors of hot papers, the 250 most-cited authors, authors of highly cited patents, and scientists who have played a key role in launching biotechnology firms.

tional relations and even foreign policy.[4] International students who remain in the United States after their studies often become part of networks that support knowledge transfer and economic development in the United States and the sending country. The networks are an important "pull" factor for students considering the United States as a destination for graduate and postdoctoral training. Those who return home after their studies or after some period of employment may go to work for US-owned multinational firms, continue research that adds to global knowledge, and form collaborations with US partners. Returnees who assume leadership positions at home may become strong foreign-policy and national-security assets for the United States.[5]

On the basis of the foregoing, the committee offers the following findings and recommendations:

Finding 1-1: International students and scholars have advanced US science and engineering (S&E), as evidenced by numbers of patents, publications, Nobel prizes, and other quantitative data.

Finding 1-2: International graduate students and postdoctoral scholars are integral to the US S&E enterprise. If the flow of these students and scholars were sharply reduced, research and academic work would suffer until an alternative source of talent could be found. There would be a fairly immediate effect in university graduate departments and laboratories and a later cumulative effect on hiring in universities, industry, and government. There is no evidence that modest, gradual changes in the flow would have an adverse effect.

Finding 1-3: Innovation is crucial to the success of the US economy. To maintain excellence in S&E research, which fuels technological innovation, the United States must be able to recruit talented people. A substantial proportion of those people—students, postdoctoral scholars, and researchers—come from other countries.

---

[4]The US Departments of State and Education host an annual International Education Week. At the 2004 event, Secretary of State Colin Powell stated, "The professional partnerships and lifelong friendships that result from international education and exchange help build a foundation of understanding and lasting partnerships. These partnerships are important for a secure, prosperous future, not only for the United States, but also for the world as a whole." Colin Powell, Statement, International Education Week 2004, Washington, DC, October 15, 2004.

[5]"Foreign students yesterday, world leaders today." Bureau of Educational and Cultural Affairs, US Department of State. Available at *http://exchanges.state.gov/education/educationusa/leaders.htm*.

Recommendation 1-1: The United States must maintain or enhance its current quality and effectiveness in S&E. A principal objective should be to attract the best graduate students and postdoctoral scholars regardless of national origin. The United States should make every effort to encourage domestic-student interest in S&E programs and careers. A study should be undertaken to examine the best policies and programs to achieve that end.

Recommendation 1-2: The overarching goal for universities and other research institutions should be to provide the highest-quality training and career development to both domestic and international graduate students and postdoctoral scholars of truly outstanding potential. Graduate admissions are directed toward fulfilling a variety of objectives, among which the education of the next generation of researchers should have the highest priority. This educational process will include research and sometimes a teaching experience. Admissions committees should keep in mind career and employment opportunities, in academe and elsewhere, when making admissions decisions. Moreover, data concerning employment outcomes should be readily available to both students and faculty.

(2) What is the impact of the US academic system on international graduate students' and postdoctoral scholars' intellectual development, careers, and perceptions of the United States? How does it differ if they stay in the United States or return to their home countries?

International graduate students and postdoctoral scholars who have trained in the United States have an opportunity to achieve careers as scientists or engineers in US universities, industries, and national laboratories.[6] A decision to stay in the United States and become a citizen can be interpreted as a measure of career success, at least in relation to opportunities available in home countries. The stay rate of international doctorate scientists and engineers has increased steadily and substantially in the last decade.[7] Plans to stay vary by year of doctoral-degree award, field, and country of origin (see Figure 1-19). The proportion of foreign-born doctor-

---

[6]N. Aslanbeigui and V. Montecinos. 1998. "Foreign students in US doctoral programs." *Journal of Economic Perspectives* 12:171-82.

[7]*International student* is usually taken to mean a student on a temporary visa, but figures sometimes include students on both temporary and permanent visas to compensate for the large number of Chinese students in the 1990s who became permanent residents by special legal provisions following Tiananmen Square. This issue is discussed in greater detail by Finn (see next footnote), who finds the stay rates of those on temporary and permanent visas almost the same.

ates remaining in the United States for at least 2 years after receiving their degrees increased from 49 percent for the 1989 cohort to 71 percent for the 2001 cohort.[8] Stay rates are highest among engineering, computer-science, and physical-sciences graduates. Stay rates varied dramatically among graduate students from the top source countries: China (96 percent), India (86 percent), Taiwan (40 percent), and Korea (21 percent). Decisions to stay in the United States appear to be strongly affected by the ability to do research in the students' home countries, which is tied to such factors as unemployment rate and per capita GDP.[9]

Decisions to establish US citizenship similarly show time and field specificity. In most fields, the percentage of graduate students who were temporary residents at the time of their degrees and obtained US citizenship was relatively constant from 1995 to 2001; in engineering, the percentages of students obtaining citizenship show marked time sensitivity (see Figure 1-20).

There is less quantitative information about the career paths and experiences of either domestic or international postdoctoral appointees than of graduate students (see Box 1-1 and the discussion of data needs in Chapter 4). Postdoctoral work has become the norm in the physical and life sciences and is becoming more common in other fields. Most postdoctoral scholars work in academe; about 10-14 percent work in other sectors, chiefly industry and national laboratories. Stay rates have not been quantified; but among postdoctoral scholars who trained in the United States, the United States was the most attractive place to settle regardless of nationality or where the PhD was earned (see Figure 1-21).

Other, more direct measures indicate that US-trained international graduate students and postdoctoral scholars gain skills that make them competitive in the US job market. Foreign-born faculty who earned their doctoral degrees at US universities have increased from 11.7 percent in 1973 to 20.4 percent in 1999. In engineering fields, they increased from 18.6 percent to 34.7 percent in the same period.[10] According to one of the

---

[8]Michael G. Finn. 2003. *Stay Rates of Foreign Doctorate Recipients from US Universities, 2001*. Oak Ridge, TN: ORISE. Although the stay rate cited in this study was defined as remaining in the United States for at least 2 years after receipt of the doctorate, Finn estimates that these rates do not fall appreciably during the first 5 years after graduation. About half the increase between the 1989 and 2001 cohorts is due to an increase in the number of PhDs awarded; the rest is from an increase in the number of new doctorate recipients deciding to stay.

[9]David L. Johnson. 2001. *Relationship Between Stay Rates of PhD Recipients on Temporary Visas and Relative Economic Conditions in Country of Origin*. Oak Ridge, TN: ORISE.

[10]National Science Board. 2004. *Science and Engineering Indicators 2004* (NSB 04-2), Arlington, VA: National Science Foundation, Appendix Table 5-24. Available at *http://www.nsf.gov/sbe/srs/seind02/append/c5/at05-24.xls*.

few available studies,[11] 32 percent of all new PhDs with definite plans to work in US industry were temporary residents at the time of graduation. That is about the same as the proportion of temporary residents in the total population of new PhDs. The proportion of new PhDs going into industry who are temporary residents is highest in mathematics (43 percent), civil engineering (42 percent), electrical engineering (41 percent), mechanical engineering (40 percent), and computer science (38 percent).

On the basis of those data, the committee offers the following findings and recommendations:

Finding 2-1: The education and training provided by US institutions afford international students the opportunity to do high-quality, frontier research and to gain the experience needed to compete for employment in S&E occupations in the United States and abroad.

Finding 2-2: Many international students and scholars who come to the United States desire to and do stay after their studies and training are completed. Those who return home often maintain collaboration with scientists and engineers in the United States and take with them a better understanding of the US culture, research, and political system.

Recommendation 2-1: Universities should continue to encourage the enrollment of international students by offering fellowships and assistantships. Universities that have large international student and scholar populations should conduct surveys to evaluate existing services provided by the institutions. Universities that do not already do so should offer orientation days for international students, train teaching assistants, update Web services, and provide professional development training for administrators staffing international student and scholar offices.

Recommendation 2-2: International postdoctoral scholars make up a large and growing proportion of the US S&E workforce, but there are no systematic data on this population. A high priority should be placed on collecting and disseminating data on the demographics, working conditions, and career outcomes of scholars who earned their doctoral degrees outside the United States. When combined with current data collected by the National Science Foundation (NSF) and professional societies, this should make possible a more complete picture of the US S&E workforce. Funds should be allocated for this purpose by Congress to the NSF or by nonprofit foundations to other organizations.

---

[11]Grant Black and Paula Stephan. "The importance of foreign PhDs to US science." In: *Science and the University*, eds. Ronald Ehrenberg and Paula Stephan. Madison, WI: University of Wisconsin Press (forthcoming).

(3) What is known about the impact of international student enrollment on the recruitment of domestic S&E talent in the United States? What is the status of working conditions for international graduate students and postdoctoral scholars compared with their domestic counterparts?

Several researchers have suggested that large numbers of international graduate students and postdoctoral scholars may have at least a mild adverse effect on domestic enrollments. As the numbers of S&E baccalaureate degrees awarded to members of underrepresented minority groups has increased, there has not been a concomitant increase in graduate-school enrollments.[12] However, it is not clear whether women or underrepresented-minority students are being displaced or are choosing other career paths. An empirical study of admissions to graduate schools showed in the aggregate a substantially higher rate of acceptance of US citizens over foreign applicants, a modestly higher rate of acceptance of women than of men in three of the fields studied, and a substantially higher rate of acceptance of members of underrepresented minority groups over other US citizens in all five fields studied.[13]

More recent studies also find no evidence of displacement of women and members of underrepresented minority groups in the graduate admissions process. For example, one study found no evidence of displacement but marked effects on educational outcomes, describing a negative correlation between the enrollment of temporary residents and US citizens in graduate programs. The most elite institutions saw the largest increases in temporary-resident enrollment and the steepest drops in enrollment of US citizens.[14] Those effects were statistically significant for white males, but not for women or members of underrepresented minority groups. It is not clear whether white males were deterred from enrolling by international students or chose other career paths for different reasons. For example, some may have been drawn to business careers during the dot.com and financial-services boom or to other high-paying professions throughout the 1990s, many of which did not require graduate training.

Other evidence suggests that there is no displacement of US citizens

---

[12]David R. Burgess. 1998. "Where will the next generation of minority biomedical scientists come from?" *Cancer* (Supplement) 83(8):1717-19.

[13]Gregory Attiyeh and Richard Attiyeh. 1997. "Testing for bias in graduate school admissions." *Journal of Human Resources* 32(3):524-48. The authors examined biochemistry, economics, English, mathematics, and mechanical engineering admissions at 48 leading graduate schools.

[14]G. J. Borjas. 2004. *Do Foreign Students Crowd out Native Students from Graduate Programs?* (Working Paper Number 10349). Cambridge, MA: National Bureau of Economic Research.

from graduate programs by temporary residents. The number of PhDs granted to undergraduates from US institutions changed little while the number of non-US bachelor's degree recipients obtaining US doctorates rose sharply. Thus, a substantial change in proportion was observed, but it was caused mostly by the expansion of PhD programs; a majority of the new slots were taken by students who had earned their first university degrees outside the United States.[15] Another study calculated that an increase of one full-time international student in an S&E graduate department is not associated with displacement of US natives or members of underrepresented minorities.[16]

A study examining possible displacement of domestic scientists and engineers from S&E describes the importance of several other factors. First, the displacement of native-born scientists and engineers occurs mostly from "temporary," not "permanent," jobs in academe. Thus, the US-born are losing academic positions that are less valued rather than highly valued. Second, that result, with the finding that displacement is largest for those in mathematics and computer science, suggests that US citizens may have been pulled and not pushed from the academic sector, at least in some fields. Those US-born scientists and engineers appear to be seeking better opportunities and higher-paying positions elsewhere in the economy.[17]

Postdoctoral work has become the norm in the physical and life sciences and is becoming more common in other fields (see Figure 1-8). Little is known about the educational background, motivations, or career paths of either domestic or foreign-born postdoctoral scholars.

Citizenship status does not seem to affect level of satisfaction with training experience (see Figure 1-11). There is a tendency for more temporary residents than US citizens to feel that their postdoctoral positions were preparing them for independent research positions (see Figure 1-12).

Another measure of working conditions is compensation. In 2002, 50.2 percent of international graduate students were supported by research assistantships (RAs); 18.3 percent were fellows or trainees, whose positions usually carry a higher stipend than RAs; and 27.7 percent of domestic graduate students were RAs and 29.7 percent were fellows or trainees.

---

[15]R. B. Freeman, E. Jin, and C. Y. Shen. 2004. *Where Do New US-Trained Science-Engineering PhDs Come From?* (Working Paper Number 10605). Cambridge, MA: National Bureau of Economic Research.

[16]Mark Regets. 2001. *Research and Policy Issues in High-Skilled International Migration,* Bonn: IZA. Drawn from data from the NSF Graduate Student Survey, 1982-1995.

[17]Sharon G. Levin, Grant C. Black, Anne E. Winkler, and Paula E. Stephan. 2004. *Differential Employment Patterns for Citizens and Non-Citizens in Science and Engineering in the United States: Minting and Competitive Effects* (Working Paper). St. Louis, MO: University of Missouri.

Similar proportions of domestic and international students were supported by teaching assistantships (see Figure 1-14). Data on support mechanisms for postdoctoral scholars are not available by citizenship (see Figure 1-15 and 1-16), but there is a significant difference in annual postdoctoral stipends, and temporary residents earned less than citizens (see Figure 1-13). That may be attributable largely to the different funding opportunities for temporary residents in that most federal training grants and fellowships are citizenship-restricted.

On the basis of those data, the committee offers the following findings and recommendation:

Finding 3-1: Recruiting domestic S&E talent depends heavily on students' perceptions of the S&E careers that await them. Those perceptions can be solidified early in the educational process, before students graduate from high school. The desirability of a career in S&E is determined largely by the prospect of attractive employment opportunities in the field and, to a lesser extent by potential remuneration. Some aspects of the graduate education and training process can also influence students' decisions to enter S&E fields. The "pull factors" include time to degree; availability of fellowships, research assistantships, or teaching assistantship funding; and whether a long postdoctoral appointment is required after completion of the PhD. The evidence that large international graduate-student enrollment may reduce enrollment of domestic students is sparse and contradictory but suggests that direct displacement effects are small compared with pull factors.

Finding 3-2: There are substantial differences among S&E fields in training and career patterns. For example, in engineering, a bachelor's or master's degree is sufficient to begin a professional career; in the life sciences, doctorates customarily spend over 4 years as postdoctoral scholars before entering the workforce. In the physical sciences[18] and engineering, most students obtain careers in industry; in the life sciences, most work toward positions in academe. Such field-specific variations are not reflected in aggregate data.

Finding 3-3: International and domestic academic postdoctoral scholars express similar satisfaction with their training experience. But ac-

---

[18]The physical sciences include physics, chemistry, earth sciences, mathematics, and computer science. In each of those subfields, there can be divergent career interests among graduates; but taken as a whole, a position in the industrial sector is the predominant career destination among recent graduates, whether or not it was the desired career at PhD inception or completion.

cess to funding sources and employment opportunities is limited by residence status. There are variable discrepancies in stipends that favor domestic postdoctoral scholars in all fields.

Finding 3-4: Multinational corporations (MNCs) hire international PhDs in proportions similar to the output of university graduate and postdoctoral programs for their US research laboratories and often hire US-trained PhDs for their nondomestic laboratories. The proportion of international researchers in several large MNCs is around 30-50 percent. MNCs appreciate international diversity in their research staff and pay foreign-born and domestic researchers the same salaries, which are based on degree, school, and benchmarks in the industry.

Recommendation 3-1: So that students can make informed decisions about advanced training in S&E, career outcomes of recent graduates should be communicated to prospective students by university departments and faculty advisers. In addition to intensive focused research work, graduate education should encompass career preparation and the development of varied skills for successful careers in S&E. Universities should develop graduate education and postdoctoral programs that prepare S&E students and scholars for the diversity of jobs they will encounter. When it is appropriate, funding agencies should provide career-transition grants for early-career researchers. The committee encourages discussion among universities, industry, and funding agencies to explore how to expand graduate fellowships and encourage women and members of underrepresented minorities to consider education and training in S&E.

(4) What are the impacts of various policies that reshape or reduce the flow of international students and postdoctoral scholars (for example, visas, immigration rules, and working conditions)?

There is increasing international competition to recruit the best S&E students and scholars. With the increasing competition, there is keen interest in why students choose to study abroad and how students choose destinations and institutions.[19] The decision of graduate students and postdoctoral scholars to go abroad for study is a combination of "push"

---

[19]Anthony Bohm and D. P. Chaudhri. 2000. *Securing Australia's Future: An Analysis of the International Education Markets in India*. Sydney: IDP Education Australia Limited, pp. 150-52. This study reports that although the United States is "an established brand, providing an excellent education across a wide array of characteristics, it performs poorly in affordability and provision of a tolerant and safe environment."

and "pull" factors.[20] Under conditions of increasing capacity among traditional sending countries, the ability of the United States to continue to attract the best students will increasingly depend on its pull factors,[21] including quality, job opportunities, convenience, and perception of being a welcoming place.

Layered on top of the globalization of competition for students is the decline in international students taking the Test of English as a Foreign Language (TOEFL) and the Graduate Record Examination (GRE) graduate-school entrance examinations (see Figure 1-7). One interpretation of the decline is that fewer international students want to study in the United States. However, the decline in TOEFL volumes is more likely to have been influenced by increasing competition from the International English Language Testing System (IELTS).[22] GRE volumes started to decrease in Asia after antifraud measures were taken in 2000. The number of students taking the GRE multiple times has decreased, and it is likely that some less-qualified students are now discouraged from taking the examination.[23] In addition, Australia, Canada, and other countries competing with the United States for graduate students do not require applicants to take the GRE.[24]

On top of that are the recent increases in security screening by US immigration officials. The United States, like other nations, must struggle to balance the need to secure technical information with the need to maintain the openness of scholarship on which its culture, economy, and security depend. The free flow of knowledge and people sometimes conflicts with the national interests of states. Repercussions that followed the terror attacks of September 11, 2001, included security-related changes in federal

---

[20]Tim Mazzarol and Geoffrey N. Soutar. 2001. *Push-pull Factors in Influencing International Student Destination Choice* (Discussion Paper 0105). Crawley, WA: Centre for Entrepreneurial Management and Innovation, University of Western Australia; Todd Davis. 2003. *Atlas of Student Mobility.* New York: Institute for International Education. Similar factors are correlated with stay rates of international graduate students (see D. L. Johnson. 2001. *Relationship Between Stay Rates of PhD Recipients on Temporary Visas and Relative Economic Conditions in Country of Origin.* Oak Ridge, TN: Oak Ridge Institute for Science and Education) and postdoctoral scholars (see Jurgen Enders and Alexis-Michel Mugabushaka. 2004. *Wissenshaft und Karriere: Ehrfahrungen und Werdegange ehemahleiger Stipendiaten der DFG.* Bonn: Deutsche Forschungsgemeinshaft).

[21]Mazzarol and Souter. 2001. Ibid, p. 17.

[22]The IELTS is owned, developed, and delivered through the partnership of the British Council, IDP Education Australia, ILTS Australia, and the University of Cambridge ESOL Examinations.

[23]David L. Wheeler. 2002. "Testing services says GRE scores from China, South Korea, and Taiwan are suspect." *The Chronicle of Higher Education* (August 16).

[24]David Payne, executive director, GRE Program, Educational Testing Service, presentation to committee, July 19, 2004.

visa and immigration policy. The changes were intended to restrict the illegal movements of an extremely small population, but they have had a substantial effect on large numbers of foreign-born graduate students and postdoctoral scholars already in the United States or contemplating a period of study here. Pre-existing immigration-related policies relevant to international student flows are international reciprocity agreements, deemed-export policies, and specific acts that grant special or immigrant status to groups of students or high-skill workers, for example, the Chinese Student Protection Act of 1992 and the policies enacted shortly after the end of the Cold War to allow scientists and engineers of the former Soviet Union to enter the United States.

Together, increased competition, decreased test-taking, increased security screening, and a soft economy have had a dramatic impact on graduate-student applications, particularly from 2001 to 2004.[25] Declines in admissions and first-time enrollments were less substantial (see Box 1-2).[26] What is the meaning of the declining enrollment numbers? Several interpretations seem plausible. First, the decline began from an enrollment peak that followed the atypical economic conditions of the late 1990s, including the dot.com boom and the doubling of the National Institutes of Health (NIH) budget.[27] The current decline could be interpreted as a return from an unsustainable peak to a point on a long-term curve that had been rising steadily for many years. A second possible interpretation is that a three-year decline is more accurately seen as a trend rather than a statistical blip. In either case, there is no evidence that the quality of graduate students or the staffing level of laboratories has suffered. S&E populations have always fluctuated, and in ways that are seldom predicted.

Throughout its history, the United States has used immigration policy

---

[25] "Survey details impact of restrictive government actions on flow of international scholars and students." NAFSA (Association of International Educators), AAU (Association of American Universities), NASULGC (National Association of State Universities and Land-Grant Colleges), and CGS. November 14, 2003.

[26] Heath Brown. 2004. *Council of Graduate Schools Finds Decline in New International Graduate Student Enrollment for the Third Consecutive Year.* Washington, DC: Council of Graduate Schools (November 4); *Open Doors Report on International Educational Exchange,* New York: Institute for International Education. *http://opendoors.iienetwork.org/;* Michael Neuschatz and Patrick J. Mulvey. 2003. *Physics Students from Abroad in the Post-9/11 Era* (Publication No. R-437) College Park, MD: American Institute of Physics. Available at *http://www.aip.org/statistics/trends/reports/international.pdf.*

[27] One review of the NIH budget concluded that its dramatic growth did not result in an increase in new US doctorates or in the number of US citizens in postdoctoral appointments even while the number of international postdoctoral scholars was rising. Howard H. Garrison, Susan A. Gerbi, and Paul W. Kincade. 2003. "In an era of scientific opportunity, are they opportunities for biomedical scientists?" *FASEB Journal* 17:2169-2173.

to manage the flow of visitors. Since the F and J visa classes were established in 1952, it has been possible to measure the impact of policies on students and exchange scholars. However, because those visa classes include students from primary to graduate school, as well as postdoctoral scholars and many other nonuniversity exchange visitors, and because graduate students and postdoctoral scholars can enter the United States with other visa classes, including the H-1b, it is not practical to try to use immigration statistics to determine anything useful about any particular level of student or trainee. That is evident in comparing enrollment patterns and visa issuance rates: if one looks only at issuance rates, the primary sending countries for postdoctoral scholars appear to be European; but enrollment numbers indicate that Asian countries send more scholars by far. There are also policy implications: restrictions applied to particular visa classes may be having unintended effects because a class includes a heterogeneous group of people.

Improvement of data on immigration and emigration has been championed for at least 20 years.[28] Coupling data inadequacies for immigration with those for the US workforce, particularly for postdoctoral scholars, and our understanding of the composition of the S&E workforce is even more limited. Moreover, there is a lack of analysis of trends and relationships among student flows, enrollments, economic cycles, and other factors. Congress and administrative agencies need better data and more analysis to craft better policies.

On the basis of the foregoing, the committee offers the following findings and recommendations:

Finding 4-1: The flow of international graduate students and postdoctoral scholars is affected by national policies. Among them, changes in visa and immigration policies since 9-11 have adversely affected every stage of the visa-application process for graduate students and postdoctoral scholars in S&E. Interagency cooperation and a willingness to work with members of the S&E community have helped to reduce some bottlenecks and improve procedures, but unfavorable perceptions remain and additional steps need to be taken. Some policies contribute to anxieties among international students and scholars and a

---

[28]National Research Council. 1985. *Immigration Statistics: A Story of Neglect.* Washington, DC: National Academy Press; National Research Council. 1996. *Statistics on U.S. Immigration: An Assessment of Data Needs for Future Research.* Washington, DC: National Academy Press; National Research Council. 1999. *Measuring the Science and Engineering Enterprise: Priorities for the Division of Science Resources Studies.* Washington, DC: National Academy Press. This study focused on the Science Resource Statistics division of the NSF and urged sufficient funding to "continue and expand significantly its data collection and analysis."

perception that the United States does not welcome them. International sentiment regarding the US visa and immigration processes is a lingering problem for the recruitment of international students and scholars. Those environmental factors discourage international students and scholars from applying to US colleges and universities and discourage colleagues who would otherwise send their students to the United States. Recent improvements in processing time and duration of Visas Mantis clearances are a positive step, but extending visa validity periods and Mantis clearances commensurate with a period of study has not been uniform across nationalities.

Finding 4-2: Large drops in international applications in the 3 years after 9-11 caused considerable concern in the university community, but their effects on numbers of first-time enrollments of international S&E graduate students were modest.

Finding 4-3: The flow of international graduate students and postdoctoral scholars is affected by institutional policies. Universities have been responsive to the needs of international students. Many have offices dedicated to international students, and several offer orientation sessions before the start of the school year and teaching-assistant training and English-language courses. Steps taken by educational and exchange institutions have mitigated some of the adverse effects of visa and immigration policies by creating resources for international applicants and establishing earlier acceptance notifications to allow more time for visa-processing. Some universities have begun to reimburse admitted graduate students the $100 Student and Exchange Visitor Information System (SEVIS) fee.

Finding 4-4: Exogenous factors, many of which predate 9-11, affect the flows of international graduate students and postdoctoral scholars. Other countries are expanding their technological and educational capacities and creating more opportunities for participation by international students. The natural expansion of education in the rest of the world increases the potential supply of talent for the United States and at the same time increases competition for the best graduate students and postdoctoral scholars. Economic conditions—including availability of university-sponsored financial support and employment opportunities—can affect student mobility, as can geopolitical events, such as war and political instability.

Finding 4-5: The inadequacy of data on international graduate students and postdoctoral scholars limits our understanding of the composition of the S&E workforce and of how it might respond to economic or political changes. Moreover, the lack of timeliness and coverage of data on US-trained and internationally trained scientists and engineers hinders our examination of trends and relationships among student flows, enrollments, economic cycles, and other factors. Congress and administrative agencies need better data and more analysis to craft better policies.

Recommendation 4-1: The United States needs a new system of data collection to track student and postdoctoral flows so that it can understand the dynamics and effects of shifting sources of talent. Funds should be provided to the NSF or other institutions to collaborate internationally to create a data system similar to a balance-of-trade account to track degree production, student and postdoctoral movement between countries, push-pull factors affecting student choice at all degree levels, and employment outcomes.

Recommendation 4-2: If the United States is to maintain overall leadership in S&E, visa and immigration policies should provide clear procedures that do not unnecessarily hinder the flow of international graduate students and postdoctoral scholars. New regulations should be carefully considered in light of national-security considerations and potential unintended consequences. Research institutions and the Departments of State (DOS) and Homeland Security (DHS) should continue their discussion on these matters.

a. Visa Duration: Recent policies to extend the duration of Visas Mantis clearances for some students and scholars is a positive step. We strongly encourage DOS and DHS to continue working toward applying those provisions to students and scholars from all countries.

b. Travel for Scientific Meetings: Means should be found to allow international graduate students and postdoctoral scholars who are attending or appointed at US institutions to attend scientific meetings that are outside the United States without being seriously delayed in reentering the United States to complete their studies and training.

c. Technology Alert List: This list, which is used to manage the Visas Mantis program, should be reviewed regularly by scientists and engineers outside government. Scientifically trained personnel should be involved in the security-review process.

d. Visa Categories: New nonimmigrant-visa categories should be created for doctoral-level graduate students and postdoctoral scholars, whether they are coming to the United States for formal educational or training programs or for short-term research collaborations or scientific meetings. The categories should be exempted from the 214b provision whereby applicants must show that they have a residence in a foreign country that they have no intention of abandoning. In addition to providing a better mechanism for embassy and consular officials to track student and scholar visa applicants, the categories would provide a means for collecting clear data on numbers and trends of graduate-student and postdoctoral-scholar visa applications.

e. Reciprocity Agreements: Multiple-entry and multiple-year student visas should have high priority in reciprocity negotiations.

f. Change of Status: If the United States wants to retain the best students, procedures for change of status should be clarified and streamlined.

Maintaining and strengthening the S&E enterprise of the United States, particularly by attracting the best domestic and international graduate students and postdoctoral scholars, will require the cooperation of the government, universities, and industry to agree on an appropriate balance between openness, mobility, and economic and national security. Making the choices will not be easy, but the recommendations provided here define priorities, data, and analyses needed to determine effective policy strategies and substantive steps that will advance the vitality of US research and attract the talented people necessary to perform it.

Appendix A

Committee and Staff Biographic Information

PHILLIP A. GRIFFITHS [NAS], *Chair,* is a faculty member of the School of Mathematics at the Institute for Advanced Study (IAS). He served as director of IAS from 1991 to 2003. He has worked in a number of fields in mathematics, and is known for introducing the fundamental notion of variation of Hodge structure. He received his BS from Wake Forest University and his PhD in mathematics from Princeton University in 1962. After appointments at Berkeley and Princeton, he taught mathematics at Harvard University from 1972 to 1983, where he was appointed Dwight Parker Robinson Professor of Mathematics in 1983. He was a member in the School of Mathematics at IAS from 1968 to 1970. In 1983, he was named Provost and James P. Duke Professor of Mathematics at Duke University. In 1991, he became the seventh director of IAS. He served on the National Science Board from 1991 to 1996. He is a member of the National Academy of Sciences and a foreign associate of the Third World Academy of Sciences. From 1993 to 1999, he chaired the Committee on Science, Engineering, and Public Policy. Dr. Griffiths is secretary of the International Mathematical Union and chair of the Science Institutes Group, founded in 1999 to provide scientific guidance for the Millennium Science Initiative.

WILLIAM G. AGNEW [NAE] is the retired director of programs and plans at General Motors. His research efforts were combustion in internal combustion engines, but at the General Motors Research Laboratories he directed research in crash injury, the effects of automotive products on health, atmospheric pollution, automotive exhaust emissions, safety, automobile use, societal cost effectiveness, socioeconomic studies, engine design, engineering mechanics, fluid dynamics, and fuels and lubricants. In recent years, he has been involved with intelligent transportation systems, accrediting and advising on engineering education, and the development of curricula to teach science and mathematics in an engineering context to K-12 students.

JOHN A. ARMSTRONG [NAE] is the former vice president of science and technology and member of the Corporate Management Board at IBM. His expertise is in quantum electronics and laser physics. He is a member of the National Academy of Engineering and a fellow of the Royal Swedish Academy of Engineering Sciences and the American Academy of Arts and Sciences. Dr. Armstrong holds an AB in physics from Harvard College (1956) and a PhD (1961) from Harvard University for research in nuclear magnetic resonance at high pressures. He joined IBM in 1963 as a research staff member. In 1976, he became director of physical sciences for the company and was responsible for a major part of IBM research in physics, chemistry, and materials science. In 1980, he was appointed to the IBM Corporate Technical Committee. A year later, he was made manager of materials and technology development at the IBM East Fishkill, NY, development laboratory, working on advanced bipolar technology and associated packaging. In 1983, Dr. Armstrong was named vice president for logic and memory, in the Research Division. In 1986, he became director of research; in the following year, he was elected IBM vice president and director of research. In 1989, he was elected a member of the Corporate Management Board and named IBM vice president for science and technology.

RICHARD B. FREEMAN is Herbert Ascherman Chair of Economics at Harvard University, codirector of the Labor and Worklife Program at the Harvard Law School, and director of the Labor Studies Program at the National Bureau of Economic Research (NBER). He is also senior research fellow in labor markets at the Centre for Economic Performance at the London School of Economics (LSE) and visiting professor at the LSE. He is a member of the American Academy of Arts and Sciences and of Sigma Xi. He has served on five panels of the National Research Council, including the Committee on National Needs for Biomedical and Behavioral Scientists. He has published over 300 articles dealing with a wide array of subjects, including the job market for scientists and engineers, the growth and decline of unions, the effects of immigration and trade on inequality, restructuring European welfare states, international labor standards, Chinese labor markets, transitional economies, youth labor-market problems, crime, self-organizing nonunions in the labor market, employee involvement programs, and income distribution and equity in the marketplace. He is currently directing the NBER/Sloan Science Engineering Workforce Project (with Daniel Goroff), and an LSE research program on the effects of the Internet on labor markets, social behavior, and the economy.

ALICE P. GAST [NAE] is the Robert T. Haslam Professor in the Department of Chemical Engineering, and the vice president for research and associate provost of the Massachusetts Institute of Technology. Until 2001, she was a professor of chemical engineering at Stanford University, professor of the Stanford Synchrotron Radiation Laboratory and professor, by courtesy, of chemistry at Stanford. She earned her BS in chemical engineering at the University of Southern California in 1980 and her PhD in Chemical Engineering from Princeton University in 1984. She spent a postdoctoral year on a NATO fellowship at the Ecole Superieure de Physique et de Chimie Industrielles in Paris. She was on the faculty at Stanford from 1985 to 2001. She returned to Paris for a sabbatical as a John Simon Guggenheim Memorial Foundation Fellow in 1991 and to Munich as a Humboldt Fellow in 1999. The aim of her research is to understand the behavior of complex fluids through a combination of colloid science, polymer physics, and statistical mechanics. In 1992, Dr. Gast received the National Academy of Sciences Award for Initiative in Research and the Colburn Award of the American Institute of Chemical Engineers. She was the 1995 Langmuir Lecturer for the American Chemical Society. She is a member of the American Academy of Arts and Sciences and the National Academy of Engineering. She served as a member and then as the cochair of the National Research Council Board on Chemical Sciences and Technology and currently serves on the Division on Earth and Life Studies Committee. She also serves on the Homeland Security Science and Technology Advisory Committee.

JOEL MOSES [NAE] is an Institute Professor, professor of computer science and engineering, and professor of engineering systems at MIT. His prior positions at MIT have included provost, dean of engineering, head of the Department of Electrical Engineering and Computer Science (EECS), and associate director of the Laboratory for Computer Science. He led the development of the Macsyma system for algebraic formula manipulation and is the codeveloper of the knowledge-based systems concept in artificial intelligence. His current research focuses on architecture, complexity, and flexibility of large-scale engineering systems. He is a member of the National Academy of Engineering and a fellow of the American Academy of Arts and Sciences, the American Association for the Advancement of Sciences, and IEEE. He was also a member of the National Research Council's Committee on Research Directions for Information Technology and Committee on Human Resources for Information Technology.

NORMAN NEUREITER received a BS in chemistry from the University of Rochester (NY) in 1952 and a PhD in organic chemistry from Northwestern University in 1957. In 1955-1956, he was a Fulbright Fellow at the Institute for Organic Chemistry at the University of Munich, Germany. He served as science and technology adviser to the secretary of state from 2000 to 2003. As an organic chemist, he has extensive experience in government and industry and a public-policy background that includes close ties to academe. From 1973 to 1996, Dr. Neureiter held a variety of positions in Texas Instruments, including director of east-west business development, manager of international business development, and manager of the TI Europe Division. As vice president for corporate staff, he was the company's principal spokesperson throughout the world from 1980 to 1989. From 1989 until 1996, he served as a director of TI Japan and vice president of TI Asia. From 1969-1973, Dr. Neureiter worked as international affairs assistant in the White House Office of Science and Technology Policy, reporting to the president's science adviser. In this capacity, he was deeply involved in preparing agreements on cooperation in science and technology initiated in 1972-1973 by President Nixon with the leaders of the Soviet Union and the People's Republic of China. In May 2004, he became the director of the MacArthur Foundation-funded American Association for the Advancement of Science Center for Science, Technology, and Security Policy. The role of the center is to provide an effective interface between the academic science and technology community and the Washington policy world.

PREM S. PAUL is vice chancellor for research and dean of graduate studies at the University of Nebraska-Lincoln. After earning a BVSc (DVM) at the College of Veterinary Sciences at Panjab Agricultural University in India in 1969 and a PhD in veterinary microbiology and virology at the University of Minnesota-Twin Cities (UMTC) in 1975, he served as a research associate for 3 years in the Department of Large Animal Clinical Sciences at UMTC. From 1978 to 1985, he was veterinary medical officer for swine reproductive diseases at the US Department of Agriculture (USDA) National Animal Disease Center in Ames, Iowa. He served on the faculty of the College of Veterinary Medicine at Iowa State University from 1985 to 2001 and conducted research on animal viral diseases. Dr. Paul held the positions of director of the interdisciplinary graduate program in immunobiology, director of graduate Education in the Department of Microbiology, associate dean for research and graduate studies in the College of Veterinary Medicine, assistant director of agricultural experiment station and associate vice provost for research at Iowa State University. Dr. Paul currently serves on the Council of Research Policy and Graduate Education of the National Association of State Universities and Land Grant Colleges and is the vice president of the Conference of Research Workers in

Animal Diseases. He has published 97 refereed journal articles, edited two books, and written several invited book chapters, including the most recent chapter on swine exogenous viruses in a book on xenotransplantation, and is a recipient of the Pfizer Award for Research Excellence. He has also served on National Institutes of Health (NIH) and USDA review panels and on the US Food and Drug Administration's xenotransplantation advisory subcommittee. His research funding includes grants from NIH, USDA, commodity organizations, and private corporations.

SAMUEL H. PRESTON [IOM/NAS] is the Frederick J. Warren Professor of Demography at the University of Pennsylvania. He served as Dean of the School of Arts and Sciences from 1998 to 2004 and has served on the school's sociology faculty since 1979. He was named Frederick J. Warren Professor of Demography in 1988. He is a demographer whose studies have focused on the causes and consequences of population change, with special attention to mortality. He has been author, coauthor, or editor of 16 books and more than 140 articles. Dr. Preston is a member of the National Academy of Science, Institute of Medicine, and the American Philosophical Society, and is a fellow of the American Academy of Arts and Sciences, the American Association for the Advancement of Science, and the American Statistical Association. He is also a member of the Population Council's Board of Trustees. He served on President Bush's Committee on the National Medal of Science and is a past president of the Population Association of America and of the Sociological Research Association. Earlier in his career, he was a faculty member at the University of California, Berkeley and the University of Washington. He was acting chief of the Population Trends and Structure Section of the United Nations Population Division from 1977 to 1979. Dr. Preston holds a BA from Amherst College and a PhD in economics from Princeton University.

ELSA REICHMANIS [NAE] is Bell Labs Fellow and director of the Materials Research Department at Bell Laboratories, Lucent Technologies, Murray Hill, NJ. She received her BS (1972) and PhD (1975) in chemistry from Syracuse University and joined Bell Labs in 1978 after completing a postdoctoral fellowship program. Her research interests include the chemistry, properties, and application of materials technologies for photonics and electronics, with a focus on polymeric and nanostructured materials for advanced communication technologies. She has published in a variety of fields from synthetic organic and heteroaromatic chemistry to radiation chemistry of polymeric systems. She is the author of over 150 publications, the holder of several patents, and editor of five books. Dr. Reichmanis received the 1993 Society of Women Engineers Achievement Award; she was elected to the National Academy of Engineering in 1995 and received the American Society for Metals Engineering Materials Achievement Award in 1996. In 1997, she was elected Fellow of the American Association for the Advancement of Science. She is the recipient of a 1998 Photopolymer Science and Technology Award, the 1999 American Chemical Society (ACS) Applied Polymer Science Awardee, the Society of Chemical Industry's 2001 Perkin Medalist, and a 2001 recipient of Syracuse University's Arents Medal. She is past chair of the Executive Committee of the ACS Division of Polymeric Materials: Science and Engineering and was a member of the National Materials Advisory Board and the Air Force Scientific Advisory Board. She is an associate editor of *Chemistry of Materials* and served as the 2003 president of the ACS.

ROBERT C. RICHARDSON [NAS] is the F.R. Newman Professor of Physics and the vice provost for research at Cornell University. He attended Virginia Polytechnic Institute in 1954-1960, where he obtained a BS and MS in physics. After a brief time in the US Army, he returned to graduate school in physics at Duke University. His thesis work involved nuclear magnetic resonance (NMR) studies of solid ^{3}He. He obtained his PhD from Duke in 1966. In fall 1966, he began work at Cornell University in the laboratory of David Lee. Their research goal was to observe the nuclear magnetic phase transition in solid ^{3}He that could be predicted from his thesis work with Horst Meyer at Duke. In collaboration with Douglas Osheroff, a student who joined the group in 1967, they worked on cooling techniques and NMR instrumentation for studying low-temperature helium liquids and solids. In fall 1971, they made the accidental discovery that liquid ^{3}He undergoes a pairing transition similar to that of superconductors. The three were awarded the Nobel prize for that work in 1996. Dr. Richardson has been on the Cornell faculty since 1967. In his more than 35 years at Cornell, he has led an active research program in studies of matter at very low temperatures. In that time, 20 students have earned PhDs while working with him. He has published more than 95 scientific articles in major research journals. He has been active in teaching introductory physics throughout his time at Cornell.

LEWIS SIEGEL is professor of biochemistry and vice provost for graduate education and dean of the Graduate School at Duke University. Dr. Siegel has published over 75 articles in bioinorganic chemistry with emphasis on mechanisms of electron transfer in metalloenzymes and on the biochemistry of the nitrogen and sulfur cycles. After receiving his PhD in biology from Johns Hopkins University in 1965, he began a National Institutes of Health postdoctoral fellowship at Duke University School of Medicine. Except for a short visiting research position at the University of Sussex in England, he has remained at Duke University for his entire career. Dr. Siegel has served as vice provost for interdisciplinary activities and interim vice provost for research. He is a leader in the national effort to reform PhD education in the United States. He serves as the chairman of the Board of Directors of the Council of Graduate Schools, which is conducting a major project on reducing attrition from PhD programs, and as chair of the Research Committee of the Graduate Record Examination (GRE) Board, which is overseeing a major restructuring of the GRE General Examination. As dean at Duke, he has been an active participant in the Responsive PhD Program and the Carnegie Initiative on the Doctorate, both of which are efforts to improve the delivery of doctoral education in the United States.

PAULA E. STEPHAN is professor of economics at the Andrew Young School for Policy Studies at Georgia State University. She graduated from Grinnell College with a BA in economics and earned both her MA and PhD in economics from the University of Michigan. Her research interests focus on the careers of scientists and engineers and the process by which knowledge moves across institutional boundaries in the economy. Her other interests include technology transfer and the role that immigrant scientists play in US science. Her research has been supported by the Alfred P. Sloan Foundation, the Andrew Mellon Foundation, the Exxon Education Foundation, the National Science Foundation, NATO, and the US Department of Labor. Dr. Stephan has served on several National Research Council committees, including the Committee on Dimensions, Causes, and Implications of Recent Trends in the Careers of Life Scientists; the Committee on Methods of Forecasting Demand and Supply of Doctoral Scientists and Engineers; and the Committee to Assess the Portfolio of the Science Resources Studies Division of NSF. She is a regular participant in the National Bureau of Economic Research's meetings in higher education and has testified before the US House of Representatives Subcommittee on Basic Science. She is serving a 3-year term as a member of the National Science Foundation Social, Behavioral, and Economic Advisory Committee. She has published numerous articles in such journals as *The American Economic Review, Science, The Journal of Economic Literature,* and *Social Studies of Science.* She was coauthor with Sharon Levin of *Striking the Mother Lode in Science,* published by Oxford University Press in 1992.

MICHAEL S. TEITELBAUM, a demographer at the Alfred P. Sloan Foundation in New York, was educated at Reed College and at Oxford University, where he was a Rhodes scholar. He was a faculty member at Oxford University and Princeton University. Dr. Teitelbaum served as staff director of the US House of Representatives Select Committee on Population. He was a professional staff member of the Ford Foundation and the Carnegie Endowment for International Peace. Dr. Teitelbaum was one of 12 commissioners of the US Commission for the Study of International Migration and Cooperative Economic Development (1988-1990). He was elected first vice president of the Population Association of America. He served (via appointment by the congressional leadership) as one of nine commissioners of the US Commission on Immigration Reform (known as the Jordan Commission after its late chair, former Congresswoman Representative Barbara Jordan), which completed its work in December 1997. He was elected vice chair by his fellow Commissioners, and served as acting chair for much of 1996. Dr. Teitelbaum is a regular speaker on demographic change and immigration, and a frequent witness before committees of Congress.

MARVALEE WAKE is professor of the Graduate School and former chair of the Department of Integrative Biology of the University of California, Berkeley. Her research emphasizes morphology, development, and reproductive biology in vertebrates with the goal of understanding evolutionary patterns and processes. She is interested in many problems in evolutionary, developmental, and functional morphology and in issues of biodiversity. She has served as president of the International Union of Biological Sciences, president of the Society for Integrative and Comparative Biology, and president of the American Society of Ichthyologists and Herpetologists. She is president-elect of the American Institute of Biological Science, a fellow of the American Association for the Advancement of Science, and a fellow and honorary trustee (for life) of the California Academy of Sciences. She was a Guggenheim Fellow in 1988-1989. She was elected to membership in the American Academy of Arts and Sciences in 2003. She is an ex officio member of the National Academies US National Committee for the International Union of Biological Sciences.

STAFF

LAUREL L. HAAK (Study Director) is a program officer for the Committee on Science, Engineering, and Public Policy. She received a BS and an MS in biology from Stanford University. She was the recipient of a predoctoral National Institutes of Health (NIH) National Research Service Award and received a PhD in neuroscience in 1997 from Stanford University Medical School, where her research focused on calcium signaling and circadian rhythms. She was awarded a National Academy of Sciences research associateship to work at NIH on intracellular calcium dynamics in oligo-dendrocytes. In 2002, she joined the staff at the American Association for the Advancement of Science and was editor of *Science's* Next Wave Postdoc Network. While a postdoctoral scholar, she was editor of the Women in Neuroscience (WIN) newsletter, and served as president of the organization from 2003-2004. She is an ex officio member of the Society for Neuroscience Committee on Women in Neuroscience, has served on the Biophysics Society Early Careers Committee, and was an adviser for the National Postdoctoral Association.

RICHARD E. BISSELL is executive director of the Policy and Global Affairs Division of the National Research Council and director of the Committee on Science, Engineering, and Public Policy. He took up his positions in 1998, having served as coordinator of the Interim Secretariat of the World Commission on Dams (1997-1998) and as a member and chair of the Inspection Panel at the World Bank (1994-1997). He worked closely with the National Academy of Sciences during his tenure in senior positions at the US Agency for International Development (1986-1993) as head of the Bureau of Science and Technology and head of the Bureau of Program and Policy Coordination. He has published widely in political economy, and he taught at Georgetown University and the University of Pennsylvania. He received his BA from Stanford University (1968) and his MA and PhD from Tufts University (1970 and 1973).

PETER HENDERSON is director of the National Academies Board on Higher Education and Workforce (BHEW). His fields of specialization include postsecondary education, the labor market for scientists and engineers, and federal science and technology research funding. He oversees BHEW's evaluation of the Lucille P. Markey Trust Programs in Biomedical Science and the assessment of NIH Minority research Training Programs; and he supervises BHEW staff working on studies that examine the community-college pathway to engineering careers and the policy implications of international graduate students and postdoctorates. He has previously contributed as study director or staff to *Building a Workforce for the Information Economy, Measuring the Science and Engineering Enterprise, Attracting Science and Mathematics Ph.D.s to K-12 Education, Monitoring International Labor Standards, Trends in Federal Support of Research and Graduate Education,* and *Observations on the President's Federal Science and Technology Budget.* Dr. Henderson holds a master's in public policy (1984) from Harvard University's John F. Kennedy School of Government and a PhD in American political history from the Johns Hopkins University (1994). He joined the National Academies staff in 1996 and is the recipient of the National Academies Distinguished Service Award (2003).

DEBORAH D. STINE is the associate director of the Committee on Science, Engineering, and Public Policy (COSEPUP) and director of the Office of Special Projects. She has worked on various projects at the National Academies since 1989. She received a National Research Council group award for her first study for COSEPUP, on policy implications of greenhouse warming; a Commission on Life Sciences staff citation for her work in risk assessment and management; and two awards from the Policy and Global Affairs Division for her efforts in dissemination of National Academies reports. Other studies have addressed human reproductive cloning, setting priorities for National Science Foundations' large research facilities, science and technology presidential appointments, science and technology centers, international benchmarking of US research fields, graduate and postdoctoral education, responsible conduct of research, careers in science and engineering, and many environmental topics. She holds a bachelor's degree in mechanical and environmental engineering from the University of California, Irvine; a master's degree in business administration; and a PhD in public administration, specializing in policy analysis, from the American University. Before coming to the National Academies, she was a mathematician for the US Air Force, an air-pollution engineer for the state of Texas, and an air-issues manager for the Chemical Manufacturers Association.

JAMES A. VOYTUK is a senior program officer at the National Academies and provides technical support and analysis for projects dealing with the demographics of the science and engineering workforce, career transitions and labor-market issues for scientists and engineers, and graduate education and postdoctoral training. His current projects involve the development of the 2005 Assessment of Research Doctorate Programs; the Study of National Needs for Biomedical, Behavioral, and Clinical Personnel; and the evaluation of the Resident Research Associateship Programs. Dr. Voytuk received a PhD in mathematics from Carnegie Institute of Technology.

Appendix B

Charge to the Committee

This committee will undertake a broad examination of the current status and role of international graduate students and postdoctoral scholars in the United States. The committee will bring together and analyze the diverse data available regarding international graduate students and postdoctoral scholars. Based on these data and other information it gathers, the committee will answer the following questions:

1. What is known about the impact of international graduate students and postdoctoral scholars on the advancement of US science, US undergraduate and graduate educational institutions, the US and other national economies, and US national security and international relations?

2. What is the impact of the US academic system on international graduate students' and postdoctoral scholars' intellectual development, careers, and perceptions of the United States? How does it differ if they stay in the United States or return to their home countries?

3. What is known about the impact of international student enrollment on the recruitment of domestic S&E talent in the United States? What is the status of working conditions for international graduate students and postdoctoral scholars compared with their domestic counterparts?

4. What are the impacts of various policies that reshape or reduce the flow of international students and postdoctoral scholars (for example, visas, immigration rules, and working conditions)?

5. What findings and conclusions can be drawn from the answers to the preceding questions? What principles should guide national policy regarding international graduate students and postdoctoral scholars?

Appendix C

US Travel and Attitudes Toward the United States

SUMMARY

Our analysis suggests that visiting the United States improves people's attitudes toward the United States. We used data from the 2002 Pew Global Attitudes Survey to relate respondents' opinions of the United States to whether they had traveled in the United States and other variables. We describe the variables that we used in our analysis, present our results, and briefly discuss their limitations.

METHODS

Our data come from the Pew Global Attitudes Survey of 2002, which asked respondents in 44 countries about their attitudes toward important geopolitical topics and asked for information about themselves, such as age and education level.[1] A list of the countries can be found below. We included several variables in our analysis, all of which are described in greater detail later: a person's opinion of the United States (USOPINION), a variable representing whether the person has traveled to the United States (USTRAVEL), whether the person admires the United States for its scientific and technologic advances (ADUSST), and the interaction of the previous two variables (USTRADUSST).

---

[1]Data from the United States were not analyzed because all US citizens have "traveled to the United States." That left 43 countries in the sample.

Definition of Variables

- **USOPINION:** Please tell me if you have a very favorable, some-what favorable, somewhat unfavorable, or very unfavorable opinion of the United States. 0 = Very unfavorable; 1 = somewhat unfavorable; 2 = some-what favorable; 3 = very favorable.[2]
- **USTRAVEL:** Have you ever traveled to the United States? 0 = No; 1 = Yes.
- **ADUSST:** Which comes closer to describing your view? I admire the United States for its technological and scientific advances, *or* I do not admire the United States for its technological and scientific advances. 0 = I do not admire the United States for its technological and scientific advances; 1 = I admire the United States for its technological and scientific advances.
- **USTRADUSST** = 1 if USTRAVEL = 1 *and* ADUSST = 1; USTRADUSST = 0 otherwise.

Countries Included in the Dataset

The dataset included Canada, France, the United Kingdom, Italy, Germany, the Czech Republic, the Slovak Republic, Poland, Ukraine, Russia, Bulgaria, Egypt, Uzbekistan, Jordan, Pakistan, Lebanon, Turkey, Guatemala, Mexico, Honduras, Venezuela, Argentina, Brazil, Peru, Bolivia, South Korea, Vietnam, Japan, Indonesia, the Philippines, China, India, Bangladesh, Nigeria, South Africa, Ivory Coast, Senegal, Kenya, Uganda, Ghana, Angola, Mali, and Tanzania.

CORRELATION ANALYSIS

We first examined the raw correlation between one's opinion of the United States and whether one has visited the United States. About 8 percent of respondents had visited the United States. Among those who had visited the United States, the mean opinion of the United States was 1.82 on a scale, described at the end of this appendix, of 0-3. Among those who had not visited the United States, the mean opinion of the United States was 1.41. This is displayed in Figure C-1.

In light of the events of 9/11, policy makers may be particularly interested in how many of those who have visited the United States have *very negative* opinions of the United States. The distribution of opinions about

---

[2]The original Pew survey coded the data differently—the most favorable opinion was coded as "1," and the least favorable opinion as "4"—but they have been recoded to make the results easier to interpret.

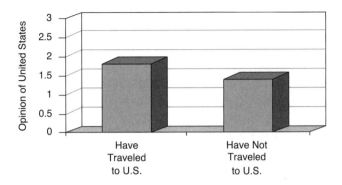

FIGURE C-1 Opinions of the United States.

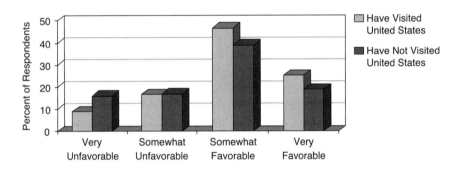

FIGURE C-2 Opinions of the United States of people who have and have not visited the United States.

the United States, by whether a person has visited the United States, is displayed in Figure C-2. Note that people who, when asked their opinion of the United States, responded "Don't Know" or refused to answer the question were excluded from the analysis.

Of those who have visited the United States, 8.8 percent have a very unfavorable opinion of the United States, but 16.0 percent of those who have not visited the United States have a very unfavorable opinion of the United States. Those who have visited the United States are substantially less likely than average to have a very unfavorable opinion of the United States, but it is important to note that a moderate proportion of people who have visited the United States still have a very unfavorable opinion of it. Visiting the United States does not eliminate very unfavorable opinions.

REGRESSION ANALYSIS

Raw correlations can be misleading, so we have also performed regression analysis to attempt to control for other factors that might influence one's opinion of the United States In these regressions, the dependent variable is a person's opinion of the United States, and the independent variables include a variable representing whether one has traveled to the United States and several control variables. The results of the ordinary least-squares (OLS) regressions in which USOPINION is the dependent variable are reported in Tables C-1 and C-2.

Robust t-statistics are stated in parentheses. The right-hand-side variables included in *all* regressions are dummy variables representing the effect of each country and controls for age, education, and whether the respondents have friends or family in the United States with whom they correspond regularly. "Extra Controls" are controls for the respondent's opinion of the dominant country in his or her region and whether the respondent has traveled outside his or her own country in the last 5 years. An observation is excluded from the regression if the respondent answered "Don't Know" or refused to give a response on any of the relevant questions.

Each numbered column represents a different regression. "N" represents the sample size in each regression (the number of people whose responses are included in the regression). "R-Squared," which can take values from 0 to 1, represents the amount of the variation in the dependent variable that has been accounted for in the regression by the variation in the independent variables. When R-Squared is higher, more of the variation in the dependent variable has been accounted for by the variation in the independent variables.

The Effect of Traveling to the United States on One's Opinion of the United States

The row labeled "USTRAVEL" displays the estimated effect in each regression (1, 2, and 3) of United States travel on a person's opinion of the United States. There are three important components of each box in this row. The first number in each box represents the estimated effect of visiting the United States on one's opinion of the United States.

In regression 1 (Table C-1), OLS regression analysis of responses to the Pew survey indicates that visiting the United States raises one's opinion of the United States by 0.109, on the scale that runs from 0 to 3. The t-statistic is in parentheses below the first number and represents how precise our estimate is. In regression 1, the t-statistic is 4.00, which is rather high, indicating that our estimate is somewhat precise. Asterisks after the t-statistic indicate whether the estimated coefficient is significantly different

TABLE C-1 Effect of Visiting on Opinions of the United States

	(1)	(2)	(3)
USTRAVEL	0.109 (4.00)***	0.122 (4.52)***	0.102 (1.98)**
Extra Controls?	NO	YES	YES
Sample	ALL	ALL	At least a college education; age strictly less than 46 years[a]
N	11,406	11,406	2,303
R-Squared	0.251	0.296	0.281

[a]All respondents in the Pew dataset were over 18 years old.

from 0. Two asterisks indicate significance at the 5 percent level; and three stars indicate significance at the 1 percent level.

The coefficient of USTRAVEL is quite significant in regressions (1) and (2). The coefficient is still significant in regression (3), but the t-statistic is somewhat smaller, probably owing in part to the smaller sample.

Our estimate of the effect of traveling to the United States on one's opinion of the United States is moderately large, but not enormous: A visit to the United States apparently raises a person's opinion of the United States by about 0.1 point on a scale that runs from 0 to 3.

Attitudes Toward US Science and Technology

Suppose we had a measure of people's attitudes toward the United States before they visited. We would be able to estimate the effect of visiting the United States on their attitudes much more convincingly. Although we do not have such data, we do have data on whether they admire United States scientific and technological achievements. People in nearly every part the world frequently come into contact with United States scientific and technological achievements (cars, for example), so it is plausible that their feelings about United States scientific and technological achievements (ADUSST) are almost fully formed by repeated experiences with products in their home countries. Perhaps, then, visiting the United States (USTRAVEL) has little effect on attitudes toward United States science and

TABLE C-2 Attitudes toward US Science and Technology

	(1)	(2)	(3)
USTRAVEL	0.14	0.10	–0.13
	(5.17)***	(2.00)**	(-1.17)
ADUSST	0.34	0.26	0.18
	(14.52)***	(4.83)***	(3.06)***
USTRADUSST			0.29
			(2.46)***
Extra Controls?	YES	YES	YES
Sample	ALL	At least a college education; age < 46 years	At least a college education; age < 46 years
N	10,492	2,272	2,272
R-Squared	0.346	0.287	0.289

technology (ADUSST).[3] Moreover, it is plausible that ADUSST is highly correlated with people's previsit attitudes toward the United States, inasmuch as we would expect people who like the United States in general also to admire United States science and technology.[4] We will therefore use ADUSST as an imperfect measure of respondents' attitudes toward the United States in the absence of visiting the United States. The results of including ADUSST are shown in Table C-2.

The coefficient of USTRAVEL is positive and significant in regressions (1) and (2). Its size—0.14 and 0.10 in regressions (1) and (2), respectively—is close to the size of the coefficient of USTRAVEL in the regressions reported in Table C-1.

In regression (3), we add a term, USTRADUSST, representing the interaction of USTRAVEL with ADUSST. The coefficient of USTRAVEL is now insignificant. It is interesting that the coefficient of USTRADUSST is positive, relatively large (0.29), and quite significant. Our interpretation is that

---

[3]This contention is supported by a regression (not shown) of ADUSST on USTRAVEL and various controls. The coefficient of USTRAVEL is –0.006, with a t-statistic of –0.45, suggesting that USTRAVEL indeed has little effect on ADUSST.

[4]Of respondents who had not visited the United States, nearly everyone who has a high opinion of the United States also admires United States science and technology, and vice versa.

people who admire United States science and technology and visit the United States improve their attitude toward the United States substantially.

LIMITATIONS

We lack data on how people's attitudes toward the United States *changed* when they visited the United States; we have only cross-sectional data on attitudes. It is therefore plausible to argue that despite the controls we have added to our regression, the "US travel" variable is still endogenous. The regressions may suffer from omitted-variable bias: Other variables that we have not controlled for, and that might not even be in our dataset, may affect one's opinion of the United States and be correlated with whether one travels to the United States. Reverse causality may be at work: Having a good attitude toward the United States may cause travel to the United States, and not the other way around. Because the data do not contain a good instrument for travel to the United States, we have tried to address the issues in the ways discussed above, but our conclusions must still be viewed with caution.

Appendix D

Bibliography

AAU, AAAS, NAS, ACE, NASULGC, NAE, IOM, NAFSA, ACS, APS, AACC, AAPT, AERA, ASBMS, ASM, CoGR, CGS, EMS, FASEB, IEEE-USA, LSA, NAICU, NPA, SAA, and SPIE. 2004. Statement and recommendations on visa problems harming America's scientific, economic, and security interests. Available at *http://www7.nationalacademies.org/ visas/Statement%20on%20Visa%20Problems.pdf.*

Agrawal, Ajay, Devesh Kapur, and John McHale. Defying Distance: Examining the Influence of the Diaspora on Scientific Knowledge Flows. *The Fourth Annual Roundtable on Engineering Entrepreneurship Research (REER) Conference, December 3-5, 2004, Atlanta, GA.* Available at *http://mgt.gatech.edu/news_room/news/2004/reer/files/ agrawal.pdf.*

Alphonso, Caroline. 2005. "Facing U.S. security hurdles, top students flock to Canada." *The Globe and Mail* (February 22). Available at *http://www.globetechnology.com/servlet/ story/RTGAM.20050222.gtstudents22/BNStory/Technology.*

Altbach, Philip G. 2004a. "Higher education crosses borders: Can the United States remain the top destination for foreign students?" *Change* 36(2):18.

———. 2004b. The past and future of Asian universities. *Asian Universities: Historical Perspectives and Contemporary Challenges,* eds. P.G. Altbach and T. Umakoshi. Baltimore, MD: Johns Hopkins University Press.

American Association for the Advancement of Science, Board of Directors. 1954. *Science* 120:958.

Arnone, Michael. 2004. "State Appropriations for higher education, 2003-4." *The Chronicle of Higher Education* 50(19):A25.

Aslanbeigui, N., and V. Montecinos. 1998. "Foreign students in US doctoral programs." *Journal of Economic Perspectives* 12:171-82.

Attiyeh, Gregory, and Richard Attiyeh. 1997. "Testing for bias in graduate school admissions." *Journal of Human Resources* 32(3):524-48.

Auriol, Laudeline. 2004a. Conclusions of Workshop (DSTI/EAS/STP/NESTI(2004)28). *OECD Workshop on User Needs for Indicators on Careers of Doctorate Holders, September 27, 2004, Paris.*

———. 2004b. Why do we need indicators on careers of doctorate holders? (DSTI/EAS/STP/ NESTI/RD(2004)15). *OECD Workshop on User Needs for Indicators on Careers of Doctorate Holders, September 27, 2004, Paris.* Available at *http://www.olis.oecd.org/ olis/2004doc.nsf/809a2d78518a8277c125685d005300b2/c3e666431ef071c8c1256f 12002dd411/$FILE/JT00169333.PDF.*

Bhattacharjee, Yudhijit. 2004. "Settling in on campus." *Science* 304:1282-84.

Black, Grant, and Paula Stephan. (in press). "The importance of foreign PhD students to US science." In: *Science and the University,* eds. R. Ehrenberg and P. Stephan. Madison, WI: University of Wisconsin Press.

Boehlert, Sherwood, Chair of the House Science Committee. 2002. Speech to SUNY Presidents on the Impact of Terrorism on R&D.

Bohm, Anthony, and D. P. Chaudhri. 2000. *Securing Australia's Future: An Analysis of the International Education Markets in India,* IDP Education Australia Limited, Sydney.

Borjas, George J. 2000. *Foreign-born Teaching Assistants and the Academic Performance of Undergraduates* (Working Paper No. 7635). National Bureau of Economic Research, Cambridge, MA.

———. 2004a. *Do Foreign Students Crowd out Native Students from Graduate Programs?* (Working Paper No. 10349). National Bureau of Economic Research, Cambridge, MA.

———. 2004b. Immigration in high-skill labor markets: The impact of foreign students on the earnings of doctorates. *American Economic Association Conference, January 7-9, 2005, Philadelphia, PA.* Available at *http://www.aeaweb.org/annual_mtg_papers/2005/ 0108_1430_1201.pdf.*

Boudard, Emmanuel. 2004. Developing an integrated information system on the career paths and mobility flows of researchers (DSTI/EAS/STP/NESTI/RD(2004)16). *OECD Workshop on User Needs for Indicators on Careers of Doctorate Holders, September 27, 2004, Paris.* Available at *http://www.olis.oecd.org/olis/2004doc.nsf/8d00615172fd2a63c 125685d005300b5/bf685d01c0e55778c1256f110055d5d8/$FILE/JT00169276.PDF.*

Bratsburg, Bernt. 1995. "The incidence of non-return among foreign students in the United States." *Economics of Education Review* 14(4):373-84.

Broad, William J. 2004. "U.S. is losing its dominance in the sciences." *New York Times* (May 3).

Brown, Heath. 2004a. *Council of Graduate Schools' Report Finds US Graduate Schools Adjusting Policies and Procedures to Address Declines in International Graduate Applications and Admits.* Council of Graduate Schools, Washington, DC.

———. 2004b. *Council of Graduate Schools Finds Decline in New International Graduate Student Enrollment for the Third Consecutive Year.* Council of Graduate Schools, Washington, DC.

Brown, Heath, and Maria Doulis. 2005. *Findings from 2005 CGS International Graduate Admissions Survey I.* Council of Graduate Schools, Washington, DC.

Burd, Stephen. 2002. "Bush may bar foreign students from 'sensitive courses'." *Chronicle of Higher Education* (April 26), A26.

Bureau of Consular Affairs. 2004. *Report of the Visa Office.* US Department of State, Washington, DC. Available at *http://travel.state.gov/visa/report.html.*

———. 2005. "Special Visa Processing Procedures - Travelers from State Sponsors of Terrorism." US Department of State, Washington, DC. Available at *http://travel.state.gov/visa/ temp/info/info_1300.html.*

Bureau of Industry and Security, Department of Commerce. 2005. *Revision and Clarification of Deemed Export Related Regulatory Requirements.* 15 CFR Parts 734 and 735.

Burgess, David R. 1998. "Where will the next generation of minority biomedical scientists come from?" *Cancer* 83(8):1717-19.

Busquin, Philippe. 2004. "Investing in people." *Science* 303:145.

Caufield, Jim. 2000. *UC Nonresident Tuition Policy: Long on Numbers, Short on Vision.* Available at *http://gsa.asucla.ucla.edu/issues/nonresident.html.*

Center for the Study of Education Policy, Illinois State University. "Grapevine." Web page. Available at *http://coe.ilstu.edu/grapevine/.*

Chander, P., and S. Thangavelu. 2004. "Technology adoption, education and immigration policy." *Journal of Development Economics* 75(1):79-94.

Chelleraj, G., Keith E. Maskus, and A. Mattoo. 2004. *The Contribution of Skilled Immigration and International Graduate Students to US Innovation* (Working Paper No. 04-10). University of Colorado, Boulder, CO.

Chiswick, Barry R. 2000. *Are Immigrants Favorably Self-Selected?* (IZA DP No. 131). Forschungsinstitute zur Zukunft der Arbeit, Hamburg.

Choi, H. 1995. *An International Scientific Community: Asian Scholars in the United States.* Westport, CT: Praeger.

Chronicle of Higher Education. 2004. "Stipends for Graduate Assistants, 2003-4." Web page. Available at *http://chronicle.com/stats/stipends/2004/.*

Clark, X., T. J. Hatton, and J. G. Williamson. 2002. *Where do US immigrants come from, and why?* (Working Paper No. 8998). National Bureau of Economic Research, Cambridge, MA.

Cohen, W. I. 2001. *East Asia at the Center: Four Thousand Years of Engagement with the World.* New York: Columbia University Press.

Commission of the European Communities. *Snapshots 'Brain drain study'*, Commission of the European Communities, Brussels. Available at *http://europa.eu.int/comm/research/era/pdf/indicators/snap6.pdf.*

————. 2001. *A Mobility Strategy for the European Research Area* (COM 2001 331 final). Commission of the European Communities, Brussels. Available at *http://europa.eu.int/eur-lex/en/com/cnc/2001/com2001_0331en01.pdf.*

————. 2004. *On the Admission of Third-Country Nationals to Carry Out Scientific Research in the European Community* (COM(2004) 178 final). Commission of the European Communities. Available at *http://europa.eu.int/eur-lex/en/com/pdf/2004/com2004_0178en01.pdf, Brussels.*

Committee on Loyalty in Relation to Government Support of Unclassified Research. 1956. "Loyalty and research." *Science* 12:660.

Committee on Science, Engineering, and Public Policy. 1993. *Science, Technology, and the Federal Government: National Goals for a New Era*, Washington, DC: National Academy Press.

————. 1995. *Reshaping the Graduate Education of Scientists and Engineers*, Washington, DC: National Academy Press.

————. 2000. *Enhancing the Postdoctoral Experience for Scientists and Engineers*, Washington, DC: National Academy Press.

Conference Board of Canada. 1999. *The Economic Implications of International Education for Canada and Nine Comparator Countries: A Comparison of International Education Activities and Economic Performance*, Department of Foreign Affairs and International Trade, Ottawa, ON.

Confessore, Nicholas. May 2005. "Borderline insanity." *Washington Monthly.*

Council of Graduate Schools. "CGS/GRE Graduate Enrollment and Degrees." Web page. Available at *http://www.cgsnet.org/VirtualCenterResearch/graduateenrollment.htm.*

Davis, Todd. 2003. *Atlas of Student Mobility.* New York: Institute of International Education.

de Solla Price, Derek J. 1963. *Little Science, Big Science ... and Beyond.* New York: Columbia University Press.

Department of Homeland Security. 2003. *2003 Yearbook of Immigration Statistics*, Office of Immigration Statistics. Washington, DC: Office of Management, DHS. Available at *http://uscis.gov/graphics/shared/aboutus/statistics/*.

Desai, Mihir A., Devesh Kapur, and John McHale. 2005. "The fiscal impact of the brain drain: Indian emigration to the US." *Journal of Development Economics* (in press).

Dillon, Sam. 2004. "U.S. slips in attracting the best students." *New York Times* (December 21), p. A-1.

DOE/NSF Nuclear Science Advisory Committee. 2004. *Education in Nuclear Science: A Status Report and Recommendations for the Beginning of the 21st Century*, Washington, DC: Department of Energy and National Science Foundation.

DTI Global Watch Stem Cell Mission. 2004. Executive Summary: Focus on Asia-Pacific. *DTI Global Watch Magazine* Available at *http://www.globalwatchonline.com/mission/tmsmrep.aspx#life*.

Ducharne, Justine. 2004. "Les universites americaines font-elles encore recette?" *Le Figaro* (June 30).

Editor. 2003. "President's science council says future health of technology sector is in jeopardy; decline of manufacturing could impact innovation 'ecosystem'." *Manufacturing & Technology News* 10 (18). Available at *www.manufacturingnews.com/news/03-1003/art1.html*.

———.2004. "A visa system tangled in red tape and misconceived security rules is hurting America. *The Economist* (May 6).

Editorial Desk. 2005. Sanity on visas for students. *New York Times* (16 February), p. A-20.

Educational Testing Service. 2004. "GRE Volumes by Country." Web page. Available at *http://ftp.ets.org/pub/gre/volumes_00_04.pdf*.

Enders, Jurgen, and Alexis-Michael Mugabushaka. 2004. *Wissenshaft und Karriere: Ehrfahrungen und Werdegange ehemahleiger Stipendiaten der DFG*. Deutsche Forschungsgemeinschaft (DFG), Bonn.

Esterlin, Richard. 1993. *Prices and Preferences in Choice of Career: The Switch to Business, 1972-1987* (Discussion Paper 2-1). Williams College Project on the Economics of Higher Education, Williamstown, MA. Available at *http://www.williams.edu/wpehe/DPs/DP-21.pdf*.

European Commission. 2002. *Towards a European Research Area. Science, Technology, and Innovation Key Figures 2002*, European Communities. Available at *http://www.cordis.lu/rtd2002/indicators/home.html*., Brussels.

European Union. "Researcher's Mobility Portal." Web page. Available at *http://europa.eu.int/eracareers/index_en.cfm*.

Expert Group on Future Skill Needs. 2004. *A Model to Predict the Supply and Demand for Researchers and Research Personnel in Line with Ireland's Strategy for Contributing to the European Research Area's 3% Initiative*, Forfás, Dublin.

Farley, Reynolds, Charlotte Steeh, Tara Jackson, Maria Krysan, and Keith Reeves. 1993. "Continuing Racial Residential Segregation in Detroit. 'Chocolate City, Vanilla Suburbs Revisited'." *Journal of Housing Research* 4(1):1-21.

Federal Republic of Germany. "Green Card Germany." Web page. Available at *http://www.green-card-germany.com/*.

Field, Kelly. 2005. "Visa delays stemming from scholars' security clearances are down since last year, report says." *Chronicle of Higher Education* (February 18).

Finn, Michael G. 2003. *Stay Rates of Foreign Doctorate Recipients from US Universities, 2001*, Oak Ridge Institute for Science and Education, Oak Ridge, TN.

Fleisher, B., M. Hashimoto, and B. A. Weinberg. 2002. "Foreign GTAs can be effective teachers in economics." *Journal of Economic Education* 33(4):299-325.

Foucart, Stephane. 2003. « Outre-Atlantique, la peur de l'etranger pourrait ralentir la recherche. » *Le Monde* (June 6).

Freeman, R. B., E. Jin, and C-Y. Shen. 2004. *Where Do New US-trained Science-Engineering PhDs Come From?*, (Working Paper No. 10544). Cambridge, MA: National Bureau of Economics Research.

Freeman, Richard B. 1971. *The Market for College-Trained Manpower*. Cambridge, MA: Harvard University Press.

———. 1980. "Employment opportunities: The doctorate manpower market." *Industrial and Labor Relations Review* 33(2):185-96.

———. 2004. Data! Data! My kingdom for data! Data needs for analyzing the S&E job market. In: *The U.S. Scientific and Technical Workforce: Improving Data for Decisionmaking*, eds. T.K. Kelly et al. Arlington, VA: RAND Corporation.

Freeman, Richard D., Eric Weinstein, Elizabeth Marincola, Janet Rosenbaum, and Frank Solomon. 2001. *Careers and Rewards in Bio Sciences*. Washington, DC: American Society for Cell Biology.

Gallup-Black, Adria. 2004. "International student mobility: Project Atlas." *International Higher Education* 37:10-11.

Garrison, Howard H., Susan A. Gerbi, and Paul W. Kincade. 2003. "In an era of scientific opportunity, are there opportunities for biomedical scientists?" *FASEB Journal* 17: 2169-73.

Gast, Alice P. 2004. The impact of restricting information access on science and technology. In: *A Little Knowledge: Privacy, Security, and Public Information after September 11*, eds. P. M. Shane, J. Podesta, and R. C. Leone. New York: The Century Foundation.

German Academic International Network (GAIN). Web page. Available at *http://www.gain-network.org*.

Goodman, Allen E. 2002. "Rethinking foreign students." *National Review* (18 June).

Goswani, Urmi A. 2005. "India fails to mature into learning hub." *The Economic Times (India Times)* (January 13). Available at *http://economictimes.indiatimes.com/articleshow/msid-98027,prtpage-1.cms*.

Government Accountability Office. 2004a. *Performance of Information System to Monitor Foreign Student and Exchange Visitors Has Improved, but Issues Remain* (GAO-04-690). Washington, DC: GAO.

———. 2004b. *Border Security: Improvements Needed to Reduce Time Taken to Adjudicate Visas for Science Students and Scholars* (GAO-04-371). Washington, DC: GAO.

———. 2005a. *National Nuclear Security Administration: Contractors' Strategies to Recruit and Retain a Critically Skilled Workforce are Generally Effective* (GAO-05-164). Washington, DC: GAO.

———. 2005b. *Border Security: Streamlined Visas Mantis Program Has Lowered Burden on Foreign Science Students and Scholars, but Further Refinements Needed* (GAO-05-198). Washington, DC: GAO.

Graduate College, University of Illinois at Urbana-Champaign. 2003. A Guide to the Campus Tuition Waiver Policy on Graduate Assistantships. *http://www.grad.uiuc.edu/Policies/TuitionWaiverPolicy.pdf*.

Greenberg, Daniel S. 2004. "What scientist shortage?" *Washington Post* (May 19), p. A-23.

Gupta, D., M. Nerad, and J. Cerny. "International PhDs: Exploring the decision to stay or return." *International Higher Education* 31 (Spring): 2-4.

Gupta, Deepak. 2004. "The Return Choice and Careers of Foreign-born US S&E PhDs." Dissertation, University of California, Berkeley.

Herbst, Christian, Michael Prellberg, Helene Laube, and Thomas Clark. 2004. "Keep out!" *Financial Times Deutschland* (June 24).

Hicks, Diana. 2004. "Asian countries strengthen their research." *Issues in Science and Technology* 2:75-78.

Hon, Chua Chin. 2005. "In a reversal of an old mindset, nine in 10 say they will go home where opportunities abound." *Straits Times* (January). Available at *http://www. straitstimes.com/sub/asia/story/0,5562,291279,00.html?*

Institute for International Education. 2004. *Open Doors Report on International Educational Exchange*. IIE, New York. Available at *www.iiebooks.org/opendoors2004.html.*

———. 2004. *Open Doors Report on International Educational Exchange: Survey of Foreign Student and Scholar Enrollment and Visa Trends for Fall 2004.* IIE, New York.

International English Language Testing System (IELTS). 2004. "Annual Review 2003." Web page. Available at *http://www.ielts.org/library/AnnualReview2003_v1.pdf.*

Italian Ministero degli Affari Esteri. "DAVINCI." Web page. Available at *http://www.esteri.it/ davinci/index.asp?lang=eng.*

Jacobs, Janice L., Deputy Assistant Secretary of State for Visa Services. 2003. Testimony on Foreign Students and Scholars. Available at *http://travel.state.gov/visa/testimony1.html.*

Jacobs, L. H., and C. B. Friedman. 1988. Students achievement under foreign teaching associates compared with native teaching associates. *Journal of Higher Education* 59(3): 551-63.

Jayaram, N. 2004. Higher Education in India. *Asian Universities: Historical Perspectives and Contemporary Challenges.* Eds. P. G. Altbach and T. Umakoshi. Baltimore, MD: Johns Hopkins Press.

Jewsiewicki, Bogumil. 2003. *The Brain Drain in an Era of Liberalism* (Millennium Research No. 9). Canadian Bureau for International Education, Ottawa, ON.

Johnson, David L. 2001. *Relationship Between Stay Rates of PhD Recipients on Temporary Visas and Relative Economic Conditions in Country of Origin* (Working Paper). Oak Ridge, TN: Oak Ridge Institute for Science and Education.

Kapur, Devesh, and John McHale. 2005. Sojourns and software: Internationally mobile human capital and high-tech industry development in India, Ireland, and Israel. In: *From Underdogs to Tigers: The Rise and Growth of the Software Industry in Israel, Ireland and India,* eds. A. Arora and A. Gambardella. Oxford: Oxford University Press.

Kelly, Terrence, William P. Butz, Stephan Carroll, David Adamson, and Gabrielle Bloom. 2004. *The US Scientific and Technical Workforce: Improving Data for Decisionmaking,* Arlington, VA: RAND Corporation.

Kennedy, Donald, Jim Jim Austin, Kirstie Urquhart, and Crispin Taylor. 2004. "Supply without demand." *Science* 303:1105.

Kerr, William. 2004. *Ethnic Scientific Communities and International Technology Diffusion* (Working Paper). Available at *http://econ-www.mit.edu/faculty/download_pdf. php?id=994.*

King, David A. 2004. "The Scientific Impact of Nations." *Nature* 430:311-16.

Koh, Hey-Keung. 2002. *Trends in International Student Flows to the United States.* IIE, New York.

Lee, Sooho. 2004. "Foreign-born scientists in the United States: Do they perform differently than native-born scientists?" Dissertation, Georgia Institute of Technology.

Levin, Sharon G., Grant C. Black, Anne E. Winkler, and Paula E. Stephan. 2004. *Differential Employment Patterns for Citizens and Non-Citizens in Science and Engineering in the United States: Minting and Competitive Effects* (Working Paper). University of Missouri, St. Louis.

Lin-Liu, Jen. 2002. "Brain Gain in Taiwan." *Chronicle of Higher Education* (October 18).

Lingenfelter, Paul. The public interest in higher education accountability. University of Texas System National Accountability Symposium, October 27-28, 2004, Austin, TX. Available at *http://www.utsystem.edu/cha/acctsymp2004/Lingenfelter.ppt.*

Lubchenco, Jane, and Goverdhan Mehta. 2004. "International Scientific Meetings." *Science* 305: 1531.

MaCurdy, Thomas, Thomas Nechyba, and Jay Bhattacharya. 1998. "An Economic Framework for Assessing the Fiscal Impacts of Immigration." In: *The Immigration Debate: Studies in the Economic, Demographic and Fiscal Effects of Immigration.* Washington, DC: National Academy Press.

Marginson, Simon. 2004. Australian higher education: National and global markets. *Markets in Higher Education: Rhetoric or Reality?* eds. P. Teixeira, B. Jongbloed, D. Dill, and A. Amaral, pp. 207-40. Dordrecht, The Netherlands: Kluwer.

Martin, Philip. 1999. Immigration and Farm Labor: An Overview. Available at *http://www. farmfoundation.org/1999NPPEC/martin.pdf.*

Martin-Rovet, Dominique. 2003. *Opportunities for Outstanding Young Scientists in Europe to Create an Independent Research Team.* European Science Foundation, Strasbourg.

Mashelkar, Raghunath A. 2004. "India's R&D: Reaching for the top." *Science* 307:1415.

May, Robert M. 2004. "Raising Europe's game." *Nature* 430:831.

Mazzarol, Tim, and Geoffrey N. Soutar. 2001. *Push-Pull Factors in Influencing International Student Destination Choice* (Discussion Paper 0105). Centre for Entrepreneurial Management and Innovation, University of Western Australia, Crawley.

Mervis, Jeffrey. 2004. "Many origins, one destination." *Science* 304:1277.

Metzke, Robert. 2000. "WANTED: 75,000 IT Pros—Germany Considers Green Card Model." *Science's Next Wave.* Available at *http://nextwave.sciencemag.org/cgi/content/ full/2000-03/02/6.*

Min, Weifang. 2004. "Chinese Higher Education: The legacy of the past and the context of the future." In: *Asian Universities: Historical Perspectives and Contemporary Challenges,* eds. P.G. Altbach and T. Umakoshi. Baltimore, MD: Johns Hopkins Press.

NAFSA, the Association of International Educators. 2004. *The Economic Benefits of International Education to the United States of America: A Statistical Analysis.* Available at *http://www.nafsa.org/content/PublicPolicy/DataonInternationalEducation/ econBenefits.htm.*

National Academies International Visitors Office. "Organizing an International Meeting in the United States." Web page. Available at *http://www7.nationalacademies.org/visas/ Organizing_a_Meeting.html.*

National Center for Education Statistics. 2000. *1999-2000 National Postsecondary Student Aid Study* (NPSAS:2000). Washington, DC: US Department of Education.

National Center for Education Statistics. 2002. *Digest of Education Statistics 2002* (NCES 2003060). US Department of Education, Washington, DC.

———. 2003. *Digest of Education Statistics, 2003.* Washington, DC: US Department of Education. Available at *http://nces.ed.gov/programs/digest/.*

National Opinion Research Center. 2005. *Science, Technology, and the Federal Government: National Goals for a New Era.* NORC, Chicago, IL. Available at *http://www.norc. uchicago.edu/issues/docdata.htm.*

National Research Council. 1985. *Immigration Statistics: A Story of Neglect.* Washington, DC: National Academy Press.

———. 1995a. *Assessment of Research Doctorate Programs.* Washington, DC: National Academy Press.

———. 1995b. *Research Doctorate Programs in the United States: Continuity and Change.* Washington, DC: National Academy Press.

———. 1996. *Statistics on U.S. Immigration: An Assessment of Data Needs for Future Research.* Washington, DC: National Academy Press.

———. 1999. *Measuring the Science and Engineering Enterprise: Priorities for the Division of Science Resources Studies.* Washington, DC: National Academy Press.

———. 2000. *Forecasting Demand and Supply of Doctoral Scientists and Engineers: Report of a Workshop on Methodology.* Washington, DC: National Academy Press.

———. 2001. *Trends in Federal Support of Research and Graduate Education.* Washington, DC: National Academy Press.

———. 2002. *Making the Nation Safer: The Role of Science and Technology in Countering Terrorism.* Washington, DC: The National Academies Press.

———. 2005a. *Assessment of Department of Defense Basic Research.* Washington, DC: The National Academies Press.

———. 2005b. *Bridges to Independence: Fostering the Independence of New Investigators in Biomedical Research.* Washington, DC: The National Academies Press.

———. 2005c. *Advancing the Nation's Health Needs: NIH Research Training Programs.* Washington, DC: The National Academies Press.

National Science Board. 2003. *Broadening Participation in Science and Engineering Research and Education: Workshop Proceedings* (NSB 04-72). Arlington, VA: National Science Foundation.

———. 2003. *The Science and Engineering Workforce: Realizing America's Potential* (NSB 03-69). Arlington, VA: National Science Foundation.

———. 2004. *Science and Engineering Indicators, 2004* (Volume 1: NSB 04-1; Volume 2, NSB 04-1A). Arlington, VA: National Science Foundation.

National Science Foundation, Division of Science Resource Statistics. "WebCASPAR Database System." Web page. Available at *http://caspar.nsf.gov.*

———. 2003. *Academic Research and Development Expenditures: Fiscal Year 2001* (NSF 03-316). Arlington, VA: National Science Foundation.

———. 2004. *Graduate Enrollment in Science and Engineering Fields Reaches New Peak; First-Time Enrollment of Foreign Students Declines* (NSF 04-326). Arlington, VA: National Science Foundation.

———. 2004. *Survey of Earned Doctorates 2002.* Arlington, VA: National Science Foundation.

———. 2004. *Survey of Graduate Students and Postdoctorates in Science and Engineering (GSS) 2002.* Arlington, VA: National Science Foundation.

———. 2005. *Science and Engineering Doctorate Awards 2003* (NSF 05-300). Arlington, VA: National Science Foundation.

Nekovee, Maziar. 2000. "Obstacles to Mobility in Europe: Young Mobile Researchers Meet EC Policy-Makers in Crete." *Science's Next Wave.* Available at *http://nextwave. sciencemag.org/cgi/content/full/2000-11/02/13?ck=nck.*

Nerad, Maresi, and Joseph Cerny. 1999. "Postdoctoral patterns, career advancement, and problems." *Science* 285: 1533-35.

———. 2000. "Improving doctoral education: Recommendations from the *Ph.Ds Ten Years Later* Study." *The Communicator* XXXIII: 2.

Neuschatz, Michael, and Patrick J. Mulvey. 2003. *Physics Students from Abroad in the Post-9/11 Era* (AIP Publication No. R-437). American Institute of Physics, College Park, MD.

Ning, Cui. 2004. "Record number of scholars headed abroad." *China Daily* (December 22) Available at *http://www.chinadaily.com.cn/english/doc/2004-12/22/content_ 042422. htm.*

Nobel e-Museum: The Official Web Site of The Nobel Foundation. "Chronology of Nobel Prize winners in Physics, Chemistry, and Physiology or Medicine." Web page. Available at *http://www.nobel.se/index.html.*

Norris, Julie T. 2003. *Restrictions on Research Awards: Troublesome Clauses. A Report of the AAU/COGR Task Force.* Office of Science and Technology Policy and Council on Government Relations, Washington, DC.

Nye, Joseph S. Jr. 2004. "You can't get here from there." *New York Times* (November 29).

Office of the Coordinator for Counterterrorism. 2001. *Overview of State-sponsored Terrorism*. Washington, DC: US Department of State. Available at *http://www.state.gov/s/ct/rls/pgtrpt/2000/2441.htm*.

Office of the Spokesman. 2005. *US extends visa validity for Chinese tourist and business travelers* (Media Note 2005/56). Washington, DC: US Department of State. Available at *http://www.state.gov/r/pa/prs/ps/2005/40818.htm*.

———. 2005. *Extension of Validity for Science-Related Interagency Visa Clearances* (Media Note 2005/182). Washington, DC: US Department of State. Available at *http://www.state.gov/r/pa/prs/ps/2005/42212.htm*.

Offices of Inspectors General. 2004. *Interagency Review of Foreign National Access to Sensitive Technology* (Report No. D-2004-062). Washington, DC: US Departments of Commerce, Defense, Energy, Homeland Security, and State, and Central Intelligence Agency.

Oltman, Philip K., and Rodney T. Hartnett. 1984. *The Role of GRE General and Subject Test Scores in Graduate Program Admission* (ETS Research Report 84-14). Princeton, NJ: Educational Testing Service.

Organisation for Economic Co-operation and Development. 1999. *Main Definitions and Conventions for the Measurement of Research and Development, 5th Edition (Frascati Manual)*. Paris: OECD.

———. 2002. *International Mobility of the Highly Skilled* (Policy Brief 92 2002 01 1P4). OECD, Washington, DC. Available at *http://www.oecd.org/dataoecd/9/20/1950028.pdf*.

———. 2002. *Main Science and Technology Indicators*. Paris: OECD.

———. 2003. *Education at a Glance*, Paris: OECD.

Paul, Lennart. 2004. "Visa-Probleme halten Gastforscher von USA fern." *Die Welt* (September 9).

Pew Global Attitudes Project. "Pew Global Attitudes Project Home page." Web page. Available at *http://people-press.org/pgap/*.

Pouliot, Joe. 2005a. "Boehlert praises improvements to visa processing." *House Science Committee Press Office*. (February 13).

———.2005b. Boehlert releases new GAO report finding reduced delays for visas for scientists and students. *House Science Committee Press Office* (February 18).

Prasad, Laxman. Employment Characteristics of PhD Holders in the Field of Science and Technology: Indian Experience (DSTI/EAS/STP/NESTI/RD(2004)23). *OECD Workshop on User Needs for Indicators on Careers of Doctorate Holders, 27 September, 2004, Paris.* Available at *http://www.olis.oecd.org/olis/2004doc.nsf/809a2d78518a8277c125685d005300b2/a7925492feb132c8c1256f0f00541a7b/$FILE/JT00169100.PDF*.

Rapaport, Alan I. 1998. *Have Forms of Primary Financial Support for S&E Graduate Students Changed During the Last Two Decades?* (NSF 99-313). Arlington, VA: National Science Foundation.

Recotillet, Isabelle. 2003. *Availability and Characteristics of Surveys on the Destination of Doctorate Recipients in OECD Countries. Statistical Analysis of Science, Technology and Industry* (Working Paper 2003/9). Paris: OECD.

Regets, Mark. 2001. *Research and Policy Issues in High-Skilled International Migration*. Bonn: IZA.

Rizvi, Fazal. 2004. "Offshore Australian higher education." *International Higher Education* 37(Fall):7-9.

Rominiecki, Joe. 2005. "North Dakota bill addresses student complaint: I can't understand my prof." *Kansas City Infozine* (February 15). Available at *http://www.infozine.com/news/stories/op/storiesView/sid/5826/*.

Rousselot, Fabrice. 2003. "Etudiants etrangers, le parcours d'obstacles." *Liberation* (September 11).

APPENDIX D

Ruesch, A. 2003. "Studium in den USA - kein Traumziel mehr?" *Die Neue Zuercher Zeitung* (November 12).

Saxenian, AnnaLee. 2001. *Silicon Valley's New Immigrant Entrepreneurs* (Working Paper No. 15). Center for Comparative Immigration Studies, University of California, San Diego. Available at *http://www.ccis-ucsd.org/PUBLICATIONS/wrkg15.PDF*.

Schaaper, Martin. OECD Methodology for Tracking Doctorate Holders and Measuring International Mobility of HRST. *Sixth Ibero American Inter-American Workshop on Science and Technology Indicators, September 15-17, 2004, Buenos Aires*. Available at *http://www.ricyt.org/interior/normalizacion%5CVItaller%5CS2_RRHH%5CSchaaper doc.pdf*.

Schmitz, Gregor. 2004. "Ihr koennt zu Hause bleiben." *Spiegel Online* (April 29).

Schneider, Lisa M., and Jacqueline B. Briel. 1990. *Validity of the GRE: 1988-89 Summary Report*. Princeton, NJ: Educational Testing Service.

Shanghai's Jiao Tong University Institute of Higher Education. 2004. "Academic Ranking of World Universities." Web page. Available at *http://ed.sjtu.edu.cn/rank/2004/2004Main.htm*.

Simon, Denis Fred. 2004. Foreign R&D and the Impact of Globalization on China's Emerging Technological Trajectory. *AAAS S&T Policy Forum, April 19-20, 2004, Washington, DC*. Available at *http://www.aaas.org/spp/rd/simon404.pdf*.

Stephan, Paula E. 2004. "What data do labor market researchers needs? A researcher's perspective." In: *The U.S. Scientific and Technical Workforce: Improving Data for Decisionmaking*, eds. T.K. Kelly et al. Arlington, VA: RAND Corporation.

Stephan, Paula E., Grant C. Black, James D. Adams, and Sharon G. Levin. 2002. "Survey of foreign recipients of US PhDs." *Science* 295:2211-12.

Stephan, Paula E. and Sharon G. Levin. 1992. *Striking the Mother Lode in Science: The Importance of Age, Time and Place*. New York: Oxford University Press.

———. (in press). "Foreign scholars in US science: Contributions and costs." In: *Science and the University*, eds. R. Ehrenberg and P. Stephan. Madison, WI: University of Wisconsin Press.

Stephan, Paula E., and Jennifer Ma. 2005. The Increased Frequency and Duration of the Postdoctorate Career Stage. *American Economic Association Conference, January 7-9, 2005, Philadelphia, PA*. Available at *http://www.aeaweb.org/annual_mtg_papers/2005/0108_1430_1204.pdf*.

Sternberg, R. J. and Williams W.M. 1997. "Does the Graduate Record Examination predict meaningful success in the graduate training of psychologists? A case study." *American Psychology* 52(6):630-41.

Stokes, Donald E. 1997. *Pasteur's Quadrant: Basic Science and Technological Innovation*. Washington, DC: Brookings Institution.

Stossel, Scott. 1999. "Uncontrolled experiment: America's dependency on foreign scientists." *New Republic* (March 29).

Straubhaar, Thomas. 2000. *International Mobility of the Highly Skilled: Brain Gain, Brain Drain, or Brain Exchange* (HWWA Discussion Paper 88). Hamburg Institute of International Economics, Hamburg. Available at *http://opus.zbw-kiel.de/volltexte/2003/695*.

Tang, Joyce. 2000. *Doing Engineering. The Career Attainment and Mobility of Caucasian, Black, and Asian American Engineers*. Lanham, MD: Bowman and Littlefield Publishers.

Teitelbaum, Michael. 2004. "Do We Need More Scientists?" In: *The U.S. Scientific and Technical Workforce: Improving Data for Decisionmaking*, eds. T. K. Kelly et al. Arlington, VA: RAND Corporation.

Thurgood, Lori. 2004. *Graduate Enrollment in Science and Engineering Fields Reaches a New Peak; First-time Enrollment of Foreign Students Declines* (Info Brief NSF 04-326). Arlington, VA: National Science Foundation.

Tremblay, Karine. 2004. Links between academic mobility and immigration. *Symposium on International Labour and Academic Mobility: Emerging Trends and Implications for Public Policy, October 22, 2004, Toronto.* Available at *http://www.wes.org/ewenr/symp/KarineTremblayPaper.pdf.*

University of Michigan Office of Budget and Planning. 2004. GSI Salary Comparison. Available at *http://www.umich.edu/~urel/gsi-sa/comparison.html.*

University of Texas Office of Accounting. 2003. Exemptions, Waivers and Third Party Billing. Available at *http://www.utexas.edu/business/accounting/sar/waivers.html.*

US Census Bureau, Foreign Trade Division. "Guide to Foreign Trade Statistics." Web page. Available at *http://www.census.gov/foreign-trade/guide/index.html.*

US Department of Commerce. "TradeStat Express." Web page. Available at *http://tse.export.gov/.*

US Department of Homeland Security. "Immigrations and Customs Enforcement." Web page. Available at *http://www.ice.gov.*

US Department of Homeland Security, Bureau of Citizenship and Immigration Services. "Immigration Classifications and Visa Categories." Web page. Available at *http://uscis.gov/graphics/services/visas.htm.*

US Department of State. "Visa Reciprocity and Country Documents Finder." Web page. Available at *http://travel.state.gov/visa/reciprocity/index.htm.*

———. 2003. *Standard Operating Procedures No 22: Revision to Visas Mantis Clearance Procedure* (Cable 04 State 153587). Available at *http://travel.state.gov/visa/laws/telegrams/telegrams_1425.html.*

———. 2004. *Student and Exchange Visitor Processing Reminder* (Cable 04 State 154060). Washington, DC: US Deparment of State. Available at *http://travel.state.gov/visa/student_exchange_reminder.html.*

US Department of State, Bureau of Educational and Cultural Affairs. "Foreign Students Yesterday, World Leaders Today." Web page. Available at *http://exchanges.state.gov/education/educationusa/leaders.htm.*

US Department of State, Directorate of Defense Trade Controls. Defense Trade Controls-Reference Library: International Traffic in Arms Regulations (ITAR). Available at *http://pmdtc.org/reference.htm.*

US Government Printing Office. "Export Administrations Regulations Database." Web page. Available at *http://www.access.gpo.gov/bis/ear/ear_data.html.*

van Hoof, Hubert B., and Marja J. Verbeeten. 2005. "Wine is for drinking, water is for washing: Student opinions about international exchange programs." *Journal of Studies in International Education* 9(1):42-61.

Wagner, Caroline S. 2002. "The elusive partnership: Science and foreign policy." *Science and Public Policy* 29(6):409-17.

Wagner, Caroline S., and Loet Leydesdorff. 2005a. "Mapping the network of global science: Comparing international co-authorships from 1990 to 2000." *International Journal of Technology and Globalisation* (in press).

———. 2005b. "Network structure, self-organization and the growth of international collaboration in Science." *Research Policy* (in press).

Walpole, MaryBeth, Nancy W. Burton, Kamau Kanyi, and Altamese Jackenthal. 2002. *Selecting Successful Graduate Students: In-Depth Interviews with GRE Users* (ETS Research Report 02-08). Princeton, NJ: Educational Testing Service.

Wang, Jessica. 1999. *American Science in an Age of Anxiety.* Chapel Hill, NC: The University of North Carolina Press.

Wheeler, David L. 2002. "Testing services says GRE scores from China, South Korea, and Taiwan are suspect." *Chronicle of Higher Education* (August 16).

Wolf, Eleanor. 1969. "The tipping point in racially changing neighborhoods." *Journal of the American Institute of Planners* 29:217-22.

World Bank. 2004. *Joint Japan/World Bank Graduate Scholarship Program Tracer Study IV.* World Bank, Washington, DC. Available at *http://www.worldbank.org/wbi/scholarships/.*

Zinberg, Dorothy S. 1991. "Contradictions and complexity: International comparisons in the training of foreign scientists and engineers." In: *The Changing University,* ed. D.S. Zinberg. Dordrecht, The Netherlands: Kluwer.

Zumeta, W. and J. S. Raveling. 2002. "Attracting the best and the brightest." *Issues in Science and Technology* 19:36-40.